HOME TO STAY

Also by Daniel Gordis

God Was Not in the Fire
The Search for a Spiritual Judaism

Does the World Need the Jews?
Rethinking Chosenness and
American Jewish Identity

Becoming a Jewish Parent
How to Explore Spirituality and
Tradition with Your Children

HOME TO STAY

One American Family's Chronicle
of Miracles and Struggles in
Contemporary Israel

DANIEL GORDIS

Previously published as
IF A PLACE CAN MAKE YOU CRY

 THREE RIVERS PRESS • NEW YORK

Published by Three Rivers Press, New York, New York.
Member of the Crown Publishing Group, a division of
Random House, Inc.
www.crownpublishing.com

Three Rivers Press and the Tugboat design are registered
trademarks of Random House, Inc.

Originally published in hardcover by Crown Publishers,
a division of Random House, Inc., in 2002 as *If a Place
Can Make You Cry.*

Portions of this book were previously published in
The New York Times Magazine.

Printed in the United States of America

DESIGN BY BARBARA STURMAN

Maps by Mark Stein Studios

Library of Congress Cataloging-in-Publication Data
Gordis, Daniel.
    If a place can make you cry : dispatches from an
anxious state / by Daniel Gordis.
1. Jews, American—Israel—Biography. 2. Jews—
Israel—Social life and customs. 3. Israel—Social
conditions. 4. Arab-Israeli conflict—1993—Influence.
5. Gordis, Daniel—Correspondence. I. Title.
DS113.8.A4 G67 2002
956.94′004924073′092—dc21
[B]   2002023725

ISBN 1-4000-4959-8

10 9 8 7 6 5 4 3 2 1

First Paperback Edition

To my brothers and their families
with admiration and with love

ולחצתיך אל לב, רעי, אחי הטוב
(חיים נחמן ביאליק, "ביום קיץ")

Elie and Avra
Tamar, Arielle, and Noah

Yonatan and Robbie
Rakeea and Melila

Je vous ai rapporté mes paroles.
Je vous ai parlé de la difficulté d'être Juif,
qui se confond avec la difficulté d'écrire;
car le judaïsme et l'écriture ne sont qu'une même attente,
un même espoir, une même usure.

I have already reported to you my words.
I talked to you about the difficulty of being Jewish,
which is the same as the difficulty of writing.
For Judaism and writing are but the same waiting,
the same hope, the same wearing out.

EDMOND JABÈS (1912–1991)

Contents

Maps

- - - - - - - - - - - - - - - - -

Because a large measure of the Israeli-Palestinian conflict revolves around the division of land, and because this book makes reference to both places shown in these maps and possible divisions of that land, the following maps are provided as a guide to the reader.

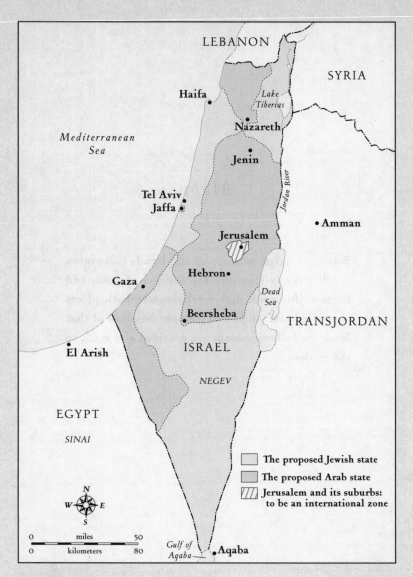

The U.N. Partition Plan—1947

This is the division of land proposed by the United Nations, which the Jewish authorities accepted but the Arab authorities rejected. Following this proposed division, the Arab forces attacked the Jewish pre-State entity. At the end of the war, Israel was victorious, resulting in a division of land that is shown on the next page.

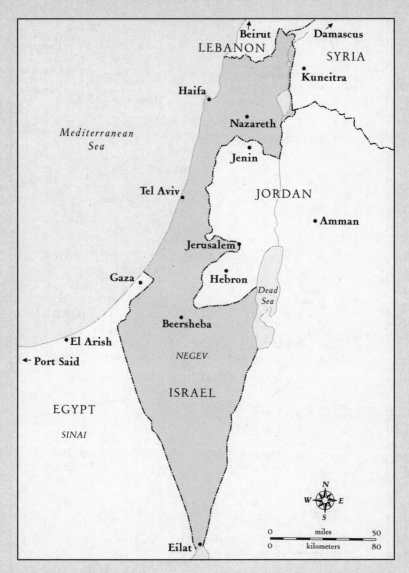

The Armistice Agreement—1949

These are the borders of Israel at the conclusion of the War of Independence. They remained Israel's borders (with a brief exception during the 1956 Sinai Campaign) until 1967, when Israel defeated Egypt, Jordan, and Syria and expanded to the borders shown on the following page.

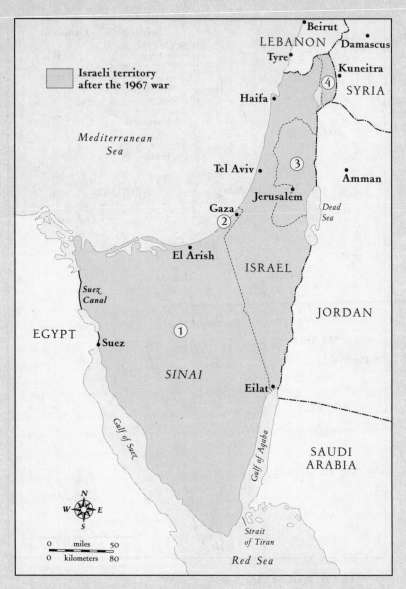

Israeli territory
after the 1967 war

Beirut

LEBANON   Damascus

Tyre   Kuneitra

(4)   SYRIA

Haifa

*Mediterranean
Sea*

(3)

Tel Aviv   Amman

Jerusalem

Gaza   *Dead
Sea*

(2)

El Arish

ISRAEL

*Suez
Canal*

JORDAN

EGYPT   Suez

(1)

SINAI

Eilat

Gulf of Suez

Gulf of Aqaba

SAUDI
ARABIA

N
W   E
S

0   miles   50
0 kilometers 80

*Strait
of Tiran*

Red Sea

The Cease-Fire Lines—1967

These are the cease-fire lines—essentially Israel's new borders—after the conclusion of the 1967 Six Day War. Israel captured four major areas: (1) the
Sinai desert and (2) the Gaza Strip from Egypt, (3) the West Bank of
the Jordan River from Jordan, and (4) the Golan Heights from Syria.

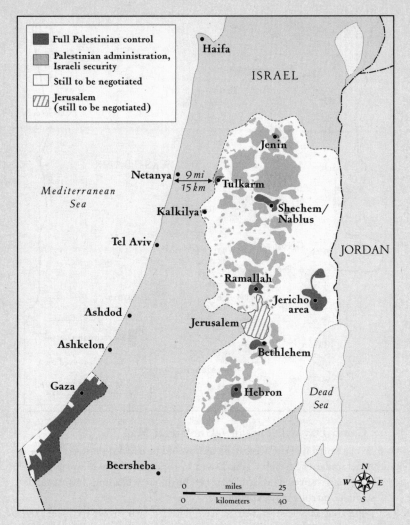

Legend:
- Full Palestinian control
- Palestinian administration, Israeli security
- Still to be negotiated
- Jerusalem (still to be negotiated)

Haifa

ISRAEL

Jenin

Netanya • 9 mi / 15 km • Tulkarm

Kalkilya • Shechem/Nablus

Mediterranean Sea

Tel Aviv •

JORDAN

Ramallah

Jericho area

Ashdod •

Jerusalem

Ashkelon •

Bethlehem

Gaza

Hebron

Dead Sea

Beersheba •

0 — miles — 25
0 — kilometers — 40

N W E S

The Oslo Agreement—1993

This map shows the portions of the West Bank and Gaza that were returned to the Palestinians after the Oslo Accords. Most of the Gaza Strip was returned, though some Israeli settlements remained, and several key cities in the West Bank (Hebron, Bethlehem, Jericho, Ramallah, Nablus, and Jenin) were also transferred to complete Palestinian control. In other areas, Israel maintained security control while giving the Palestinian Authority jurisdiction over civil matters. The remainder stayed in Israeli hands pending a final settlement.

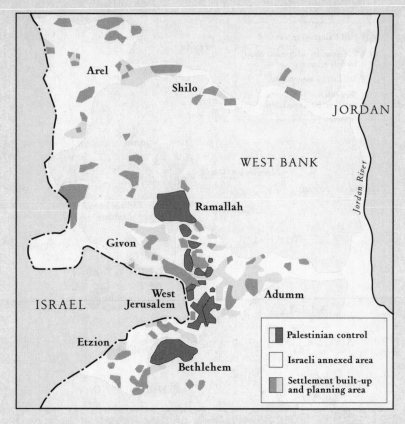

Camp David Proposals—Unofficial Map

A map of a portion of the West Bank as it would be divided between Palestine and Israel under the Israeli Camp David 2 proposals. The map was prepared by Palestinian sources. The significance of the different shadings in areas under Palestinian control is not explained.

Note that Israel is claimed to have retained two broad strips of land, dividing the new Palestine into three noncontiguous areas, something that the Palestinians felt they could not accept. Shortly after negotiations over these maps stalled (among many other critical issues, such as Jerusalem and the right of Palestinian refugees to return to Israel), the Al Aksa Intifada erupted.

Prologue

SEPTEMBER 11, 2001

JERUSALEM, ISRAEL

It's been two hours since the World Trade Center disaster. I was at my office with Talia, our fifteen-year-old daughter, when a colleague called to ask if I'd heard the news. I hadn't—I'm sick of the news. I try to log on to some decent web site, but there's no way to get in. They're jammed. I pack up my briefcase and we run home.

We're glued to the TV. Talia and Avi, our twelve-year-old son, are silent, taking in the images that are beyond horrible. Micha, our eight-year-old son, eventually wanders in, and we explain what's happened. To our surprise, he watches for a few moments and then bursts into tears. My wife and I follow him into the living room and sit on the couch with him. He says he's crying because when he was in New York two weeks ago, he wanted to go to the top of the World Trade Center, but we said we didn't have time. Now, he says, he'll never get to go.

But we know it's not really that. This is the New York City from which he has just come, the place where he was safe from all this. Central Park. Ice skating in Chelsea Piers. Now he knows—there's really no escape. He's only eight years old, and he has nowhere to run to.

"Is Uncle Elie OK?" Avi wonders. We've been trying to call the States nonstop, but there's no getting through. We try e-mail, but have yet to get answers. We assure him that Uncle Elie, my brother, is fine. "But how can you be sure he didn't go down there for a meeting?" he asks. We can't of course, but there's no way to reach him. Avi goes to sleep on the verge of tears.

Mostly we're watching CNN. But we occasionally take a look at Israeli TV, which in addition to the news from New York is showing celebrations in the West Bank. In Nablus, Palestinians are giving out candies in celebration, and gunmen are firing assault rifles into the air to applaud the deaths. In the refugee camp of Balata, and in the Palestinian cities of Tul Karm and Bethlehem, similar celebrations.

It feels as though we're surrounded by evil, everywhere. Micha's right—there's no escape, and it seems almost impossible to sustain the optimism that everything will one day be OK. We're just back from our summer vacation, and already I desperately need a break. I realize that I'm ready for the holidays, for the beginning of a new year. Of course this past Rosh Ha-Shannah was the beginning of all the horror, so it's hard to know how optimistic to be. But still, as I look out the window at the beauty of Jerusalem, even in the dark of night, a city that's survived attack and siege for thousands of years, despite everything, hope still seems to win out over despair. Maybe, just maybe, next year will be better.

SEPTEMBER 20, 2001
JERUSALEM, ISRAEL

I've learned a few important things in the days that have passed since September 11. I've learned what it is that our family in the States lives with each time a bomb goes off here. Phone lines jammed, no way to get in touch. And the inevitable calculations. Where was he supposed to be now? Would he have any reason to be in that neighborhood? Who's called in? Who hasn't been heard from? And after a couple of days, this time, who will in all likelihood never be heard from?

And in the States, they've learned those feelings that Israelis live with each time something happens: the panic, the confusion, the anger, the pain, the fear. New Yorkers, now nervous each time a subway train stops, are tragically learning what it is to be on edge all the time. Take the tunnel, or is the bridge a better idea? Should we stay away from major centers? The questions that change an entire way of life, questions that Americans are now, like us, tragically beginning to ask each day.

And I've learned that you can't really leave a homeland. We came here three years ago with no real ambivalence. We weren't angry at America—on the contrary, we knew full well all it had given us. But Israel always felt like home in a way that the U.S. didn't, so we took the plunge. Now, each time I fly back to the States, I fill out the little customs slip you give in at passport control. *Country of citizenship: USA,* which allows me to enter on the fast line. *Country of residence: Israel.* Each time, the U.S. customs officer looks at me, the passport, the clearly filled out slip, and says, "Welcome home." And each time I'm tempted to correct him, to tell him that it's not home anymore, but I say nothing.

Now, I know he's right. It is home. With each singing of "God Bless America" on CNN, it's more clear. It is, indeed, my "home, sweet home." I have two homelands, and now they're both under attack. And I find myself grieving for what's happening to each.

A few days ago, on the first day of Rosh Ha-Shannah, as the five of us were walking home from lunch on a gorgeous Jerusalem afternoon, Micha pointed to a blue and white bumper sticker. It read, *"Ha-tzionut Tenatze'ach"*—Zionism Will Prevail. "What do they mean by that?" he asked. "It means that Zionism will win, in the end," I tell him. "No, I understand the words, Abba, but what do they mean by that?" And without thinking, I tell him, "It means that Israel will always be a safe place for the Jewish people."

"Well, that's wrong," he replies without missing a beat. Shocked at suddenly realizing what all the talk of winds of war must sound like to him, I hold his hand as we're walking and tell him clearly, "No, it's not wrong. We really are safe here. It will be all right."

But that night, as I'm putting him to bed, I can tell that he's not convinced. I sing to him and rub his back, assuring him that Israel is strong, that the United States will help protect us, and that we're always going to take care of him. I bundle him up against the surprisingly chilly night, and all that's sticking out of his covers are his head and his hands, which, I suddenly notice, aren't little boy hands anymore—they're getting to be big boy hands. I'm struck by the incongruity between his big boy hands and the way he's desperately clutching his blanket, with its worn corner, the blanket that he'd almost given up in the last few months but now seems to need more than ever.

My God, I say to myself. He's only eight years old. Why does he have to go to sleep worried about missiles and gas masks? "Everything's going to be fine," I whisper to him as he relaxes and begins to fall asleep. "Nothing bad is going to happen to us. We're going to be fine."

He falls asleep, and I wonder: Does he believe me? He's so little. He deserves to believe that things will be OK, doesn't he? At least for now?

NOVEMBER 7, 2001

MANHATTAN

It's been just under two months since the attacks on the World Trade Center. I've been to New York a few times for business since September 11th, but I haven't yet had time to go to Ground Zero. Today I have a few extra hours before my flight to Tel Aviv, and a friend—a rabbi who's been very involved in the relief effort and has a pass to get into the police-protected barricaded area itself—agrees to take me down. I haven't explained why I want to go down there, but he knows about my cousin who did not survive in the second tower, and he knows what we've been living through during the past year. With no questions asked, he agrees to take me.

He picks me up on Eleventh Avenue in the early afternoon, and we drive south towards where the World Trade Center used to be. As we get closer, there are people on the sides of the streets holding up large placards—"God Bless You," "God Bless America," "God Bless the Rescue Workers"—and I'm struck by the fact that almost two months after the attack, people are still so moved. Back home, we sweep up the glass, bury the dead, and clean off the street so that by the next morning, or the day after at the latest, there's little record of what happened. The glass merchants are used to replacing an entire storefront at the drop of a hat, and you can get your store painted at virtually any hour of the day or night. There's something healthy here, it strikes me, about recognizing what a sickening assault on life these attacks are, no matter where they happen. We're not even at Ground Zero yet, and in a way I didn't even remotely expect, I feel a pang of jealousy for how new this is here, for the sense of outrage. It must be nice not to be used to this.

We park the car and take vests, helmets, and breathing apparatuses out of the car. Even here, a few blocks away, there's a stench in the air that makes it hard to breathe. Helmets on and masks over our mouths and noses, we begin to walk to "the pit." I'm struck by the calm, the cleanliness, the order. Newly installed chain-link fences everywhere, signs indicating who can and cannot enter each area. Soot-covered windows, most of which now have phrases etched with someone's gloved fingers: "We Will Never Forget." "God Bless America." And deference. Men in suits speaking respectfully to the hard hats. The hard hats nodding to us. Everyone making room for everyone else. It's a construction site now in many ways, but there's an abiding awareness of what happened here, and none of the typical shouting and crassness that you expect at a construction site. This is a people newly touched by this sort of evil, and they seem humbled, deferential, respectful. This is, quite clearly, now holy ground.

We reach the edge of the pit and just stand there. Despite the fact that I'd been down to the WTC more times than I can count, I now can't figure out exactly where I'm standing. With the Towers gone, it's impossible to get my bearings. I remember bringing Avi to New York City last May for the birth of my newest nephew, and taking him down here. It was a cloudy day, so we decided not to spend the money to go to the observatory at the top; instead, I took him to the base of one of the Towers and showed him how to look all the way up to the very top. As the clouds moved slowly by, the building had seemed to be moving, that if we weren't careful, it would actually fall over.

Now I try to envision exactly where we were when we were here, the last time I was down here. And I cannot figure it out. All that's left is a huge pit, where the Towers used to be, and buildings all around with their facades blown off. I somehow feel like a voyeur peering into the rooms of those buildings; something about them, unexpectedly exposed without the outer wall, makes them seem like an innocent person unexpectedly stripped of their clothes. Desks, chairs, computer monitors just sitting there, thirty floors up. All normal, except the wall is gone, completely blown off, and of course nothing is normal. I turn away and look into the pit.

Cranes are still working to get enormous steel girders out of the tangled pile and onto trucks waiting to cart them away. I watch as the gigantic crane reaches down, grabs a piece of steel, lifts it up, and begins to swing it over to the truck. And to my amazement, as this happens, the air is suddenly filled with a thick black plume of smoke and soot. Even with the mask over my nose and mouth, the stench is revolting and it's hard to breathe. The air is black now, but aside from me, no one seems particularly surprised by this. The firefighters along the edge of the pit are ready, and as the smoke fills the air and blocks the view of the sky, half a dozen fire hoses drench the area where the crane is digging, and gradually the soot stops rising. Mesmerized, I watch this ritual for a while. A piece of metal hoisted up, black smoke blocking our view of the clear blue sky. Firefighters and their hoses, and the gradual return of the blue.

I find myself staring up, searching for the blue sky in the midst of all this. Every few minutes, the gentle New York breeze shoos the soot away and the blue returns. There's an eerie peace and tranquillity here, a predictability of the process that will continue for days to come. Metal will be moved, the fires will smolder. Someone will hose down the work area, and within a few minutes the blue sky will return. The smoke will be gone.

And in a strange way, I find myself jealous of that normalcy that is bound to return, even to here. Yes, this is a changed country, a wounded city, and some things will never be the same. The loss of life was beyond horrendous, the suffering of those left behind virtually indescribable. But here, the president assured his nation that this won't go on, that he will stop this. At home, our prime minister gets on TV and tells us "we must prepare for a long and drawn-out conflict. This will not be over soon, and we must be strong." Here, security is much tighter. The evil that did this is being pursued across the world, and the sheer size of the rest of the buildings downtown seems to say, "Wounded, but not destroyed." This city will bounce back, and I wonder, after whatever is built here is built, how much will really be different? Was this about a horrid attack, or a changed way of life? I suspect that it was the former, and I feel guilty for the envy that I can't push away.

The World Trade Center was attacked because it's a symbol. That does not detract from the horror or the evil, but it does mean that most Americans are basically safe. I suspect that if you're having pizza in Madison, Wisconsin, or sipping coffee at the 7-Eleven in Boise, Idaho, you're OK. Unwittingly, I wish we had places like that where I live, places that, because they're not symbolic, are not on anyone's list of targets.

The problem, of course, is that our whole country is a symbol. And no place is safe anymore.

After a while, we make our way back to the car, walking but not talking. There's virtually nothing to say. We go to the trunk, return our vests, helmets, and masks, and drive away. I'm off to a meeting at Forty-eighth and Park, and my friend drops me off nearby. Now I'm in a different world. A world seemingly untouched by everything that happened down there at that pit, a world in which life has apparently returned almost to normal.

Except I still can't breathe. The stench won't leave my nostrils. I buy a Coke from a street vendor, figuring that might make a difference. It doesn't. Two months later, and the fire is still smoldering. Two months later, and the remnants of that sheer evil still block out the sun, still make you gasp for breath.

I glance at my watch. Just about bedtime for the kids in Jerusalem. And I wonder: How do you put out a fire that spews forth from deep in the land, a fire that seems willing to burn forever? How do you extinguish the smoldering ruins of what used to be, before they hide clear blue sky forever?

HOME TO STAY

Introduction

In the summer of 1998, my family and I embarked on what we thought would be a one-year sabbatical in Israel. We'd been living in Los Angeles for just about fifteen years, and it was time for a break. Our kids were growing up quickly, and we thought that a year away would be good for all of us. At work I'd been building a new school for the training of rabbis, the first such school to be founded in the United States in many decades. It was very exciting work; I enjoyed watching the students grow; I loved the teaching that I was doing. But it was also all-consuming work, as I crisscrossed the country recruiting faculty and students and doing the political work that getting our new school accepted in the "mainstream" required. It was exhilarating but exhausting, and—as my wife constantly reminded me—it was time to take a break and regroup. Otherwise, she said, the kids would be out of the house before I stopped to breathe.

Just as Beth and I were talking more and more about our need for some time away, I was invited by the Mandel Foundation to be a Fellow at the Mandel Institute in Jerusalem for the next academic year. The Foundation is an internationally respected organization that trains advanced Jewish professionals in a variety of programs, and they made me an offer I couldn't refuse: Come to Israel. We'll give you a stipend you can live on, assign you an office, a computer, and a secretary, and you can write anything you'd like, read anything you want to read, study with our faculty in any way that appeals to you, and use this year to think about how you'd like to develop the rabbinical school you're running. Then, after the year, you just pack up and go home. No strings attached.

It was a fantastic offer and the timing was perfect, so we jumped at the opportunity. We assumed that this year would give our kids a chance to learn some Hebrew and to experience a culture very different from the one they were growing up in in West Los Angeles. The year, I imagined, would give me a chance to think, to read, and to write a couple of books I'd been planning for a long time. And I'd get to study with a world-renowned faculty in an institute that had an international reputation for excellence. Then, we assumed, we'd go back to Los Angeles and get on with life.

We took that trip, and spent the year in Jerusalem. I wrote one of the books that I'd planned, and though I didn't get around to writing the other one, I wrote a lot. Jerusalem is a city that seems to overwhelm its inhabitants, and there are few places in the world more complex and interesting than Israel. So, as we lived through that year, I instinctively chronicled many of our experiences in e-mails to friends, some letters to my family, and many other little vignettes that I didn't actually send anywhere, but just wrote for the sake of making some sense of everything I was seeing and feeling.

Different people do different things to relax and to process their lives. I write. It's what I love to do, and throughout that sabbatical year in Jerusalem, I found myself writing about our experiences late at night, early in the morning, and once or twice even on the laptop as we drove in the car.

But early in our year, in ways that we certainly didn't expect, we found ourselves falling in love with life in Israel and thinking seriously about staying beyond the one year, and even for good. On many levels, Israel felt like home in ways that America never had. Living in Jerusalem afforded us a chance to be at center stage during one of the most dramatic episodes of Jewish history—the creation of the first modern Jewish state. And perhaps most important, Israel seemed to us a virtually perfect place to raise our children.

Coming from Los Angeles, our kids couldn't believe how accessible and safe Israel was. In L.A., we scarcely let them cross the street by themselves, much less take the bus to the mall or roam around for hours when we had no idea where they were. But Israel was completely different. It was, and still is, a society in which children are much more independent, in which everyone, from all socioeconomic levels, rides the city buses, where our kids could play in the afternoon for hours without telling us where they were going, where they could go to the market and "buy" some food just by signing for it and by telling the merchant that their parents would come by later and pay, where our then-twelve-year-old daughter could—and did—come home by herself from a friend's house at one-thirty in the morning without us having any reason at all to worry about her.

And Israel is a stunningly beautiful country. The deserts, the mosques, churches, and synagogues that are hundreds of years old, waterfalls when you least expect to find them—we drank all this up during that "vacation" year, like kids in a candy store. But most important, of course, during the year that we were on sabbatical in Jerusalem, Israel seemed poised for peace. Prime Minister Benjamin Netanyahu, who had alienated the Palestinians, the American president, and much of the Western world, was voted out of office, and Ehud Barak, a popular former general and army chief of staff, was voted in. Barak promised that peace was at hand, and no sooner than he had been elected, ran off to Syria and then to the Palestinians to close what he thought would be rather quick deals to end the decades of war.

It was, in short, a virtually idyllic time. Our children were thriving, the country was beautiful, work was great, and peace was at hand. What more could you ask for?

So, several months later, after seemingly incessant discussions and late-night conversations, we decided to "pack it in" and to try to make a life in Israel. We sold our house in Los Angeles, left the jobs we'd been planning to come back to, shipped all our earthly possessions to Israel, and started out anew. What followed were two great years, years in which our kids grew and learned a new language, years in which I adjusted to a new professional life after almost fifteen years in my previous place of work, years in which we were buoyed by the excitements and challenges of creating a new chapter in our life as a family, years in which Israel thrived and moved slowly towards peace with her Palestinian neighbors. In many ways, it seemed that things simply couldn't have been better.

And then everything came crashing down.

At the end of September 2000, just as we were beginning our third year of life in Israel, hostilities broke out between the Palestinians and Israel. People referred to this period in different ways. Some called it the "second Intifada." Some called it the "El Aksa Intifada," after the name of the mosque that Ariel Sharon had visited just days before the violence broke out. But no matter what people called it, it was a war. It was a low-grade, drawn-out war of attrition, which left us in a country radically different from the one we had moved to. Suddenly we discovered that we'd taken our kids from the comfort and security of suburban life in Los Angeles not just to the Middle East, but to a Middle East ravaged by war, still consumed by a conflict that is the world's oldest, still beset by a conundrum that simply defies solution.

Particularly during that year, I wrote a lot more. I wrote e-mails to friends about what was happening. Sometimes, late at night, after the evening news made it virtually impossible to fall asleep, I wrote little pieces that I just kept on my computer but never showed to anyone else. With time, the e-mails that I wrote to a group of thirty or forty friends began to take on a life of their own. Friends forwarded them on to others, a few national Jewish organizations sent them to *their* e-mail lists, and with time it became clear that the letters that I was writing to a few dozen friends were being circulated to literally thousands of people. Eventually a few of those e-mails were forwarded to an editor at the *New York Times Magazine*, and excerpts were published there, too.

In some ways, of course, it was a little strange that personal notes I'd first been sending just to friends were getting such wide attention. At times my wife was a bit concerned that we were living in a fishbowl as the details of our lives were forwarded back and forth across the globe, but by the time I realized how widely these letters were being distributed, I'd come to feel that they were potentially important, that they told a story about Israel and her citizens that the press and journalists were simply not telling. For what mattered, I felt then and still feel, was not only who was killing whom, but what all this meant for the lives and dreams of the people who lived here—people on both sides of the political divide. So I kept writing and e-mailing.

As this e-mail phenomenon began to take off, a few friends suggested that I gather the material into a book. At first I resisted the idea, but with time I began to reconsider. Eventually I decided to give it a try. Fortunately, even though I hadn't saved many of the letters that I'd sent out, my brother, Elie, and some close friends had saved virtually everything, and over the course of a few months, I was able to retrieve most of those letters. What follows here are portions of that material. Some of this book is comprised of the e-mails that I sent out over those years, some to groups of friends, others to my brother. Other chapters are pieces that I wrote and never sent anywhere. Still other sections consist of material that I wrote after the fact to give a context for what had been happening back when I'd written those letters so many months earlier.

As I gathered all this material, I realized that these letters and ruminations tell a story about a seemingly endless struggle. Specifically, they show how we and many others like us slowly came to the painful realization that peace was not just around the corner, as we had thought, but quite the contrary, was actually further away than it had ever seemed. In some ways, this book is a chronicle of a loss of innocence—ours, and that of our children.

There is nothing sadder in war than the children who are its victims. And this war has had more than its share of child victims. Many Palestinian children, urged by leaders in their community to leave school and throw stones and Molotov cocktails at Israeli soldiers, have tragically died in the conflict. And Israeli children have died too. They've been killed by snipers, by suicide bombers, by rock throwers, by enemies they didn't even know they had.

With time, though, I began to realize that our children, like all their Israeli friends and like many other Israeli children, were also victims of this war. They weren't killed or injured, thankfully, but they slowly grew to understand that there were actually people in the world who were searching for an opportunity to kill them. As the war unfolded from October 2000 on, I watched the subtle but undeniable impact that this year was having on our kids. They'd moved from the protected and secure environment of West Los Angeles, where all the adults they knew cared about them and loved them, to Israel in 2000–2001, where they were suddenly very real targets. That changed much about the way they saw the world. For me, this is one of the most harrowing parts of this story. That, I still believe, is the part of the story that will leave its deep and ugly scars well into the next generation.

So as I began to gather the letters and the vignettes that I'd written, I focused mostly on the material that dealt with children. Our children, "their" children. Dead children and living children. But children all, children whose lives and whose outlooks on the world would never be the same. This is the story of what Israel was, and what Israel became, seen and heard through the eyes and ears of our kids, or through our own eyes and ears as we thought about our kids and the battles into which we'd unwittingly brought them.

It's the story of a time in which peace gave way to war, when childhood innocence evaporated in the heat of hatred, when it became difficult even to hope. Like countless other Israeli parents, we tried to make our kids' lives manageable and meaningful, despite it all. What our children learned, what they lost, and how, in the midst of everything, they taught us all over again what it is that really matters—that's what this book is about.

Before

It's a Strange Story We Tell

- - - - - - - - - - - - - - - - - -

It's a strange tale we Jews tell, this story about a call that only one man can hear. The call to go to a new place. To leave everything, and everyone, behind. We tell it so often, hear it so regularly, know it so well, that there doesn't seem anything particularly peculiar about it. But there is.

> 12 *The* LORD *said to Abram, "Go forth from your land, the place of your birth, and from your father's house to the land that I will show you.*
>
> *²I will make of you a great nation,*
> *And I will bless you;*
> *I will make your name great,*
> *And you shall be a blessing."*
>
> *⁴[So] Abram went forth as the* LORD *had commanded him, and Lot went with him. Abram was seventy-five years old when he left Haran. ⁵Abram took his wife Sarai and his brother's son Lot, and all the wealth that they had amassed, and the persons that they had acquired in Haran; and they set out for the land of Canaan.*
>
> —BOOK OF GENESIS

Why do people do such things? Leave their home, the place where they were raised, the place from which their parents came, to go to some unseen destination, "the land that I will show you"? America is a country of immigrants, of course. Many of our grandparents, great-grandparents, and great-great-grandparents did exactly that, but they could tell you what they sought in the United States. A better place. A more secure life. They were looking out for themselves, to be sure, but mostly for their children. They left everything behind in order to give their kids a better tomorrow, a future with more hope. Would they have possibly dreamed of going to a place where their children would live with less security, with more danger, with nightmares that were real?

This story we tell doesn't talk about that. Or does it? It seems to promise Abram—not only the first Jew, but the first wandering Jew—something better, more secure, more ideal. "And I will make of you a great nation, and I will bless you. I will make your name great, and you shall be a blessing."

So Abram heeds the call and sets out. The future will be bright, he is assured—he cannot yet know the cost. We, too, prefer happy endings, so we usually stop telling the story there, so that everything more or less works out. But deep down, we know that *that* call was only the prelude. The cost was yet to come.

22 *Some time afterward, God put Abraham to the test. He said to him, "Abraham," and he answered, "Here I am." ²And He said, "Take your son, your favored one, Isaac, whom you love, and go to the land of Moriah, and offer him there as a burnt offering on one of the heights that I will point out to you." ³So early next morning, Abraham saddled his ass and took with him two of his servants and his son Isaac. He split the wood for the burnt offering, and he set out for the place of which God had told him.*

—BOOK OF GENESIS

Again God calls Abraham, and again Abraham heeds the call. Now, for the second time, Abraham willingly goes to God's destination, "one of the heights that I will point out to you." Again he sets out for the place of which God had told him, but this time it is not with his entire family, but only with his son. Today he heads not to the future of a blessing that beckons, but to the sacrifice of his child, his very key to that future.

The tradition says, of course, that Abraham passed the test with flying colors. In the end, the angel tells him not to sacrifice his son and points out a ram stuck in a thicket that Abraham can offer in his stead. But did he truly pass the test? Is this really what God wanted? Can this be right? Is this what a parent—any parent— should do? Is it ever OK to sacrifice your child? For anything at all?

Most of us are convinced that we would do differently. We would not heed a call that demanded the sacrifice of our children. No matter where the call came from, or what it said. But what would happen if we woke up one day and found ourselves in that very same land, and it suddenly dawned on us that even without knowing that we'd heard the call, we were actually sacrificing our children? We would leave, right? Wouldn't that be the only sensible thing to do? Leave and save the children. That's what we'd have to do, no?

Or perhaps not. Could it be that there is something so subtle, so magical, so intoxicating—and so dangerous—about this land that it leads parents to willingly sacrifice their children?

July 1998: Landed

Weizman Urges Arafat to Meet with Netanyahu

President Ezer Weizman yesterday called on Palestinian Authority Chairman Yasser Arafat to meet with Prime Minister Binyamin Netanyahu to show he is committed to furthering the peace process.

JERUSALEM POST: Thursday, July 21, 1998, page 3

Dear Elie:

We're here, and just wanted to let you know that we made it safe and sound. Hard to believe we're here, but we are. And it feels great. I've got to admit, Jerusalem is still a thrill, no matter how often I fly over here. After all those hours of flying, when the descent starts and you can see the Tel Aviv shoreline from the plane, it's still home in some strange way. I hope that the kids will learn to love Israel as much as we do. If that's all they get out of the year, it will be well worth it.

To tell the truth, the trip wasn't half bad. Neither of us was terribly looking forward to the transatlantic flight with three kids, but I have to admit that it wasn't nearly as bad as we expected. The plane was filled with quite a few groups of teenagers headed to Israel for one summer program or another, and even though Beth said, upon surveying the crowd we'd be sharing air and space with for twelve long hours, "Oh, no, I hate teenagers," the truth is that the teenagers saved the day. Sitting behind us were a pair of sisters from the Bay Area, each

14

with her own Game Boy, which they were amazingly enough eager to
share with Tali and Avi. So the big kids were in heaven for many
hours, and even Micha got befriended by a different kid on the flight
and was happily engaged. It was still a long haul, of course, but the
kids were great, and we found free baby-sitting. What could be bad?!

As you can obviously tell, we're also hooked up to e-mail, so
we're now reachable. Pretty amazing. The person that I'd arranged to
have meet me at the house so I could buy a used monitor from him
(didn't seem worth dragging the good Trinitron here for eleven
months) was right on time, and with one phone call I got an account
with what seems to be the popular ISP around here. So far, so good.
Maybe this isn't the Third World, after all.

The relative smoothness of the whole affair kind of reminded me
of our getting here twenty-nine years ago with Mom and Dad.
Remember any of it? I remember very little (except, of course, for hating the whole two years here, but that's a different story!). But Dad
still tells that story about how they got lost on the way to finding the
Merkaz Kelitah [Immigrant Absorption Center] where we were to be
staying and asked a passerby how to get there, to which the reply was
"I don't know, but I'll tell you." So far, we haven't had any of that classic Israeli nonsense, though I suppose it's not far off.

But to tell you the truth, none of that worries me very much.
They were moving here for good, and barely knew the city. We know
the city, and are just here for the year. Dad had to deal with the complex world of academic medicine in Israel, and I'm on sabbatical—no
new work culture to have to get used to.

The truth is, though, it's more than that. Each time we come here,
I'm struck by what a different country they went to. Kind of backward,
at war (and not only technically) on a variety of fronts, and still in its
very nascent stages. I suppose I'll get a better sense of this in the weeks
to come, but Jerusalem seems different now. For one thing, I've got my
e-mail, and there are many fewer soldiers on the streets. Feels more like
Europe than the Middle East (except for the heat, which is pretty bad
right now). Remember how Mom and Dad were told they'd have to

wait eighteen months to get a phone line—another of Dad's favorite peeves three decades later? That era seems gone, if my experience of getting an ISP account in one day is any indication. We wanted some cash, so we went to an ATM right around the corner, stuck in our card from our Los Angeles Home Savings checking account, and voilà! The money still looks fake and amateurish, but well, we got it without any of those legendary bank lines that I still remember from when we were kids, so who's complaining? I wonder what would have happened if this was the country we'd moved to in 1969. Think we'd still be here? Hard to know.

Either way, though, I'm excited for the kids to have this experience. They're actually outside now, exploring the neighborhood, and looking at them from the window up here, I was reminded of us here, at almost the same ages, living only a mile or two away. I hope that this will be good for them. I think it will. Tali's a bit nervous, but I don't think that the boys have figured out yet that school will be in a language they don't speak. Well, we'll get there when we get there. Thank God for summer vacation!

That's about the story here. We're off to stock the kitchen, show the kids around a bit, take them out to dinner, and get this little adventure under way. Mostly, just wanted to give you this new e-mail address and let you know we're here. We'll be living in Mom and Dad's apartment for the first few weeks until our rental is ready (hard to believe that they've held on to a place here for thirty years—I guess for them, too, connections here run pretty deep).

Drop a line. Miss you already. Off to brave the heat.

Love,
D

August 1998:
Throwing Out a Childhood

Hey, Elie:

Glad all's good on your end and that the summer house is working out well. We could use a little beachfront property here! It's been so damn hot, I can't tell you. Each day hovers at around one hundred degrees or a bit more, and at night it seems to cool down to a balmy ninety-five. Even Jerusalem is that hot, something I didn't remember, and it's not dry, either. I hate the heat—always have, probably always will. You walk outside, and even before you get to the car, it's like a wall of heat is blocking your way, and if you push yourself to make it through, you're drenched and disgusting. I'd be perfectly happy hanging out at the Jerusalem pool or taking it easy, but we've been touring around as much as possible.

As you recall, the apartment doesn't have any air conditioning, so we leave the windows open at night to get at least a bit of a breeze in here. It helps a little, and it adds a quaint dimension to the very early mornings here. With the windows open, I sometimes wake up very early, so I make myself a pot of tea and sit in the living room and read. In the very early hours of the morning, when there are still very few cars on the road, I can hear the muezzin chanting out their call to worship from one of the mosques, probably near or in the Old City. And then, a few moments later, I hear the church bells from the Dormitian Abbey on Mount Zion, just as the chants of the local Sephardic synagogue down the street come wafting in. The chorus of the muezzin, the chimes, and the Sephardic melodies is a great way to wake up and be reminded how different is the place you are now from where you were just weeks ago.

But leaving the windows open also has its downside. We've now been woken up a few times at about 2:00 A.M. with kids playing soccer on the street in front. At first I thought it was outrageously inconsiderate that their parents let them play soccer on the street in the middle of the night, but now I think it's kind of cool that parents can let their twelve- and thirteen-year-old kids play outside in the middle of the night with not a single worry. It might not be the neighbor-conscious approach that we're used to from L.A., but then again, in L.A. we didn't let the kids out of our sight on the street; here, if Tali or Avi had any inclination to play on the street at 2:00 A.M., there'd be no rational reason not to let them.

That's the big difference between Jerusalem and Los Angeles, between Israel now and Israel back when we were kids here. Do you remember how Mom and Dad were always telling us that we couldn't pick up anything interesting that we saw lying on the ground because it could be rigged to a bomb, and how they explained that children were getting killed by bombs that were attached to toys and other items that appeared to have been abandoned? I remember it clearly, and still find myself shying away from anything left on the ground.

But now things are different. No one seems to worry about that anymore. Each time Micha bends over to pick something up, I have an instinctive reaction to grab his hand and to remind him that it's dangerous. But it's not. It's a stupid little thing, but I think it gives a sense of how different things are now. The business with the Arabs probably isn't completely over yet, but at least kids don't have to live in fear of toys on the ground. Life here is getting normal. Not your average American suburb yet, to be sure, but it's getting there. Kind of nice, after all these years.

The kids are doing great, by the way, though even they, who had seemed immune to the heat at first, are now beginning to melt. Beth is on this intense "we've got to see something new each day" kick, I suppose because she realizes school is going to start soon, my work is going to get a bit more serious, and we've only got a relatively few months to get the kids to have a feel for Jerusalem and the rest of the country. The kids are making fun of her and saying, "Time to get in the car—Ema heard about a rock we haven't seen yet." But it's in good humor. They actually do seem to enjoy most of the places she drags them to.

Actually, though, what I think she wants is for them to have more than a feel for Israel. She wants them to love it here the way she does. It's just in her bones—in a way that it's still not in mine, as much as I love seeing Tel Aviv from the plane as we land. With her, it's different. She just adores this place. I'm having a great time with her and the kids, but even though it *is* very different from the place that I remember as a kid, and there's obviously much to love, I don't begin to match her infatuation with it.

In all, we're having a great time. It's amazing what being on vacation can do for you. Even when I've taken a month off in the past, I was always on the phone with the office, checking e-mail, getting faxes, planning what was going to happen when I got back. A year's a totally different experience. This time I've completely let it go, and the relief is unbelievable. I'm already getting a bit worried about what it will be like to go back at the end of the year, though as this is only August, spending more than a moment on that concern seems a bit premature!

Unfortunately, though, I'm actually heading out to the airport in a few hours for my trip back to L.A. to get the academic year started there. I'm not much in the mood to leave Beth and the kids, and as we've only been here for a few weeks, I don't feel the need to get out of Israel or to recharge my U.S. batteries. But there's no choice in the matter, so I'll try to make the best of it.

So here's the main reason for this note. The day that I get back to Jerusalem after this jaunt, we're moving to our rental apartment in Bakk'a and are heading out of the apartment Mom and Dad have held on to all these years. (That means that Beth will more or less have to pack up the place on her own, though after what we did to prepare to leave the house in L.A., repacking our ten duffel bags probably won't seem like much of a big deal.) Since we're leaving Mom and Dad's apartment and it's now going to pass on to other people, it seems we're going to have to throw out a bunch of their stuff.

In ways that I didn't anticipate, it's going to be strange to leave this apartment. It's still filled with lots of the detritus from thirty years ago. For example, some of their furniture from the living room is still here. Remember that classic '60's stereo cabinet? Still there. The plates are the same ones from back then. Lots of Dad's paintings are here (I took a few and put them in my office at the Foundation), and there are some other interesting things, too. Letters from Mom to Dad when he was traveling during their two years here, checkbook stubs and receipts—a life. That old black dial telephone that they liked so much (and that Dad still wants us to hold on to). A good number of Sabba [*Sabba* is Hebrew for "Grandpa"] Meir's books, too.

Now that Yoni's moving out, we have to get rid of lots of this stuff. Yoni [the author's youngest brother] doesn't want it in his new place, quite understandably, and we don't have room either. Mom and Dad said that they don't care about most of it (aside from the telephone, and a few other odds and ends), so a lot of it's going to get trashed.

Which is sad. I'm a bit surprised at how attached I feel to this apartment—even though I never lived in it—and to all the things in it that Yoni moved here from their previous apartment years ago. After all, I was the one who disliked being here for those two years as kids. I still have an incredible amount of respect for Mom and Dad and their taking a shot at living here, but I still hated it. I remember despising school, not liking the kids in the neighborhood, always feeling that I was slightly out of it because I never fully got the language. I hated being stuck between secular Israelis who thought we were religious fanatics and religious Israelis who thought we were some strange version of secularists. I remember the day that Mom and Dad told us that we were moving back to the States, how you and Yoni cried, and how I was secretly thrilled but didn't want to say anything.

And still, despite all that, it's hard to part with all the reminders of those years. I was glad we left, have resisted Beth's desire to move here for years, and still—I realize how much of who I am was shaped by that experience. The strangest part of the whole thing is the fact that we're now bringing our kids to have exactly the same experience that I did. Go figure.

Well, c'est la vie. Back to the apartment packing—it's a dirty job, but somebody's got to do it! If there's anything in the apartment that you remember that you want, let me know and we'll put it aside for you. Truth is, there's not lots of the kids' things here anymore. I don't know if Mom and Dad threw them out when we left after two years, or whether they brought them back to the States, or if they've gradually gotten thrown out over the past twenty-something years. But if there *is* anything that you want, we're happy to hold on to it for you. You can pick it up when you come for Tali's Bat Mitzvah in a few weeks, or we can stash it for you for the year and deal with it at the end when we pack up. I just don't want to dismantle your childhood without your consent. (After all, you were the one who liked it here.)

Anyway, off to the airport. I'll be in L.A. in two days, and will be there for about two weeks. My office number's the same as it always was, and I'll be staying at Josh and Bonnie's house in the evenings. I'm sure I'll talk to you in the next few days.

Love to all your girls,
D

September 1998:
Deaths in the Family, and a Very
Different Rosh Ha-Shannah

Hi, everyone:

A brief (or not so brief) note before I get back to real work (I absolutely *must* make some progress on the book I'm trying to finish) in a few moments. Yom Kippur begins tomorrow night, so I thought that I would write an update about life here over the past two weeks.

I think that the major impact during this time has been that our kids, especially the older ones, are getting a clear glimpse of how very different life in Jerusalem is, for better and not. It started most clearly at a Shabbat dinner three Friday nights ago.

We were invited to the home of some people we didn't know

well, but whom I had briefly met once. We went to their house after shul, and as our kids were exploring the apartment during the evening, they came across a picture of a soldier in uniform who looked a lot like the father in this family, but was clearly not him. One of our kids asked who it was, and the dad said it was his brother. Then, after an awkward pause, he added that the picture was taken shortly before his brother was killed in action in Lebanon about ten years ago. I don't think our kids had ever met anyone who'd lost anyone that close in any war, and they were clearly impacted. I wouldn't necessarily say shaken, but something got in about how immediate things are here.

Then, the next Friday night, we were invited across the hall in our apartment building to the home of people that we *really* didn't know. What the hell—one more Shabbat of not cooking, so we took it! They turned out to be lovely people, with six kids in an apartment just like ours, which our kids think is a tad tight with three kids. During the meal, as our kids were trying to learn all the other kids' names, one of the parents said that a certain child was named Boaz, and someone from our family (I no longer recall who) said that they liked that name a lot. The father said, "We like it too, but he's named for Michal's [his wife's] brother, who was killed in the army when she was two months pregnant."

The look on our kids' faces was pretty remarkable. Avi had a puzzled look, as if he were thinking, "Is this going to happen *every* Friday night?" What could we say? It won't, but it'll happen a lot more than anyone would like to believe. That verse from Exodus about the tenth plague, which speaks of the smiting of the firstborn and says that "there was no house in which someone wasn't dead" came to mind. It's true here, and the kids are learning that as a fact of life; tragically sad, but not abnormal in the way that it would be in the States.

The clincher occurred a few days later, though, after Beth and I had spent some time telling the kids how brave these two young people had been, how much they loved Israel, and how they were willing to give everything for the Jews to have a place to live. (Academics here are big-time into post-Zionism, a radical critique of the mythologies that once lay at the heart of Zionism, such as the idea that the Jews were always militarily outnumbered here, that we acted only in defense, or that Palestine was basically uninhabited when we arrived on these shores decades ago. But at home, we're still using the mythology of the previous generation; it's a lot simpler.) Anyway, a friend of ours comes over and somehow the weird coincidence of these two Friday nights comes up in conversation. Our friend, who knows both families, says, "Those two deaths were particularly bad."

It turns out that the first person, who was killed on his twenty-fifth birthday shortly after making aliyah from the States, was part of a platoon in Lebanon. They had sent a scout up to check something out, and when they heard shooting, they realized he had been ambushed. Our friend's brother went to get the scout. As he was trying to get to him, he was killed, and moments later, two others who went to get *him*, including the medic of the unit, were killed.

That was bad enough. But then our visitor tells us that the brother of our next-door neighbor, who was killed when he was eighteen, was coming off a watchtower on his base and was met by another group of soldiers on a training exercise. The officer of that group, in complete violation of policy, had his safety off and his finger on the trigger. Seeing someone on the watchtower he just didn't expect, he instinctively opened fire, killing Boaz (our neighbor's brother) on the spot.

Explain *that* to your kids. Tali hasn't said much about it, but Avi doesn't stop asking. He doesn't understand how an officer could get something like that wrong, why he didn't know that it *had* to be an Israeli on an Israeli tower, etc. But what he's obviously trying to figure out is how one mentally processes the absurd loss of life. In the States, he never heard anyone talk about someone dying, and here, he's looking for a family that hasn't had to deal with it. This sort of life makes no sense to him. What do you say? I have no idea. He's such a sensitive kid, and he doesn't get it. It doesn't scare him; it just makes him incredibly sad. I suppose that's what we'd want if we had to choose, but it's hard to watch.

Then I had occasion to take Avi to daven at a shul in the neighborhood, one I've liked for a long time and wanted him to experience. We were sitting towards the front next to the wall, and Avi happened to be sitting under a sort of poster that had the prayer for the welfare of IDF [Israel Defense Forces] soldiers on it. A man came over and asked Avi to move so *he* could sit there. Avi did, and afterwards I had to explain to Avi the story that I knew about that man (I'd heard it last year sometime). He was the one who bought that plaque/poster for the shul, shortly after his son was killed. Avi, now alert to the idea that this is not a simple business, asked how he was killed. I said nothing, but a friend sitting next to me decided not to mince words and told Avi that the boy had been part of one of two elite units in Lebanon that simply miscalculated. Each thought that the other was a group of terrorists trying to get across the border, and unleashed everything they had. Both units suffered horrible casualties, and this father sits under that *tefillah* every morning when he goes there to pray. What do you say to a nine-year-old about *that*?

Thankfully, we haven't had many more of those encounters lately. We went right from that to Rosh Ha-Shannah, which was great (in no small part because services were over at 11:55 A.M.). But it was there that the kids got to see a very different side of the country. They got to see that it's more than the fact that there are a lot of Jews here—it's a Jewish place.

We only had a ten-minute walk or so to shul in the morning, but even in that short time, we passed at least six or seven other services in progress. The entire neighborhood was filled with the sounds of Rosh Ha-Shannah. It was a very powerful experience. Everywhere, people were dressed in their finest. Life itself was Rosh Ha-Shannah. On the way home, since we got out a little earlier than the others, we could hear *shofarot* being sounded from every direction. Even Micha thought that was neat. Like a little kid watching fireworks and eager to see what the next ones would look like, he kept looking in every direction to hear where the sounds were coming from.

I was struck by how different this was from "High Holidays" in

Los Angeles, or in Dallas, where I used to work for Rosh Ha-Shannah and Yom Kippur. There, the synagogue was a refuge from the larger culture. We gathered together, brought in the new year with elegance and decorum, then emerged out of the synagogue into a mostly non-Jewish culture in which Rosh Ha-Shannah basically didn't exist. Here in Jerusalem, it was virtually the opposite. Decorum was nowhere to be seen (this is Israel, after all) and there was very little attention to elegant dress beyond a white shirt and nice pants, but the entire city seemed to breathe the air of Rosh Ha-Shannah. Even kids from non-religious families, riding their bikes around on the streets, seemed part of an atmosphere that was completely different from other days of the year. No matter who you were and what you were doing, this was Rosh Ha-Shannah. There was no escaping it. I think that our kids, each in their own way, saw that here you didn't fit Rosh Ha-Shannah into life—here, life itself *was* Rosh Ha-Shannah.

The other thing that the kids picked up for the first time was that only here, services in Hebrew are effectively services in the vernacular. I think that the older ones picked up how great it was to daven with several hundred people, all of whom understood exactly what we were saying. That, too, was part of what made this feel like home during these recent days. I've always been envious of my Protestant friends who can go to church and worship and know that everyone there is actually saying something they understand. Here, especially at moments when the liturgy was about restoring Jews to Jerusalem, the singing was unbelievable. As much as I liked getting out before noon, I could have stayed much longer.

Before I go on too long about this, a brief comment about the day after Rosh Ha-Shannah. In shul, they announced on both days that on the day after Rosh Ha-Shannah, which is the Fast of Gedaliah, a group called Oz Ve-Shalom (religious Zionists for giving back land for peace—a rather small group, as you can well imagine in this country of extremists) was having a morning service at Kikar Rabin, the square where Rabin spoke right before he was murdered. I decided that I definitely wanted to go, both to see what would happen and to show support. I imagined that it would be this huge mass of people and convinced a couple of friends to go with me.

We drove up to Tel Aviv, and when we got to Kikar Rabin, it was empty. There was not one person in the whole plaza. We were obviously in the wrong place, but parked and eventually found a small lobby in an adjacent cultural center. There were only about seventy-five people there, which I thought was kind of pathetic in a country of slightly under six million Jews (there's an ironic number, no?). What was immediately interesting, however, was that in the middle of all these obviously mainstream religious people (though with very leftist politics if they were there), there was a group of kids wearing t-shirts of the youth movement of the Labor Party. These kids were not at all religious. The girls were wearing pants (horror of horrors!); the boys didn't have their heads covered. For the life of me, I couldn't figure out what they were doing there.

Suddenly, in the midst of the very small group, I recognized Rabin's son, Yuval. He had obviously been asked to come, and these kids came to basically keep him company, as the religious crowd is definitely not his. But seeing him there at this service in memory of his father moved the whole experience to a different level.

When we got to the Torah reading, he got the third and final aliyah. When he was called up simply as "Yuval ben Yitzchak," it was enormously powerful. You could have heard a pin drop. After the end of the Torah reading, someone did an *El Maleh* [memorial prayer] for Rabin. The language was changed from the usual to *"hu yizkor et nishmat Yitzchak ben Nechmiah ve-Rosah, Rosh HaMemshalah ve Sar Ha-Bitachon, she-nirtzach ve-nishmad al yedei ben avlah . . ."*—"May He recall the soul of Yitzchak son of Nechemiah and Rosa, the Prime Minister and the Minister of Defense [Rabin had both portfolios at the time], who was murdered and obliterated by a son of evil." Again, the silence was unbelievable. It was also poignant to be at this service with all these nonreligious kids. They obviously don't go to such services very often, or probably ever, but ironically it was the loss of Rabin that got all these people together for that morning.

There were a few other interesting people in this very small crowd. Such as Yoel bin Nun, one of the founders of the Gush Emunim, a group that supported building settlements on the West Bank so it couldn't be given back. Bin Nun has since changed his tune and believes that the whole thing was a mistake. He typically walks around now with two full-time bodyguards because his former compatriots have threatened to kill him.

Why, you might ask, would they want to kill him? After Rabin was killed, bin Nun claimed (truthfully or not, no one knows) that he had a list of rabbis who had declared Rabin a *rodef* (something akin to traitor—the exact legal status would take too long to explain here), which in Jewish legal terms effectively made Rabin a legitimate target for murder according to that group's reading of Jewish law. Bin Nun, to my knowledge, never did divulge the list (if he indeed had it), but the reputation that he has for having even mentioned the idea that he might divulge the names of those rabbis means that to this day he still needs bodyguards at all times.

Menachem Froman was also in attendance. He's a very right-wing rabbi from a settlement called Teko'a, who also changed lately. He says that he tired of having his Yeshiva students come back from the army in body bags; it's just not worth it. He continues to live over the green line but also meets with Palestinians—including Yassir Arafat—to try to figure out some way to achieve peace (others say he just loves the publicity—who knows). He, too, is shunned by his community; politically, there's some reason that the residents of Teko'a can't depose him as rabbi of the settlement (I don't fully understand the politics of that). So he stays as a matter of principle, and they ignore him as a matter of principle. What a place this is.

After the end of the service we went outside, to the exact spot where Rabin was shot. I was struck immediately by how ugly the alley was. It's one of those half alleyway, half parking lot areas that are so common to Tel Aviv, and the sheer incongruity of the "nothingness" of the place seems wholly incommensurate with the magnitude of what happened there. On the ground, there's a small memorial that among other things reads, *"kan, ba-makom ha-zeh, nirtzach . . ."* "Here, on this very site, was murdered . . ." The repetition, it seemed to me, suggested the incredulity of the whole thing.

Minutes later, when we were a small group of about fifty people (some had left—this was a regular workday in downtown Tel Aviv), someone started to sing Hatikvah. On the street right by us, cars, trucks, and buses were careening by, but a few pedestrians did stop to see what the gathering was about. The singing of Hatikvah was moving beyond words. It's hard to describe how sad the whole thing was, how much has gone wrong with the country since that horrible night, and what a difference three tiny bullets can make in the course of a people and a country. Even after the crowd dispersed, my two friends and I just hung around a bit. There wasn't much that we could say; the tragedy and loss defy words. We drove back to Jerusalem without talking much.

The only other thing that I noticed was the graffiti on the wall of the alley. There are some "pop art" pictures of Rabin, and hundreds of slogans with sayings like "Peace, we miss you," "Shalom, Chaver," and most important, "Yitzchak—how can you ever forgive us?"

Good question, I thought. Whom do you begin to blame when a whole society is afire with extremism, when out of millions of people, only about seventy-five thought that his memory was worth recalling that day? It wasn't a hopeful moment.

But then again, someone told me later that the attendance this year was twice last year's, and four times that of two years ago. It'll take a lot of years, even at that rate, for the crowd to grow to make a difference, but maybe we're moving in the right direction. I don't know.

A brief conclusion regarding our gardener. We have a little garden in the back of the apartment we're renting, for which we needed to get a gardener. Someone in the building recommended an Arab man named Ahmed, so I told him to tell Ahmed to come by. It was supposed to happen yesterday, but Ahmed never made it. Turns out he's Palestinian. Because tensions are running high with the Palestinians and Hamas has "promised" to blow up an Israeli public bus, Israel has sealed the borders airtight. So Ahmed can't get here.

Of course, vignettes like Ahmed's are just one small glimpse into a much larger conflict that doesn't seem to want to end. Five years after the signing of the Oslo peace agreements with the Palestinians, the process of returning land to them is way behind schedule. Prime Minister Netanyahu claims that he believes that any territories turned over to the Palestinians will become bases for Hamas operatives, and when Hamas threatens to blow up buses, they play right into his hands and convince Israelis that maybe it actually is a good idea to hold up the process. But holding up the process creates extraordinary frustration among the Palestinians, frustrations that sometimes turn into violent, terrorist rage. They don't believe that there's anything they could do to convince Netanyahu that he's wrong, and that in effect Israel is scuttling the peace agreement now that Rabin is dead. Settling this ancient conflict is proving not so simple.

All that is a long way of explaining why Ahmed can't make a living and we can't get our garden weeded. Seems to me he gets the shorter end of the stick. I mentioned to Beth last night why the gardener didn't come, and she got mad. She said that she never agreed to hire a Palestinian, and she doesn't want to. Why? Because she thinks that hiring a Palestinian to do Jews' manual labor just intensifies the hatred and enmity between the two groups.

I, too, would rather have a Jew do the work. Part of the mythology of Israel that I was raised on was the notion that Jews would do all manner of work, that there would be no *avodah shehorah* [roughly translated as "dirty work"] that would be beneath us. We'd be the garbage collectors, the masons, the bricklayers, and the road-builders. That, we were told by Zionist ideologues like David Ben Gurion and A. D. Gordon, was what having a Jewish state meant. But that dream died a long time ago, and after the first Intifada, when it became dangerous to hire Palestinian workers, Israel began to grant workers' visas to hundreds of thousands of workers from Thailand,

Romania, the Philippines, and other countries where people are willing to travel in order to find work. Nowadays it's a combination of Arabs and other foreign workers who work the farms and do the manual labor.

But as much as I might not like the fact that the idealistic vision of a Jewish state (in which we share the responsibility for doing the manual labor) has long since died, I see no reason not to hire Ahmed. It seems to me that if he wants work, we actually help him by giving him an income, and it's not a bad thing for him to meet religious Jews who aren't (yet) crazed fanatics. Beth says absolutely not. No Palestinian gardener. So we compromised. I'll cancel Ahmed if she can find a Jewish gardener before he can get into the city. My prediction: Ahmed will be here in a few days. Life is complicated.

As if you didn't know that! Anyhow, with Yom Kippur just around the corner, our wishes to everyone for a year of all good things, but mostly peace. Pursuant to the dictates of the Mishnah, though I'm not sure the Mishnah would permit this via e-mail, all the Gordis clan deeply hope that we didn't do anything to hurt or offend you during the past year. If we did, we beg your forgiveness, and hope that the spirit of forgiveness that will be the subject of the liturgy this week will actually spread to the hearts of this people, who need it so desperately.

Gmar chatimah tovah,
D, B, and the kids

Unanswered Questions in
Moscow and Los Angeles

There's something strange about this year in Jerusalem, something eerie about how easy it was to get here, how natural living here sometimes seems. It's almost uncomfortable when I think about those people who desperately want to come here but cannot, and the ease with which I could move here if I wanted to, but don't. Some days, when I least expect it, I think of two very different memories of talking to people about the possibilities of making a life here.

The first is of a trip we took shortly after Beth and I got married. It's January 1982 and Beth and I are in Moscow. Like lots of our friends, we've signed up to visit Soviet refusnik families, to bring them books and other items their community desperately needs, and equally important, to smuggle out of Russia the names and addresses of others who want to leave but need to be "invited" in order to apply. Using those names and addresses, the Israeli government will see to it that they receive an "invitation" from a "relative."

Professional spies we're not, but in all, we've been pretty well prepared by our contact. We've been told to expect to be followed, which refusniks will be harder to find or reach, what kinds of things I should teach if we can get a study group together, what to bring for the bitter Moscow winter. We're a bit scared, but feeling good about this adventure.

On one of our first nights there, we meet a Moscow family on our list. We huddle in their tiny and freezing apartment, where they introduce us to their infant, who's in a stroller outside on the porch (the cold air makes babies healthy, we're told), and offer us some fruit compote or similar concoction. We pass along the books we've brought for them and then, ill-equipped as we are, try to encourage them and to bolster their morale. That, after all, is the task. We get to talking.

"When are you going to leave America and go to live in Israel?"

Uh-oh. Not one of the questions we were prepped for. It would be easy to lie and say something like "in two more years, when we finish school," but somehow, lying to people in their condition—out of work, hungry, spied on, harassed, all because they applied to leave the Soviet Union—seems a bit sick. But honesty here doesn't work much better.

"We're still thinking about it."

"Thinking about what?"

"About whether we're going to move to Israel." It's a bald-faced lie, and it fails miserably. We're not thinking about it at all. Beth would go in a second, but after my two years there as a kid when my parents made a stab at living in Israel, I've done my time. The way I see it, my sentence was commuted for good behavior. If I were stuck in this Moscow hell-hole, I'd go to Israel. But leave Manhattan, where we were living then when we were both in graduate school, and American Jewish life for that? No thanks. The issue of moving to Israel is not on our radar screen at all—and they can tell.

Now it's their turn to be incredulous. They don't say much, but we can both tell what they're thinking. You, you who have the option to go at any minute, just don't want to? What does *that* mean? How could you not want to be there?

I don't want to discuss it, and I don't want to be in the apartment any longer. They've written us off as phonies, it's clear, and a breath of the freezing Moscow night air would be better than this. We're out of their apartment not too long afterwards.

That night has stayed vivid in Beth's memory, and in mine. Often, when we find ourselves in some freezing city, one of us jokes and says, "Time to put the baby out on the porch." But for me the jokes are still a bit uncomfortable, almost twenty years later. Even now, whenever I think of them and their infant on the porch (and wonder if he survived that health spa), I recall the shame I felt at having no answer to their question. We're spoiled, I find myself thinking. They, who had nothing, wanted nothing more than to be allowed to live in Israel. They, who lived in constant fear, still opened their apartment to secretive Jewish study because they were desperate to fill their lives with Jewish words and tradition, all as a preparation for moving to the Jewish homeland.

And what about us? We, who have everything, don't want to make do with less than we have. Despite everything I write and teach about the Jewish experience in the modern world, am I afraid to face the logical conclusion of all those arguments and simply move here? What is it that I don't want to give up? Two cars? A big house? A great job? Physical safety? Since when has Jewish life been about being safe? In the scheme of Jewish history, how important are all the things that are keeping us in L.A.?

The other memory that now pops up frequently with that Moscow scene took place years later, in Los Angeles. It's somewhere in the early 1990s, probably '93 or '94. Shawn, a student of mine, is about to graduate from rabbinical school, and we're talking about some of the things that worry her. Like lots of about-to-be-rabbis, she's nervous about what to tell people when they ask questions she can't answer. "Tell them the truth," I try to reassure her. "Tell them you don't know, and then tell them why you don't know."

"I suppose," she says, sounding rather unconvinced. "After all, that's what you did with me."

"I did?" I had no idea what she was talking about.

"Years ago, when I first started school here, I was just back from two years in Israel, feeling very guilty about having left. Looking to make myself feel a little better, I asked you how you came to terms with not living in Israel."

"What did I say?"

"You said you had no good explanation, and that you struggled with it."

I certainly had no good explanation, but I don't remember struggling with it. In retrospect, the "struggle" line sounds a bit gratuitous, and again, I'm not feeling too great about my stance here. Shawn's married now, living and working in Los Angeles, and we're in regular touch with her, her husband, and her three boys. No longer students, they've become good friends. But seeing her consistently reminds me of that comment about still struggling with where I lived. It wasn't entirely true, I think. It's a lot easier to say that you're struggling than to genuinely be struggling.

I wonder, sometimes, which one of us I was deceiving.

November 1998:
Brewing Fanatics?

Hi, everyone:

The big news on this end is that we celebrated Tali's Bat Mitzvah a few weeks ago. It was a great day, but a subject for a different time. That major happening aside, I think we've having the most fun watching the kids, and seeing how quickly they're learning to view the world in an entirely different way. Until we got here, they assumed that life in L.A. as they know it is simply how life is supposed to be. Now, I think, they're beginning to see just how different other places can be.

The kids are doing fine. School is coming along, and they're beginning to make some nice friends. Talia made a lot of pleasant acquaintances at the beginning of our stay, but good friendships were obviously a little slower in following. Not surprisingly, Israeli kids are very reticent to befriend the American kids who are only here for a year. They get attached to someone who comes for a short period of time, and then the friend just disappears back to the States. It's understandable, but obviously hard for our kids. For they *will* disappear back to the States, but in the meantime, they need friends as much as anyone else. So it's nice to see them finally breaking into the social scene.

The older kids, Talia and Avi, are quickly becoming real Zionists! We're delighted about that, but the tendency to extremism here in this country, even with kids who are only visiting, is a bit disconcerting. Two quick examples of how this country can make you an extremist without your even trying:

On the night of Simchat Torah, I took Avi to "Yakar," one of the happening shuls in town. It's one of those modern-Orthodox synagogues known for being packed, for great singing, for a serious social consciousness, and for good intellectual fare during the week in classes and lectures. Over the past years, this has become the place to be and I like it a lot, even if most of the crowd is younger than I am.

Anyhow, on this particular night the street was packed with people dancing, and at one point, Avi and I had gotten out of the circle to chat with some friends. We were surrounded by hundreds, many hundreds, of men dancing in the street and women dancing inside the building, all in good spirits and a festive mood. To me, it seemed pretty idyllic. Thus I was a bit surprised when, in the middle of the conversation, Avi exclaimed, "Look, Abba, that's the most disgusting thing I've ever seen!" Imagining that he'd spotted a dead cat (there are lots of those here) or some such thing, I looked for something disgusting. Finding nothing, I asked him what he was talking about. He said, "A car driving on the same street where we're trying to dance!"

I thought that it was a very interesting phenomenon, this little boy who thinks that a car on the street disturbing Simchat Torah dancing is disgusting. On the one hand, it's great that this is a country in which religious life pervades things so completely that it seems normal to expect that on Simchat Torah, "of course the streets were meant for dancing. What else could they be for?!" But at the same time, I realized, it's not a far jump from there to objecting to cars driving on Shabbat, not just on holidays. How do you preserve the sense of the religious quality of a society without getting to a place where you think it's OK to impose it on other people? Not an issue that Israel's done a very good job with thus far, and I couldn't believe how quickly Avi had gotten immersed in all that. And this from a kid who's from a relatively moderate home.

The second time I got a sense of the feverish passions that modern Israel evokes, even in kids, was in response to TV and its coverage of the Wye Plantation negotiations a few weeks ago. The country was very tense about those negotiations, as it seemed here that the entire peace process—and Israel's international standing—was at stake. The peace process, to which Netanyahu had been opposed ever since the deal was signed in Oslo (because he doesn't trust Arafat or the Palestinians, and fears that Israel will give back land and then face a mortal enemy from a much worse strategic position), was stalled. So Clinton had basically forced Netanyahu to show up, but the prime minister wasn't prepared to make any serious concessions.

Without concessions, of course, Netanyahu would look inflexible, America would begin to pressure Israel even more, the Palestinians would (rightly?) cry foul, and the Israeli left would be more convinced than ever that as long as Netanyahu is prime minister, there is no hope for peace. But if Netanyahu did give in to pressure and did make concessions, he faced an extraordinary backlash from the right wing of the Knesset, including his own party. It appeared to be a virtual no-win situation with only the potential to ignite the region (politically, or worse), and the entire country seemed fixated on the news, every hour on the hour.

We were watching TV at home in our apartment while the negotiations were unfolding in Maryland. On CNN, some commentator pointed out that the pressure on Netanyahu was enormous, since if an agreement about how to move the peace process forward wasn't reached, Arafat would simply declare Palestinian statehood this May.

Avi said that he didn't understand, so I explained the whole thing very clearly and very carefully several times. After that, he still said, "Abba, I just don't get it." Somewhat exasperated, I asked him what he didn't get. He said, "I just don't understand how he can declare a state in the middle of *our* country!" Even after all my explanations about how Israelis and Palestinians both claim that this is their home, Avi still sees this as a place that is naturally ours, naturally Jewish, as if the Jewishness of the land is part of the state of nature. That's the danger, and that's the miracle. He feels that this whole place was made just for him and people like him. The miracle is that even though he doesn't even live here, he senses that Israel is home.

You don't have to think too long about what happened to world Jewry just over fifty years ago in Europe, or the way the British treated the Jews who tried to escape from Europe to Palestine, to appreciate what an extraordinary thing it is that Jews finally have a place where being completely at home seems natural. But the danger is that we can so easily forget that it's not just *our* home. Our kids live in a house where they hear constantly that Palestinians also have a legitimate right to a home, to a place that they, too, could call their own. We show our kids the ancient sites that are sacred to the Arab population here, and try to create for them some semblance of a balanced picture. We encourage Tali to learn Arabic well, because there is another people here that has to be taken seriously and understood. Our kids never hear any of the derisive comments about Arabs that I assume are uttered in other sorts of communities in Israel. But the danger is that no matter how much we try, I'm not sure how much of that is genuinely seeping in.

At the end of the day, there's something about having a home that simply seems overpowering. Avi senses that this is "his" home, and nothing else that we've explained seems to have had the same impact. Is the same thing happening in Arab homes not far from here, just in the opposite direction?

Well, so much for the two older children. Micha, on the other hand, is quickly becoming an ardent supporter of the Palestinian

Authority. He's not much enamored of the Jewish state. For the life of him, he can't figure out why we left a house with enough bedrooms, closets, showers, all his toys, his friends, all to go to a country where his school doesn't speak his language, it's hot in the day, cold at night, the car isn't fancy, etc. I think that he believes we've gone bananas. He's not miserable (or so we try to convince ourselves), but he's hardly in love with life here.

One cute moment. Micha has a friend who has *pei'ot,* those long curly sideburns that are typically seen in the Hassidic community. A really cute kid. His dad's the one who insists on the *pei'ot,* while his mom is much more modern about these things. So she has the kid's hair cut so that it leaves a tail in the back. Thus the kid is probably the only one on the planet with *pei'ot* and a "rat" tail. Micha asked Beth what the *pei'ot* were, and Beth explained the whole idea behind it. After which, Micha asked, "Do they always come in threes?"

So there's still room for hope. He's making some friends, learning a tiny bit of Hebrew, and dealing. Last night he asked Beth as he was going to sleep, "If we're Jewish, how come we don't live in Israel?" Out of the mouths of babes . . . I'm glad he didn't ask me. I've been asked that question before, and have never had a good answer. He's a smart kid, and you can't get much by him.

Beth is having a blast. She's studying every day at MaTaN, her women's yeshiva, and she and I are also getting to spend time together like we haven't been able to in almost seventeen years. Today, for example, we kept our afternoon schedule clear, went out to lunch, then walked to an artists' colony near the Old City to look at the many *Hannukiyot* [Hanukkah menorahs] that are now on display all over the country. Then we just took our time walking home (empty-handed, since the *Hanukkiyot* we had seen were mostly priced in the $2,000–$5,000 range).

We're also enjoying the freedom that not needing a baby-sitter is giving us. Our baby-sitter exists—in the form of a cell phone. It's pretty common here to leave the kids alone at night, and they have our number. In Jerusalem you can't be that far away, and one of the nice things about apartment living is that our kids could turn to almost anyone in the building to come help out. But of course, that hasn't been necessary, and we're feeling liberated by being able to just pick up and go out for coffee at night.

So, in all, we're having a great time. But still, there's some "getting used to" to be done. Suffice it to say that (truthfully) I had a dream last night that Beth and I were exploring our apartment, and we came across a walk-in closet we hadn't known was here. Freud, schmeud! But we're learning to do just fine with a lot less, and I think that the experience is healthy for the kids. They're learning that life can still be meaningful in a beat-up old car, a small (but admittedly very cute) apartment, and no extra space. We're all pretty spoiled Stateside, and I think that they'll now have an appreciation for how fortunate all of us are to live that sort of life.

Well, enough for now. Hoping that your year is also getting off to a good and successful start, and for those of you who observe it, that you'll have a good Yom Kippur. *Ketivah va-chatimah tovah.*

If a Place Can Make You Cry

With all the discussions of the Wye Plantation negotiations, land for peace, and the like, Israelis are on edge but obviously excited. True, Netanyahu's getting pressed hard, but we're going to have peace. Sooner or later, but not too much later. Anticipation is in the air. At cafes and restaurants, wherever the hourly news is broadcast, the entire crowd falls silent waiting for the latest update. Something, it seems, is about to happen. Could the fighting really be over? It's pretty amazing, given how different things were just a few decades ago.

All this constantly reminds me of a vivid memory from November 1977. Sadat was coming to Jerusalem. I had no TV in my Columbia University dorm, so my grandparents invited me over to watch with them. We sat on the long sofa, facing the television, and the drama unfolded. A plane from Egypt crossed the border, landed, the stairs rolled up. Handshakes all around. A band began to play. And suddenly, with Begin and Sadat standing at attention, the sounds of Hatikva, Israel's national anthem.

It was an awesome moment, watching the president of Israel's enemy standing at attention for her anthem. I listened intently, taking it all in, when suddenly another sound registered. I turned to my grandfather, a tall and large man, and the first thing I noticed was his wet shirt. Only then did I see the tears flowing.

In all the thousands of hours we had spent together, reading, studying, arguing, laughing, it was the first time I'd ever seen him cry. Suddenly I realized what this all meant. A lifetime of believing that this could never have happened was suddenly proven wrong. Could this have meant the end of the dying in a century bloodier than any our people have ever known? I don't know how much of that I understood then, but now I think I have a sense of why he was crying.

Even after a quarter of a century has passed, whenever someone mentions Sadat's coming to Jerusalem, my first thought is "It made my Sabba cry."

. . .

Eighteen years after Sadat landed, eighteen years to the month, I was in my parents' house. I was in Baltimore to give a talk but knew that it wasn't going to happen. No one would show, and I didn't care. Rabin had been shot two days earlier, and no one—including me—had any interest in my talk. Sitting on a couch once more, this time watching the Rabin funeral for the umpteenth time on tape. Speeches, of course, and military pomp and circumstance. But in the end, it boiled down to the simple truth. A body, wrapped in a *tallit*, is placed in the ground, and all the hopes of the last eighteen years seem to be buried as earth is shoveled into the grave. The army cantor begins to chant the *el maleh rachamim*, the traditional memorial prayer, and only when I accidentally brush my hand against my face do I realize that I've been crying.

. . .

Now, six years later, in this tempest-tossed city, I'm struck by everything I never let those memories teach me. By all the questions I never let those moments ask me. In retrospect, I'm amazed that never once during those moments did it occur to me to actually *go live* there, any more than it occurred to my grandfather, for that matter.

For after all, if there's a place in this world that can make you cry, isn't that where you ought to be?

November 1998:
Thanksgiving, After All

Without Joy, Netanyahu Wins Vote to Adopt Peace Agreement

Israeli Parliament approves American-brokered peace plan by significant majority, reflecting widespread, pragmatic acceptance of partitioning the Land of Israel; Prime Minister Benjamin Netanyahu, whose Likud Party was created to defend Jewish homeland from territorial compromise, turns his back on his party's founding credo.

New York Times: Wednesday, November 18, 1998, page A1

Hi again! Hope that everyone's Yom Kippur was meaningful and pleasant. Things here continue to be fascinating, so another few vignettes of life in Israel in the brief period since I last wrote:

Yom Kippur #1   Yom Kippur was fascinating. The services themselves were fine, but nothing out of the ordinary. What was most interesting was what happened outside of shul. When Kol Nidre was over, an announcement was made that there'd been a problem the previous year with religious Jewish kids from neighborhoods adjoining ours throwing rocks at Arab cars at one of the main intersections not far away. The person making the announcement said that our synagogue

45

was among those that had committed to putting an end to this custom this year. People were urged to put their kids to bed, and then to come out en masse to the intersection to make sure that no rocks were thrown. He also said that if anyone had a weapon at home (that elicited a laugh, since virtually *everyone* has a weapon at home!), some people should bring theirs to make sure that things didn't get out of hand. Struck me as being a bit like the Wild West. I had no gun, and opted out.

Yom Kippur *#2*   Instead of playing sheriff and policing those kids from the nearby neighborhoods to make sure that they didn't throw stones, we took our kids to Emek Refa'im, the main thoroughfare on the other side of our neighborhood. There's a custom among the non-religious kids to turn the road into a Rollerblading festival of sorts. As there is literally not a single car on the streets in Jerusalem on Yom Kippur, the many main drags become bike-riding, Rollerblading, and stroller-pushing fiestas. Our kids had a blast. They were obviously not Rollerblading on Yom Kippur, but they were awed by the sight of hundreds of people simply strolling down the middle of a street that is normally clogged with buses, trucks, etc. It was quite a scene.

Beth said that it depressed her. She was distressed that all these nonreligious people couldn't think of anything to make of Yom Kippur other than a roller derby. I suppose she's right, as usual, but I chose (also as usual) not to be as contemplative as she is. I think that I tend to be more immediately moved by the sight of Jewish life thriving in this country; she sees the long-term implications of what's happening here, sometimes for good, sometimes not. So on the eve of Yom Kippur, I was thrilled to see an entire city "shut down" by the holiday, making the streets safe for kids of all sorts. She, on the other hand, sensed that the complete secularization of Yom Kippur and its banal expression bespoke the beginning of the end of a Jewish consciousness in contemporary Israel. Maybe she's right. For all that we're enjoying this year of being together, it's also becoming clear how differently we see life here, and indeed, much of the world.

Gardener   Remember the gardener episode from the previous e-mail? There was a Palestinian gardener who was supposed to weed our backyard, but who couldn't get into the country. Well, it turns out that he never got in. The yard got to look horrendous, so eventually we hired a Jewish gardening company. Shortly after that, the gardener did get in, only to find that all his accounts had turned elsewhere in the meantime. I heard this from his contact in our building. Pathetic. Six kids, no money, and now no clients, because the border had to be sealed. It *did* have to be sealed, I think, but the mostly unmentioned human toll is beyond sad. You don't have to wonder too much about what his hungry kids think about Jews.

Bombs   The border had to be sealed recently because a few factions of Palestinians are still trying to set off bombs here. You obviously know about the bombs that exploded in Machaneh Yehudah a few weeks ago. I was at the Mandel Institute office, where the general rule is that quiet is a must. No loud talking, no stereos, etc. It's like a monastery in there, which is great (if you like working in silence, as I do). Anyway, there I was typing away at my computer when I heard a radio blaring downstairs. I said to myself, "They're going to get fired if 'so and so' hears this," but when I heard "so and so" down there with them, I got curious. I ran downstairs, and the whole office (fifteen or twenty people) was huddled around a radio. From the news broadcast, it was clear what had happened. A few of the people in the office were crying; the rest stood grimly by. I glanced at my watch; good—kids in school and not on buses. Gradually the details leaked out, we knew the basics, and people went back to their workstations, shaken but not terribly surprised.

That night, Friday night, the people in shul were experiencing a kind of unspoken euphoria. The attackers had been the only ones killed. Some people, I know, thought it was a genuine miracle (whatever that means). Everyone else admitted we were lucky. But I thought about the strange phenomenon of a city being ecstatic that someone blew themselves up while trying to blow us up. In most places, people would be horrified that someone tried to blow them up in the first place; here, that's not news anymore.

Gas Masks No sooner had the last of our family headed back to the States after Talia's Bat Mitzvah than Beth said to me, "Now we'll get to live a normal Israeli life for a while." First it was summer and getting used to the place, then the school strike, then the beginning of school, then the holidays, then the Bat Mitzvah. Now, we figured, life would be normal.

Enter Saddam. The next morning, the front page of the paper said that everyone should get their gas masks fitted, and those who didn't have them should visit the local dispensing site to get some. (We, as non-citizens, weren't eligible for free ones.) We decided to tell our kids about this before they went to school, since we knew they'd hear about it there. We explained to them that this was just a precaution, that we'd look into it, and we'd do whatever was necessary.

Avi was actually more upset than we expected. Every day, he asked what was going on with Saddam. He wanted to know how nerve gas worked, how gas masks worked, which room we'd convert into our "sealed room," etc. We kept telling him not to worry, and then he finally said, "If you're not worried, how come you're on the phone all day trying to find out where to buy gas masks?"

He was right, I realized. We were lying to him. So we gave up on the gas masks. That wasn't actually any more honest, but it seemed less upsetting to him. I told him we wouldn't need them, and the proof was that we weren't even going to get them. Somehow, that actually seemed to reassure him. It kind of reassured me, too (and resolved the question of whether to pay a thousand shekels—about $250—for something I didn't want to need and am convinced wouldn't work anyway). After all, in the Gulf War, no one died from nerve gas, but several kids did suffocate from masks that malfunctioned. We'll do without them, unless we absolutely need them. If we're too late, I guess we'll only know that for a couple of minutes.

Guess Who's Coming for Shabbat   A few weeks ago, they announced in shul that there was going to be a Shabbaton (a kind of Shabbat-long mini-convention) with our synagogue and some twenty Palestinian couples from Gaza. The guests were to come for Friday and Saturday, and would engage in some dialogue groups and some communal meals. The catch was that you could only attend these sessions if you hosted one of the couples at your home for a couple of meals, and gave them a place to sleep.

I very much wanted to do this. I've been frustrated by not meeting as many people from the "other side" as I'd like to, and I figured that such a gathering would also give us a chance to get to know better some politically like-minded Israelis. So I tentatively signed us up pending Beth's approval. Big mistake.

Beth was none too happy about this and adamantly refused to participate. She said that as "guests" in our apartment building, we had no right to invite a Palestinian family to sleep over, not having any idea how people in the building would feel. She said that she didn't want to be marginalized during our year here by being seen by the rest of the neighborhood as some "crazy left-winger." And, she admitted, she was scared, because we really knew nothing about these people. I tried to put up a good counter-argument, and though I didn't actually convince her that this was a genuinely good idea, after some very lengthy "discussion" (major euphemism), she agreed that we could host them.

But in the end, unfortunately, it didn't happen. The official explanation was that participants on both sides had received death threats. But we were on the public list of Jewish participants, and no one threatened *us*. I suspect that it was the Palestinians who were threatened, but no one wanted to say that publicly.

Miracles   All that notwithstanding, there's no getting around the fact that Israel is a miracle. I was talking to a student of mine the other day, and in the course of a long and meandering conversation, she told me that she wasn't going to say Hallel on Yom Ha-Atzma'ut [Israel's

Independence Day] later this year. The physical place, she said, is holy, but the country isn't. Therefore she wouldn't recite prayers (like Hallel) that were meant to mark religious and sacred moments on a day that she thinks should be seen simply as a day marking a nationalist occasion. Religion and the sacred, she seemed to be saying, had nothing to do with the modern state of Israel.

I thought about it for a second, and told her I disagreed with the analysis. After all, Jews celebrate other instances of Jewish national sovereignty as miraculous, no matter how short or imperfect they were. Isn't that exactly what Hanukkah is all about? No one says that the dynasty that the Maccabees created (part of what we celebrate on Hanukkah) was holy, either; but we still say Hallel on Hanukkah. The claim, I think, is that the Maccabees' establishment of an independent Jewish political entity after they successfully fought the Greeks in 164 B.C.E. was considered miraculous, even if what they ended up creating here was very flawed and ultimately did not last very long. Given what's happened to the Jews over the past three thousand years, our people have come to see every instance of Jewish political independence in this small land as a miracle worth describing in religious terms, even if we are not wholly satisfied with what was created during those periods.

And I think that's still true, even in this highly imperfect place we call Israel. The older I get, the closer 1942 seems. When I was a kid, the Shoah* seemed like ancient history. Today, when I realize that my parents were teenagers even as Auschwitz was operating, Nazi Germany seems eerily recent. And daily life in Israel just reinforces that sense for me. There are too many elderly people walking around here with numbers tattooed on their forearms to ignore what this country was created out of.

In the 1940s, the world basically conspired to let the Jews become extinct. Germany and the Axis powers murdered them. The

---

Shoah, in Hebrew, means "calamity." "Holocaust" is an English word that means "burnt offering" or "sacrifice to God." The Jews of Europe in the 1930s and 1940s were not sacrificed—they were murdered. There is a tremendous difference, so I use the word "Shoah" in order to take that difference seriously.

U.S. and Canada (with a long list of associates) closed their borders so that Jews on the run had nowhere to go. The British closed the shores of Palestine. Now we know that even the Swiss, long considered the sainted neutral party, stole from the Jews' estates and admitted nothing for decades. A third of the Jewish people was exterminated, and it came close to being much, much worse.

I think of that, and how recent it was, every time something happens here that other people would think was terribly annoying. Long lines at the checkout stand in the grocery store? I can live with it. "Too many Jews in Jerusalem" still seems pretty amazing to me, given the fact that just over fifty years ago, the British kept them all out and sent refugees back to Europe, only to have the boats filled with survivors of the Nazis sink and many of the dispossessed people drown on the way.

Long lines of cars during rush hour trying to get up the hill and through the entrance to the city? It's fine with me. After all, all along the road are the (now carefully preserved) burnt-out trucks that were used to convoy food and water to the Jews of Jerusalem, surrounded and besieged by the Jordanians, in 1948. We came close to losing Jerusalem, too, in 1948. (That's why Jerusalem isn't even mentioned in Israel's Declaration of Independence. In the days just before the state was declared, the authors of the declaration couldn't be certain that Jerusalem would be part of Israel, so they left any mention of the city out of the document they were writing.) When I think of all that, I can deal with the traffic. It seems like a problem we're lucky to have. And I'll say Hallel on Independence Day with no qualms at all.

Thanksgiving   Tonight's Thanksgiving. Thursday night. Had we been in the States, we'd be doing our regular jaunt to San Diego with the friends we spent all Thanksgivings with, people we miss dearly this year. Beth and I were conflicted about whether to celebrate it tonight. We decided not to. It would only make our kids homesick and conscious of how much they miss their friends, we figured, so we blew it off. We're just having turkey tomorrow night for Shabbat. Enough.

Then Micha had a play date after school today. Around dinnertime, the kid's father came around to pick him up. We got to talking and invited him for dinner. He talked a lot—about being a Russian refusnik for twelve years, about how the Soviets desecrated his mother's grave when he applied to leave, about how they wouldn't let him take most of his books with him when he finally got to leave Russia and move to Israel.

And then he began to muse about life here, too. He talked about what it's like to do thirty days of reserve service, body-frisking Arabs for arms and explosives at traffic checkpoints, only to come back to work the next day and have to sit at construction sites (he's a road construction engineer), having coffee and drawing maps with the very same people he'd body-searched the day before (Arabs do most of the construction here). Over some good (kosher) French wine, he talked about how crazy it all makes him, but how after twelve years of waiting in Kiev, there's still never a moment that he's not grateful to be here.

Seems to me, we ended up having a Thanksgiving dinner anyway.

On to Hanukkah.
Love from all of us.

A Morning Ultimatum, A Memory, A Nightmare

A morning ultimatum: Despite the political tension in the country, there's still something idyllic about the life we're living. The kids are adjusting to school, I'm working and getting a good deal of writing done, Beth is loving her classes—and we're spending more time together than we have in years. The apartment we've rented is adorable, with lovely art. It's pretty quiet, and a large window in the master bedroom lets the light flow in during the morning, making the room a great place to hang out in the quiet hours after the kids have gone off to school. And why not? This is a sabbatical year, isn't it? We're supposed to relax.

So one morning, we get up with the kids, get them all packed for school, serve them breakfast, and send them on their way. Then we decide to be delinquent. Beth has no classes, and I'll take the morning off from writing. We're each in the middle of a good book, so with a few quiet hours at our disposal, we clean up from breakfast, climb back into bed, and begin to read.

I've read only a couple of pages when Beth breaks the precious silence and says, "You know I'm not leaving, don't you?"

"Leaving where?"

"Here. Israel."

"Who says you have to leave?"

"I mean at the end of the year. I'm not going back to the States."

"You're funny."

"No, I'm not, and I'm not kidding. You can go back if you want, but I'm staying here. And frankly, I have no idea why you'd want to go back."

No idea why I'd want to go back, I wonder? Let's see. How long do you have? Well, I lived here for a couple of years as a kid, and I hated every waking moment of it. We've got a huge house in Los Angeles that we can afford, and lots of friends. I've got a great job there that I'll never be able to reproduce here. I'm a known quantity there, sought after on the lecture circuit, with large numbers of professional connections. Here, we'd have no house, we know virtually no one, I'd be either a professional nobody or a has-been, or both. No idea why I'd want to go back?

But I don't say any of that because I can tell that she's serious, and I don't want to have an argument. Not this morning. And, I suddenly realize, I'm not sure that I want to go back either. I can list many more reasons to go back than to stay, but whereas I've resisted this conversation for the almost twenty years that we've been married, this time I'm willing to have it. Maybe there's something to this.

"OK—I like it here, too. I'm willing to talk about it."

"You are?"

"Why, did you expect me to say that there's no way?"

"That's what you've been saying since the day I met you."

"Let's think about it, OK? And for now, let's just read?"

The silence returns, but I notice that neither of us is turning many pages. The wheels are churning. Is it possible that some line in the sand has just been crossed?

. . .

A memory: For the next several days, I keep revisiting that conversation. Walking to the office, when I'd normally be processing what I was about to write or what I'd just written, I think about what we're going to do with our lives. On the basketball court the next Friday morning during my weekly game, Levi, my regular one-on-one partner, glides right by me and sinks an easy layup.

"Do you want to call it a day?" he asks.

"No, why?"

"You're not here. You're not playing any defense. You OK?"

"I'm fine. Let's go. Your ball."

"What are you thinking about?"

"Nothing."

Everything, actually. And I'm wondering, why am I not resisting this time? This country's gotten under my skin in a way that I've never let happen before, but it doesn't feel new. Instead, it feels like an old relationship restored, and I find myself trying to understand why I feel such a deep attachment to this place. Why does it seem so much a part of me, a piece of myself that I'm no longer anxious or willing to abandon?

I am not sure of the answer, but a memory I haven't thought of in years keeps coming to mind. It's the first week in June, 1967. My brothers and I are still young. I'm almost eight, Elie's six, and Yoni's three. But we're old enough to know that something is wrong. Very wrong. The television in the kitchen is on nonstop, which is not usually the case. But even more noticeably, something's very different at the dinner table. Normally, we have our more-or-less regular seats at the table. My parents each have their spot, and each of the three kids has his. Tonight, though, as has been the case for a couple of days, my parents are home but not sitting at the table. My mom serves us dinner, and while we eat, my parents are pacing around the kitchen, watching the evening news. "Why are you not eating?" we want to know. "We're OK. We're just not hungry."

Gradually we learn that Israel is at war, and that for the first day or two, the fate of the entire country hangs in the balance. Even the exceptionally good news from the first hours of the war—such as the destruction of almost all of Egypt's air force on the ground by an Israeli preemptive attack—does little to convince Jews across the world that the danger is over. It will be many years before I understand what the war was about and how Israel managed to defeat so many other, larger armies in just hours and then days. But I still remember—much more vividly than I remember almost anything else from that age—that when Israel was threatened, my parents couldn't eat. When Israel was threatened, the very fabric of our family was ripped asunder, because my parents didn't have dinner with us.

Israel was threatened and something was very wrong in our family. That's it, isn't it? This isn't about moving to a new country. It's about the idea of coming home.

. . .

And a nightmare: There's a reason that I was never able to answer those questions in Moscow or Los Angeles about why we didn't live here. Knowing what I do about Jewish history, feeling the way I do about the lessons that the twentieth century should surely have taught us about the need for a Jewish homeland, I don't know how to justify living anywhere else. That's not to suggest that I think that *all* Jews should live in Israel. I've never thought that. But for *me*, given how *I* see the world, nothing else makes sense. This is the first chance in two thousand years to make the prayers I recite daily come true: "Bring us together from the four corners of the earth." "When will You rule in Zion?" Do I mean all those words that I recite daily and weekly, or am I just kidding myself?

And what, I ask myself, will I do towards the twilight of my life, when I know that the end is at hand? As I look back on my life, whether I'm in my forties or my nineties, and I face the fact that I was fortunate enough to be born during the first generation or two of Jews in over two thousand years that had a chance to build a uniquely just and caring Jewish society—what will I do with the guilt I know I'll feel when I have to admit that I chose to be on the sidelines, that I chose not to be part of making Jewish history?

How will I live with myself for those minutes, or hours, or days? Will I feel that my life—no matter what else I accomplished—was wasted because I chose not to be part of the unfolding of my people's story? It's the first time that my mortality has worried me in any serious way—not because I'm going to die, but because of the possibility that before I do, I'll regret the way I lived.

. . .

I keep thinking about that morning conversation when Beth said that she wasn't leaving. And I wonder: Maybe Beth isn't pressuring me. Is it possible that she's saving me?

When the Maccabees Blew Up the
King David Hotel

- - - - - - - - - - - - - - - - - -

In the weeks preceding Hanukkah, the entire country takes on a pre-holiday aura. Stores run special sales, gas stations advertise that you can get a free this or that for Hanukkah if you fill up your tank beyond a certain amount (at about $4.00 a gallon, hitting that mark is never all that difficult), storefronts are decorated, and of course kids in school are taught the story of the Maccabees over and over again.

In a country like this, the message behind that oft-repeated lesson isn't that hard to divine. Hanukkah celebrates two different stories. There's a story about oil that should have lasted only for one day but lasted eight days until more pure oil could be prepared for the Temple, and the more mundane story about how a band of Jewish warriors, the Maccabees, successfully fought the Greeks (actually they were the Seleucids, but no one seems to worry about that technicality here) and evicted them from large parts of the country. Hanukkah is the story of Jewish warriors recapturing this land and making it theirs, so for obvious reasons, our kids are learning and relearning the story in school. Because Hanukkah is, when you come right down to it, just an earlier version of what's happened here in the past few decades.

This is our sabbatical year, and Beth has a very clearly defined division of labor. I get some time off, she gets some time off. And the kids have to go on one little educational expedition with each of us once a week, even if it's in the city. The other afternoon was my turn, but I was anxious to buy an upgrade to a CD database that I use regularly, an upgrade that I had just seen advertised on sale for Hanukkah. I knew that would never pass for a legitimate outing but figured that I'd come up with something. So off we went—me with three kids in tow—down King George Street to the software store. I found the CD, bought it, and started home, when suddenly I remembered that Beth thinks we're on some father-children educational expedition. Death itself would have been preferable to the treatment I'd have received if I hadn't done *something* educational with the kids.

Down the road I saw Agron Street, which I knew we could take to the left and go directly to the King David Hotel. Salvation. The kids and I hung a left on Agron, walked down to King David Street, and turned towards the hotel. The boys, especially, were ecstatic. The King David Hotel, to them, is Jerusalem's Taj Mahal, and even though they'd passed it hundreds of times, we'd never gone in with them. They couldn't believe their good fortune. This was much better than those boring archaeological tours their mother makes them do.

Inside the ornate (and, I think, ridiculously overdone) lobby, Avi looked around with awe and said, "Wow, this is even bigger than Josh and Bonnie's house." That's right, Captain Obvious, I thought. This is a hotel; they're one family. We meandered around, looked at the reading rooms and lobbies, the staff dressed in their fancy outfits, and then I took them out to the back veranda, overlooking the Old City. I started to explain how Menachem Begin—then a member of the Jewish underground fighting to get the British out of the country, and later Israel's prime minister—blew up one of the wings of the hotel. I pointed out the wing that was destroyed (and which has, of course, been completely rebuilt) and explained about the long Zionist campaign to get rid of the British.

Duly educated, the kids took one more look around, and we headed for home. Having completely forgotten the software store, they were bubbling with stories about the King David when we got home, and I was quite the hero.

An hour or two later, we sat down to dinner. Our outing had long been forgotten until Micha, now five, suddenly asked, "Abba, can you tell me the story again about how the Maccabees blew up the King David?"

We all laughed, but it hit me. In some ways, he got the story wrong, for the Maccabees fought here two thousand years before Begin orchestrated the bombing of the King David Hotel. But on another level, he got it right, and it made no difference that he'd confused the two stories. For him, for them—and maybe for me— Israel is one long continuous story. It doesn't really matter whether it was the Maccabees or Menachem Begin. Whether it was the Greeks or the British we've tried to evict. This place isn't a city, or a country—it's a story. A story we tell, and a story we live. A story about trying to have our one little place on the globe and for it to be just ours. Precisely because he doesn't yet know the difference between ancient Greeks and the British Mandate, Micha understands that.

For the first time, he's beginning to understand that his life is part of a larger story. And I wonder if there's anything more important that he can learn this year.

Gas Masks in the Toy Department

Well, our decision to put Avi at ease by not getting gas masks may have made sense from a parenting point of view, but the government now says that it no longer makes sense from a safety standpoint. We're all supposed to get masks—Israelis who have old ones are to upgrade theirs, and now even tourists, who are not normally eligible for them, are supposed to pick them up. Things with Iraq and the U.S. are heating up, and Saddam is rattling his sabers. When he fought the U.S. during the Gulf War, he *did* fire missiles at Tel Aviv, and a couple hit. There's no telling whether he'll do it again, and there's no reason to be confident that he won't use chemical or biological warheads. So, during what in the States is the week before Christmas, we're shopping around to find out where we can pick up five gas masks.

The tourist pickup site is in the Mashbir, Jerusalem's biggest department store, smack in the middle of downtown. We're supposed to go upstairs a floor or two, bringing our American passports and cash for the masks. We're told we have to bring the kids with us, for reasons that are not clear.

Anticipating the standard Israeli bedlam and chaos, we try to get there relatively early, but are not nearly the first ones in line. The place is packed, and things are moving slowly. Most of the room seems filled with what our children call "yeshiva kids," the eighteen-year-old high school graduates here for a year of religious study before beginning college. The "yeshiva kids" are bantering about; some seem a bit unsettled by the prospect of getting a gas mask, while most seem content to have the time to chat.

As our children get fidgety, we let them wander farther and farther away from us. It turns out that this floor of the store is also the toy department, so they're more than happy to be checking out all the shelves lined with stuff they want. There's something surreal about the scene, our kids frolicking around the shelves of toys while we wait in line to make sure that they'll stay alive (maybe) if we're bombarded with poison gas in, by the way, a place we've chosen to relax in for the year.

We finally get to the front of the line and hand the woman behind the table our five American passports. She turns to the back page of each and stamps it with an *M* in a circle, indicating that we've been given a mask. No getting two, apparently, as if you'd want to. We fork over the cash as she's stamping the passports, and she places five boxes, each just a little bit smaller than a shoebox, on the table, along with a receipt for the cash. Two are adult sizes, three are for kids. The warning on the boxes clearly says not to open them up until instructed to do so by the radio, and that premature breaking of the seal will limit their effectiveness.

I look at my kids, and it strikes me that there's no way that these three different faces will all fit into the same size mask. "Doesn't he need the smaller size?" I ask, pointing to Micha, who's now come up to the table.

"No, what I gave you will be fine."

"But look, the three kids are different sizes. She's twelve years old, and he's just five. How can one size fit all for something like this?"

"Believe me, this will be fine."

"Well, do you at least have a sample one open so we can put it against their faces and see?"

"No, we don't have any samples," she says with growing irritation. "Just take these," and she throws them into two big shopping bags (as if we'd bought something at the store itself) and hands the bags to us. "Next in line?"

"What's that?" Micha suddenly wants to know.

I realize we haven't told him the reason for our visit to this store. But I don't know what to say. "Well, there's this bad guy out there who hates Jewish people and Israel, and now we think that he might try to kill us so the newspaper said that we have to get these little gas masks so if he fires missiles at us we can put these masks on you and we'll be OK, assuming that the lady's right that these are all the right sizes, and assuming that these things actually work, which they didn't during the Gulf War" doesn't seem like a reasonable response. Truth is, I have absolutely no idea what to say. I don't think I'll be able to bear the response, or the next question. And besides, I'm beginning to cry.

"Did you see anything fun in the store?" I ask instead.

"Yeah, I want to show you something I want." We walk over, and all three kids actually have their eyes set on "stuff." But they know that we never cave in like this in toy stores, and I can see they're getting ready to be told that they can't have the toys.

"OK, why doesn't everyone pick one thing that they want and we'll go to the cashier and pay for it?"

Stunned, the kids can't believe their good fortune and, with a relative minimum of fuss, pick out their toys. Walking out of the store, onto the sunny sidewalk on King George Street as we head for the car, I can tell they still can't believe we bought them the things they wanted. And I can tell that Beth is also amazed that I didn't resist. But she also knows exactly what happened.

. . .

Life's short, kids, and it's really not that fair, either. "Nasty, brutish and short" is what Thomas Hobbes called human life in the state of nature, a state it seems we're veering closer to every day. Tali's friends in the States don't say things like "nasty, brutish and short." They say, "Life sucks, then you die." Kind of the same thing, it seems to me. But bottom line, little kids shouldn't have to go to buy gas masks. It's just not what you should have to know about when you're that little.

You want some toys? Really, why the hell not. . . .

December 1998:
The First Night of Hanukkah
and Present-Day Miracles

In Jerusalem, Clinton Visits a Fellow
Embattled Leader

President Clinton, forced to confront issue of impeachment, reluctantly interrupts efforts to rescue Middle East peace plan during visit to Jerusalem.

New York Times: Monday, December 14, 1998, page A1

Regards from a paralyzed city, where the much beleaguered president of the United States and his entourage have brought traffic to not a virtual standstill, but a complete one. What a mess. The papers this morning said that there are tens of thousands of Israeli police and soldiers assigned to trying to keep him alive, in addition to the Secret Service, who are all over the place (their black four-by-four Broncos, or Jeeps, or whatever they are, are rather conspicuous in a country of tiny white cars!). If this is what it takes, it's obviously worth it, but what a complete and utter mess.

Some imam (as Muslim clerics are called) on the Gaza Strip told some Western reporter tonight that he wouldn't personally ask anyone to assassinate Clinton, but that if someone did, he'd be "very happy." That's only been shown about 150 times tonight on Israeli television.

Anyhow, it's the first night of Hanukkah, which is always special here, so a brief note or two.

I'll start not with Hanukkah, but with our little visit to the emergency room this past Shabbat afternoon. We were home, having a nice Shabbat lunch with my dad (visiting here to do some teaching at Ben Gurion University in Be'er Sheva) and another family, when all of a sudden, Avi got terrible stomach cramps. We put him to bed, but he was in agony. After a series of examinations by my dad (a former pediatrician) and our guest (a current ob-gyn), they decided he needed to go to the hospital. As the pain was on his left side, they were more concerned about a twisted bowel than appendicitis, but as either would require surgery, I was not pleased.

So off we trot, in the middle of Shabbat. I carry a moaning Avi to the car, and my dad (who's worked in hospitals here) comes along to negotiate with the natives. We happened to know that the hospital on duty for emergencies that afternoon (there's one hospital picked each day, and it's listed in the paper) was Sha'arei Zedek, a religious hospital more or less on the opposite side of town.

I was driving rather rapidly (that's a bit of an understatement) to get there the most direct way I know how, when all of a sudden, to my utter amazement, I saw a main thoroughfare completely blocked off by police barricades. I drove up to read the sign, which read *"ein kenissah be-shabbat ve-chagim"*—"no entry [to cars] on Shabbat and Festivals."

I was incredulous. This was by far the most direct route to the hospital, and for the first time, we'd confronted head-on the battle for the streets between the religious and the nonreligious (for whom I suddenly felt great sympathy). This was the sort of religious coercion I'd always associated with backward cities like Teheran, the kind of thing that I assumed was seen about Israel only when CNN was looking for dirt. But here it was—undeniable, and very much in the way.

I started a U-turn, to go a different way, when I suddenly said to my dad, "To hell with it; I'm going through this." Dad was a bit nervous, and feared that we'd be stoned (by rocks, that is), but I figured that since I was still in my "Shabbat uniform" (dark pants, white shirt, white *kippah*), they'd see that I wasn't the normal "neighborhood violator" and we'd be OK. (Our car also has plastic windows, the glass having been removed by the previous owner for just such occasions, though the rocks anticipated were supposed to be thrown by Arabs, not Jews—but rocks are rocks, I figured.) I raced through the neighborhood and ultimately got to the barricades at the other end. There we were met by a group of kids, looking rather surprised to see a car moving in their neighborhood. I got out to move the barricade and explained (in their native tongue) that there was a sick child in the back of the car who was going to the hospital.

One of them said, "So he's sick—this is how you spend Shabbat?" I was so appalled that I had no idea what to say. Their black-and-white view of the world (no pun on their dress intended) is so absolute that they don't even accept that Jewish tradition allows people to drive for medical emergencies. Nor did they seem to care about the kid in the back. They saw only a religious issue, not a person.

The beauty of our tradition is so overwhelming at times.

We finally made it to the hospital, registered Avi, and got him seen by all the various people (nurses, doctors, surgeon, chest x-ray, blood test, urine test—the works). The care was actually good if not with all the bells and whistles. It was interesting, in the midst of everything, that the language of discourse amongst most of the nurses and many of the doctors was Russian—quite a change from a few years ago. A brief reminder that this is still a country of immigrants.

But there was this incredible religious cognitive dissonance even in the hospital. At first blush, it seemed that Shabbat *was* clearly suspended in the hospital. All the doctors were writing in charts, the x-ray machines were working, people were doing whatever they had to. Except, of the fifteen elevators, eleven were shut down and the remaining four were on "Shabbat mode," which means that the elevator goes from the bottom to the top without stopping, and then stops at every floor on the way down. It *does* get you where you need to go, but it's incredibly slow, and extremely frustrating when you're trying to get your sick kid looked at. At one point I had to take Avi for a chest x-ray, and the elevator was so slow, and he was so scared, that he didn't want to wait. So I carried him up the four flights of stairs, wondering the whole time what exactly was accomplished by shutting off the elevators once people already had to do without Shabbat in the hospital setting anyway, and how the nonreligious staff (which was the majority, by far) felt about having to deal with this all day long.

The phones, by the way, were also shut off. Every single pay phone in the hospital was disconnected. I found that rather amusing; my father was livid. I guess he was right. What if someone needed to call a family member and happened to be the only Israeli without a cell phone? The violation of personal decision-making was about as aggressive as I've seen, and all this in a place where Shabbat is violated as a matter of necessity anyway. Yet this wasn't Meah She'arim, the ultra-Orthodox section of Jerusalem, either. Instead, it was a major hospital in the "modern" part of the city. Sometimes it seems like Israel is part New York, part Paris, and part Teheran.

Though I was mostly relieved that Avi was OK (apparently it was one of those strange cases where a strep infection actually invades the stomach and causes severe cramping), I couldn't help but realize how far we've yet to go in this country. This was one of those instances that proves that it was much easier, or at least simpler, for Jews to be a religious community when we didn't run the show, when the world was non-Jewish and we had to carve out our little niche in the midst of a society that we didn't control.

Then, the hospitals did what they pleased—it wasn't up to us. The elevators weren't ours; the phones weren't ours. And the roads weren't ours. Now they are. But now that they are, it's clear that the Jewish religious tradition has no idea how to create significant religious space without invading the autonomy (and safety) of those who either see the world differently or are dealing with an emergency.

But raise that issue here, and you're a heretic to some. Or a dullard to the rest, who believe that the obvious answer is a wholly secular state, with little or no Jewish qualities. But then, I ask myself, what's the point of all the effort we've spent in building this country? Why were all the lives lost? To create another Belgium or Holland? A sobering reminder of all that's yet to be done.

It's obvious these days, of course, that the problems here aren't only internal, between Jews. The problems with the Arabs seem more insoluble as time goes on. Part of the problem is that with Netanyahu in power, it often does seem as if we're "home alone," with no real adult in charge! He obviously detests the Arabs, and though he speaks in terms of security, it's clear that he's not looking for a solution. And he antagonizes them in the worst possible ways, doing things that are totally unnecessary, and without any political savvy whatsoever. He's authorized the building of a huge Jewish housing complex, called Har Homa, in a neighborhood that the Palestinians call Ras al-Amud and consider theirs. It's just on the outskirts of Jerusalem, not in a densely populated Arab area, so I don't know if he's right or wrong to build there. But the brash and insensitive way in which it was announced was designed to infuriate them. It worked.

And the same was true when, in September 1996, he allowed the opening of a tunnel that had been dug as part of an archaeological dig but which opened into the Muslim Quarter of the Old City. It's the kind of thing that probably could have been handled with some sensitive backstage diplomacy and bartering, but no, not Bibi Netanyahu. He just opened the tunnel, right in the middle of their quarter of the city, prompting massive Palestinian demonstrations to which Israeli security forces responded with force. A number of people were killed, and scores were injured.

Whether the Jews have a "right" to open that tunnel or not is not the question. Even those Jews who want to take over the Muslim Quarter (and I'm certainly not one of them) ought to admit that there are smart ways and dumb ways to interact with the Arab population there. We're just infuriating them left and right, but technically the peace process is still on.

So we're sort of lurching, or not lurching, towards peace, but the pace seems to get slower and slower. These last few weeks have been incredibly sobering. As you've undoubtedly read, Lebanon has become very dangerous. Hezbollah is trying to make the cost of the occupation of South Lebanon high enough that Israelis will pressure the government to withdraw. (Once they do that, of course, Hezbollah probably thinks that they can then do the same with mainstream Israeli cities, which is why a lot of people here don't think we can leave Lebanon.)

But the cost of staying there is getting to be terribly high. Quite a few soldiers have lost their lives over the past couple of weeks. Hezbollah actually left a video camera by the road where they'd planted a mine, so that Israeli television viewers got to see a small group of soldiers get blown up over and over and over again. Why did the media choose to show it? Because they want the IDF to pull out of Lebanon. Sound familiar?

One interview with a parent was particularly harrowing. The mother of one of the soldiers killed said tearfully, but without crying, "We send them off to the army so tall, six foot, or six foot two. And then they come home in such small boxes." I watched our kids one evening a few days ago as that was played on the radio in the house, and they didn't say or ask anything. I wasn't sure if they didn't understand the Hebrew, or if they chose not to process that one. I chose not to raise it with them.

I've come to realize that living here is a reminder of how non-ideological American life is, for better or for worse (probably for worse, though I'm not always sure). The battle lines here are about much more immediate issues. I remember that on November 4th (the secular anniversary of his murder), we had a memorial for Rabin at work. Everyone was basically expected to go. Technically, you had a right not to show up, but it would have been considered very gauche. All offices shut down, and a brief and rather moving ceremony was held. In America the dais would have been "staffed" by three people—Reform, Conservative, Orthodox. Here it was three others: religious, nonreligious, and Arab.

Each of the three spoke briefly, but I thought that the Arab woman was by far the most insightful. She's a student in one of the Mandel programs, though I've never met her, and an Israeli citizen, born and bred in Israel, living in an Arab village. She spoke of her sadness at Rabin's death, but also at the sense of relief that she and her fellow Israeli Arabs feel at having a day of commemoration that does not exclude them. After all, she said, all the holidays in this country (and there are many) are either religious holidays from the Jewish calendar, or days associated with Jewish history (Yom Ha-Shoah, etc.), or days linked to Israel's military victories. The first two, she said, don't speak to them in the least. They're Muslims, after all. And the last, though they're Israeli citizens, are still problematic, since those days are celebrations of Israel's defeat of *her* people. "How can we celebrate the independence of our own country," she asked, "when it's really a celebration of *your* having defeated *us*?"

What Rabin's memorial afforded her, she said, was a day to mourn *with* Israelis, a day to mourn the assault on democracy, which is sacred to both communities. Again, a reminder of how far there is to go. When peace finally comes (and I'm still among those who firmly believes that it will), there's going be a lot of internal work to do here. That work I don't believe we'll live to see finished.

This passionate, ideological element of the country (the part that's so different in so many ways from our lives in the States) was apparent even at a parent-teacher conference we went to last week. It was for Tali's school, and as a high schooler (they start high school now with seventh grade), she has lots of teachers that we had to see. We're fortunate to have a daughter who's a very good student, so we weren't particularly worried about what would be said. But neither were we prepared for what did get said. As if it had been scripted, each teacher started with "Tali's such a wonderful girl. It's too bad you're only staying a year. It's terrible. This country needs children like her." And then they went on with the grades, the homework, etc.

I told Beth that I felt like we'd walked into a Zionist ambush. Obviously it was comforting and fun to hear nice things said about our kid, but I was struck that all the teachers couldn't help but see a nationalist issue as being perfectly appropriate to this meeting. And I wondered, when our Israeli friends who come to the States for a year (and who also have kids who are good students) go to teachers' conferences at public schools, do the American teachers talk to them about our country needing more kids like this? I kind of doubt it. Strangely, that's part of what we're going to miss about being here.

Actually, the more I thought about this kind of pressure, the more I liked it, which is new for me. Such pushing always made me uncomfortable in the past, probably because I didn't think we had a very good reason for *not* living here. But I wasn't nearly as offended this time; I thought it was wonderful that these people (not all Israelis would agree, of course) seemed to believe that the place where they live is important, that it's an experiment with cosmic significance. In a way, I was kind of jealous. Do most of us believe that about our communities? Our lives? I wondered.

Which leads me to the radio tonight. I dropped off my dad at his hotel, and then meandered my way back home through the traffic jam brought to us care of the U.S. Secret Service. Bored, I turned on the radio, and on each station heard something about Hanukkah. And I remembered again what an amazing thing it was to have a country that's so very Jewish at the core. It sounds obvious, of course, but it's not. Many (most?) of the windows tonight had candles burning in them. There was "holiday season" music, but it was Hanukkah music. There was a lot of religious programming, but it was in Hebrew, and it quoted the Siddur [the prayer book], the Talmud. People at the office, religious and not, and *Jewish* and not, said *"chag same'ach"* at the end of the day. For once, our kids feel that their culture is the majority culture; that being what they are and who they are is normal, natural.

As the road turned higher, giving me a view of the whole southern half of the city, the radio station turned to a candle-lighting ceremony somewhere, and someone sang the *berakhot* [blessings]. The first one, and then the second, which I noticed used a known but less used formula. Instead of *"she'asah nissim la'avoteinu, ba-yamim ha-hem, ba-zeman hazeh"* ("who performed miracles for our ancestors in those days, at this season"), he said *"U-ba-zeman hazeh,"* making it mean "in those days, and in our own time."

To my right, the whole southern half of the city flickered and pulsed with light, a modern Jewish city, completely alive, wholly Jewish, a city to which the leader of the free world had come because it's a place where the Jewish people are finally secure and have some say about their own future. And I thought of what Palestine was like when my dad was born, how few Jews were here, how little Hebrew was a spoken language, how so few even dared dream there'd be a Jewish state, and, of course, how little people understood the full extent of what was just beginning to happen in Europe.

The blessing's completely true, I realized. There *have* been miracles for our ancestors here—in days of old, yes, but no less in our own time. They are real miracles, miracles we don't usually think about. I think that tomorrow I'll say Hallel [a series of Psalms praising God] with particular intensity.

And yet, of course, there are other miracles still to come. There's something rather universal about having your child be sick. Signing out of the hospital at the end of a long and nerve-wracking day, I was in line with two other families. One was a completely secular Israeli family, who normally regard people dressed the way I was as "the Neanderthal enemy." And the other family was Arab, a young couple with a sick little baby. They were scared, and they could tell I felt bad for them. There we were, all three of us, taking care of paperwork, feeling for the other. Without labels, without roles—just people who understood one another and wished we could have helped each other.

If only it didn't take emergency rooms for that to happen, I thought. What's going to happen to all that hate? Where will it possibly go?

Are there still more miracles to come? One can only hope.

Happy Hanukkah from all of us.

Aerogrammes and Rubber Stamps

Virtually living on e-mail this year, connected to work, to friends, and to family by a modem more than even a telephone, I'm struck by the fact that we hardly get any "real" mail. We rarely even bother to check the mailbox. It occurs to me that unlike our extended visits to Israel in years past, we haven't even bought one aerogramme. Why would we? But still, it's funny what memories living here for a year can dredge up.

Almost immediately after I was born, my maternal grandfather left his family in America and moved to Israel. He had vowed to make aliyah ever since the Depression had eroded his faith in America, and eventually he did. He waited for me, the eldest child of his only daughter, to be born, and then left to begin a new life. He asked my grandmother if she would come with him, but she declined. So he said goodbye to my grandmother, my mother, and her older brothers, picked up, and was gone.

Shortly after he arrived in Israel, he had a rubber stamp made up, which he used at the top of every air-letter he wrote for the next fifteen years. It was in Hebrew. Translated into English, it read: "Jews! Come to Israel, so that you may live and we may live."

It became a kind of fixture, that little imprint at the top of all his letters. We'd open up the air-letters, trimming carefully around the edges, and unfold the top. It was always there—I guess he really believed it.

I, though, never did. Cute, I thought, appropriate to the aging grandfather who loved to walk the Jerusalem forest each day, but hardly life advice that one had to take seriously. As I got older and the letters kept coming, I even began to laugh at that silly rubber stamp.

A quarter of a century later, he's gone, buried not far from here just outside Beit Shemesh. I think of him often as I pass Beit

Shemesh on the way to Tel Aviv or the airport, and I smile as I remember that stamp I thought was so naïve. I wonder if he knows that little by little, family by family, a large number of his descendants gradually made their way here. I wonder if he knows that of his seven grandchildren, four (including my brother Yoni and me) now live here. Or that of his fifteen great-grandchildren, eleven now live in Israel.

And, I wonder, who's laughing now?

January 1999: We Told 'Em

Dear Elie:

A quick note before I head to the airport. Tried calling you at home a few minutes ago, but got your machine, so I assume you guys are out. It's just after Shabbat here, and I'm getting picked up by the taxi in a few minutes, but wanted to drop you this line before heading out so you'll be "in the know."

Last night we told the kids about our decision to stay in Israel for good. They weren't exactly surprised, as we'd been hinting at it for a long time, but neither were they expecting it. It was actually quite a scene. Bottom line, the deed is done.

Kind of hard to believe. Seems like a momentous decision to take in the space of just a few quick months. I guess it is pretty major. I'm not sure why we're not terrified. Maybe we're just too stupid to be scared. Maybe I'm so nervous about the whole process of letting my

Los Angeles work know and disengaging from that whole scene that I'm not yet thinking about what this means for our lives. In any event, the kids know, and I'm headed off to L.A. to get the second semester started there and to let them know formally that I'm not coming back.

I'll try to give you a call when I get in. My number at work should be the same—assuming that they still let me use the phones!

Talk to you soon.
D

January 1999:
Next Year(s) in Jerusalem

Hi, everyone:

As some of you have undoubtedly heard by now, the Gordis family is embarking on a longer adventure than we had originally planned. After a great deal of consideration, a good bit of anguish, and a lot of excitement, we've decided to try to make a go of it here in Israel. This is in a lot of ways a dream we've had for a long time, and completely unexpectedly, things this year have made its realization possible. So, given an opportunity we never imagined we'd have, we've decided to stay beyond this year, to try to set down roots and make a life in Jerusalem.

To start at the end, here are the basics: Some time after I began my fellowship at the Mandel Foundation this year, it became clear that there might be a possibility of the fellowship developing into something more long-term. What were originally just preliminary and purely exploratory discussions gradually became more specific and serious, and on Friday morning just a week and a half ago, we crossed all the "t's" and agreed to stay. We told our kids that Friday night (more on that below), and then I flew to Los Angeles on Saturday night to give formal notice at the University (they'd been apprised of this possibility for quite some time) and to spend some time with my students, who were understandably quite taken by surprise and concerned about the future of their studies.

Anyway, at this point it's a done deal. I'm going to stay on with the Mandel Foundation, involved with a variety of educational ventures, most specifically with the Jerusalem Fellows, our program that brings senior Jewish educators from around the globe for two years of intensive study in Jewish and general philosophy, philosophy of education, public policy, and the like. In some respects, it will be work similar to what I was doing as dean of the rabbinical school in Los Angeles—working with students (we call them "Fellows" here, as their work is much more independent than that of a student in graduate school), working with the renowned faculty associated with the Foundation, recruiting, assisting the Fellows as they move out of the program back into the work world, and thinking strategically about the directions the program should take in the next few years.

In other ways, though, the work will be different in a manner that I already find fascinating. The Fellows come from all walks of Jewish life. Unlike the students in any one rabbinical school, who tend to represent one spot on the religious spectrum, these Fellows span the spectrum from Haredi ("ultra-Orthodox") to completely secular. They also come from a variety of countries around the globe (France, England, Russian, Ukraine, Australia, Argentina, Israel, the United States, and others). Many are very advanced in their fields already—a good number have Ph.D.'s, others are rabbis, all are proven professional successes.

It's an opportunity to work with people at a different stage of their careers; I feel ready for that variety and the challenges it will bring. After working in one movement for a very long time, the diversity of this world is exceptionally appealing to me.

Beth is going to explore a variety of professional opportunities over the next few months, and the kids are eventually going to calm down and grow up normally (we hope). (Contributions for their long-term therapy funds are being gladly accepted by the "American Friends of the Beleaguered Gordis Children," a newly registered 501C3.)

The big question, of course, is "why?" The real reasons are all those things I've been writing about ever since we got here. My parents made aliyah in 1969, and though we only stayed for a couple of years, it was enough to get all of us (parents and brothers) speaking Hebrew reasonably fluently and, perhaps more important, to feel in ways that words can't fully express that Israel is home.

Beth, too, has a long history with the land of Israel. She came as a high school junior and lived in an Israeli dormitory and with a wonderful Israeli family with whom she's still in touch. (Twenty-something years later, they actually came to Tali's Bat Mitzvah a few months ago—it was a wonderful reunion.) Beth hoped to return to live in Israel after graduating college, but life took its twists and turns. So, twenty-four years later, we're back and ready to pick up where she left off.

Actually, coming to Israel was part of the prenup that we would have had if we'd had any assets to protect. When we decided to get married (one begged, one consented—you guess), Beth said that a "condition" of said partnership would be to come here to live. One of us (not Beth—you guess which one it was) said that wasn't very likely. After all, what was a rabbi who didn't want to be a "real" rabbi going to do in Israel? There were already a lot of people selling tomatoes at the corner fruit markets.

So we eventually settled on the idea of spending a year here, but even that kept getting postponed. There was the Ph.D. to finish, work at the University, books to write that weren't yet completed—the whole nine yards. We'd all but given up on this whole plan when the Foundation invited us for the year's sabbatical. We jumped at the chance, since the kids were the perfect age, figuring a year was what we'd get, and that even that was a tremendous gift.

But all of a sudden, it seemed that a rabbi who didn't want to be a real rabbi could actually get a job in Israel! And given that new reality, we had to decide whether we were kidding ourselves all those (more recent) years when we'd said we'd do it if only we could or were actually serious about it.

In a lot of ways, as strange as moving to the Middle East sounds to most people, this feels very natural to us, and in some ways the next logical step in our (almost) forty-something lives. It seemed to us (at different moments, and in different ways) that if we always loved coming here and were always sad to leave, we should think about that seriously. When we went out for dinner for Beth's birthday in September, we were in a restaurant with a whole variety of couples: an Ethiopian couple, some Russians, an Israeli couple, us, and selected others from all over the place. Beth remarked that the whole country was a modern-day miracle, and then asked, "If you have a chance to live your life as part of a miracle, how do you walk away from that?"

The Hebrew language, the city of Jerusalem, the idea of a Jewish society in which the successes as well as the failures are our own responsibility and no one else's—all these have become part of what we love about living here.

In ways that are pretty hard to express, we feel connected to this land. Part of it is history; the fact that so much history has unfolded here makes Israel profoundly compelling to us. When Micha asked the week before last how come the Maccabees blew up the King David Hotel, he didn't have the details quite right, but he got the point. He has already intuited that different groups of Jewish people have struggled to make a homeland here; we sense that our kids have begun to sense that they, too, are part of that continuing saga.

There are probably few, if any, Jewish parents who relish the fact that their kids will have to go into the army; but there's also something about the fact that Jews have their own army in their own country, and defend their own state on their own terms, that is critically important after the history of the twentieth century. And the fact, of course, that the whole army scene may soon be diminishing in importance, with peace so clearly on the horizon, makes this issue less central than it might have been for us a few years ago.

Because of all this, I even love the street signs in this country. There's no "Second Avenue" or "Maple Street" in Israel. Virtually all the street names, particularly in the large cities, are taken from history. In Jerusalem, it's King George Street and King David Street that make up the heart of downtown; streets named after the twelve biblical tribes of Israel make up our neighborhood. The names of non-Jewish heroes of the Jewish people—David Lloyd George (the British prime minister at the time the British issued the Balfour Declaration in 1917, expressing their support for the creation of a Jewish state), Jan Masaryk (the Czech leader who saved Jews during the Second World War and was supportive of the budding Zionist enterprise), Émile Zola, and others—are at the heart of the shopping district just a few blocks away.

In Tel Aviv, I love happening upon the major downtown intersection between Herzl and Ahad Ha'am Streets. It always strikes me as ironic that the streets named after the two men intersect. Herzl, the father of political Zionism, knew little about Jewish culture and was no fan of what he did know. Ahad Ha'am opposed the creation of a political homeland, and wanted Israel to be a spiritual center for the Jewish people. They are rumored to have disliked each other intensely, but there they are in downtown Tel Aviv, locked in a figurative embrace as thousands of people cross that intersection each day. I don't know how many Israelis actually think about the irony of that crossroads as they walk there, but I do. The fact that the two of them, different though they were, are major arteries in Tel Aviv today reminds me of the exciting and passionate dialogue that has always taken place about what Israel should be, and that continues. Now we'll get to be part of that from the inside.

History's not all of it, of course. We think that this is a great place for our kids. We especially love the way Israel and Israeli society have allowed our older kids to blossom. They are independent here in ways that they could never be in the U.S. of the 1990s. We love the fact that Tali and Avi both navigate their way to school on the public bus, and that they can just hop on a bus to go shopping, to buy pizza, or just hang out with a friend at the last minute. We let both Tali and Avi walk alone at night to their youth group meetings; Tali had a sleepover with her youth group and came home in the early hours of the morning, let herself into the apartment with her own house key, and went to sleep! We had long since gone to bed, and it never occurred to us to wait up for her or to ask her to wake us when she got in. It's just that there's nothing to worry about. They have the confidence and self-assuredness to get places on their own and to see this town as theirs—it's wonderful to watch.

There are a myriad of other things—in addition to the history and the kids—that draw us here as well. It's a frantic place in a lot of ways, but an exciting kind of frenetic energy. People are always on the move, and seem never to stand still. The newspapers never lack for some crisis or misstep to highlight—there's a histrionic quality to the press here that can get exhausting, but which speaks to the high stakes of virtually all decisions that are made in a country as young as this. And yet, as frantic as Israeli life can be, its pace seems slower than the pace in Los Angeles. People work hard, and they work long hours, to be sure; but you see many more parents taking their kids to school, fathers in the markets at the end of the day, people hanging out on their porches, sitting in cafes, living life. Israelis socialize at all hours of the night, weekday or weekend. People come over for coffee or tea at the drop of a hat, and sit chatting until the early hours of the morning without anyone thinking much of it. Perhaps it's the history that's been lived here that has taught people to enjoy life while they can; but whatever the cause, there's a joie de vivre here that we love.

Thus I expect that I'll see a lot more of the kids here than I did in the past few years. While my job will undoubtedly involve some travel (recruiting for the program will probably take me to Europe, South America, South Africa, and the former Soviet Union within the next few years, and there will be much work in the U.S. as well), the pace of constantly being on airplanes, hopping from one state to another, only to come back on Sunday night to teach on Monday morning, will subside. More than has been the case for many years, our kids will now have a chance to continue what they've gotten used to this year— going to sleep with both of their parents actually in the house at the same time.

There's an emphasis on family here that we cherish. We went to Avi's school today for a Tu Bi-Shevat celebration, and almost all the kids had both parents in attendance. It's accepted to leave work for a kid's performance or celebration, even if that means changing a class or missing a meeting. Beth is off from school next week, so we're going to take the kids out of school for three days so we can go to Eilat. I'm going to be gone from the office, and when I've told people I'll be away, the response was that this was perfectly natural—families just go away sometimes. It's hard to articulate, but life here has a way of strengthening our bonds, to each other and to the community at large.

Finally, even though moving to the Middle East is a daunting prospect in many ways, it's also one of the exciting dimensions of this whole decision. This is a much more civilized and settled Middle East than it was only a few decades ago, but there's still much that hasn't been tamed that I love. Israel is an amazing mix of the most sophisticated dimensions of Europe and the ancient traditions of the Middle East. Within a short time, you can still drive from Israeli's high-tech "silicon valley" just outside Tel Aviv and get to the West Bank, where life is entirely different. The kids still get a kick out of our having to stop the car on the way out of Jerusalem towards Jericho when a shepherd is moving his flock across the road. It can take a long time, but their interest at watching someone who lives almost exactly the way his ancestors did hundreds of years ago is fascinating. They see kids their own age out tending flocks, responsible for an entire herd with no adult to supervise. Our kids are beginning to see how very differently various cultures live and raise their younger generations. I hope that they never lose that interest in all this.

In certain parts of the country, the bazaars, the fruit peddlers selling their wares off carts that are pulled by donkeys, the Arab men sitting in their traditional garb, playing backgammon and occasionally interrupting for commerce, all lend Israel and the Middle East an aura of "authenticity" that I still love. Not long ago, Beth called me at work from her cell phone, laughing hysterically, just to inform me that on the main street not far from our apartment, she'd watched a policeman on foot chasing a donkey that had somehow gotten away from its owner. As far as she could tell, the donkey escaped.

Some of this remains in the Jewish parts of Israel as well. It's not at all unusual to see Ethiopian women walking through town wearing their traditional garb and headdresses, or the radically different cultures of the elderly German couples sitting in cafes and the more recent Russian arrivals struggling to bring a bit of Moscow or Kiev to Israel. Russian theater, contemporary Israeli pubs trying to be very "London" or "New York," a reasonably sophisticated classical music scene, and a population that seems to be reading all the time—all of this is what contributes to the mix and energy of this tiny country.

Then there's also the physical beauty. There's a raw magnificence that the desert has, and time hasn't touched it. The different-colored sands that make up the mountains outside Eilat, the gentle rolling dunes on the road from Jerusalem to Jericho—there's a tranquil quality to the scenery that I love, and that sometimes strikes me as incredibly sad, given the not-at-all tranquil things that happen there. The Galilee and its trees are by no means redwood forests, but they're glorious in their own way. The Sea of Galilee, somehow much larger than I expect each time I see it, retains its biblical beauty. You probably don't move to a place just because it's beautiful, but the beauty certainly adds a layer to the love that both of us feel for Israel.

And yet, despite all these attractions and many more that we haven't mentioned, we don't expect that this experiment of ours is going to be easy. It is the Middle East, after all. There are Saddam-initiated moments when we have to make sure to tell a baby-sitter where the gas masks are. Many of the conveniences of American life don't exist here; we'll be moving from a six-bedroom house to an apartment; we'll be far from family and friends; there's a new language to teach and to write in; a new society to figure out, etc. Lots of our friends who've come here earlier are tired; most are not leaving, but it's easy to see that they've lost some of the energy and enthusiasm that they came with years ago. Ironically, that doesn't make us want to be here less; it makes us feel more of a responsibility to do this. We're new blood, and that's what Israel needs to survive.

To be honest, it would be somewhat of an exaggeration to say that our kids share this sense of responsibility. When we told them last Friday night that we were planning to stay, their reactions were interesting. Micha had a complete tantrum, threw some things around the apartment, yelled, "*You* can stay here, but I'm going back to America," and then just calmly walked back to the table to ask if he could play with Lego. Obviously we said yes, and since then he's been unbelievably calm and much happier than before. The end of months of uncertainty has relieved him. Last night, he told us that he wanted to be either an "army guy" or an astronaut. I told him that he definitely would be a soldier, to which Micha asked, "Why?" When I explained that all Israeli boys go into the army, Micha asked, "Am I Israeli?" "You will be, we hope" was the answer. Beth was virtually apoplectic that I had initiated that conversation; we were headed out to dinner at the King David Hotel and she couldn't believe that we'd "dump" that on him five minutes before we left. But Micha was actually thrilled.

At the same dinner that Friday night when we told the kids and

Micha had his tantrum, Tali had a fever of 104. She didn't even want to come to dinner, but we asked her to join us (knowing what we were going to talk about). When we told them (after each of us saying to the other, "No, *you* tell them"), Tali lethargically looked up from her soup and mumbled, "Oh, I kind of expected that. It's OK. I kind of like it here, and besides, next year my immune system will be used to all these Middle Eastern germs." We decided that we like her best when she's feverish and docile, and thought seriously about not giving her any more Tylenol.

Avi's had the hardest time, since he had started to miss his Los Angeles friends in a big way in the past month or so. But he's dealing with all these changes, and doing fine. He has up days and down days, but our family and close friends have been writing him very supportive e-mails, often including stories of their own moves here. Those have been helping quite a bit. He's hanging in there.

I'm not sure that the kids understand this move yet, but I hope that one day they will. For me, the reason for this decision crystallized in a recent conversation with the woman who will be my boss at the Foundation. When we were negotiating the terms of our arrangement, there was a point when I said that one particular detail didn't matter that much, and then added, "This whole thing is so irrational anyway." My boss, herself an immigrant from Belgium, responded, "True, it *is* irrational, unless you factor in destiny."

And that's the issue—destiny. It's about feeling that we belong here, fit in here better than we ever did in the States. The States was a great place to live, and both of us love a lot about it. But it always seemed to us that we were tolerated there—the Protestant tolerance for the Jews and all that—while here, the place is made for us. It's the difference between being a guest and being home. I hope our kids will come to appreciate that. Sometimes I worry that we'll have taken them out of the States too early for them to know how much one can feel like a guest in one's country of birth.

One of the things that's been most reassuring over the past week and a half has been the reactions of various people who've heard that we're staying. People who've done this before feel tremendously validated when someone else does something equally insane, we've discovered. Israelis who have heard via the Jerusalem rumor-mill that we're staying just come up to us on the street to say *"mazel tov,"* and our kids' teachers have been incredibly supportive. We even got an Israeli discount at the hotel in Eilat (you need an Israeli identity card to get the cheap rate, or it triples for Americans) just by telling the reservations clerk that we were staying. "Really?" she asked. "That's wonderful. Don't worry about the paperwork—I'll put a note in the computer." Yesterday, one of the secretaries at the Mandel Foundation who recently heard about our decision came into my office (unusual, since she's not my secretary) to say *"mazel tov."* She said, "It's going to be great," to which I said, "Let's hope so." She looked a bit stunned, and said, "It *will*—this is a wonderful home."

It's not, of course, that we think that this is the only place in the world to live a meaningful Jewish life. We have a lot of friends here who say that they couldn't wait to leave the places that they left. We don't feel that way at all. (It's understandable with the Russians and the Iraqis, obviously.) We're not running *from* anything, but moving *to* something. We've always disliked those lectures one gets from Israelis about how Jews "should" live in Israel; that's not where we're at, at all. We'll be leaving a great country with a deeply entrenched democratic tradition, a fantastic community, wonderful friends, teachers. We'll probably never be able to replicate the friendships that we've had in all those different places; some of those relationships are twenty-something years old, others go back more than thirty years. We've been blessed to be part of the communities that we've lived in; that's the part that we know we'll miss the most.

Work, too, is going to be hard to leave. It was hard to be at the University of Judaism last week, knowing that I was walking away from a fantastic project like building a new rabbinic school. As much progress as we've made, and we've made a lot, there's still a lot to do, and there's no doubt that the school's greatest days still lie ahead. It was painful to see how much the students have been learning and growing, and to know that I won't be a part of the rest of their journey. But even in the midst of all those powerful feelings, this decision felt right. Other than that, we have no idea what's in store. Time will tell, we imagine.

So this is a "conversation" that needs to be continued, but this is at least a start.

Shabbat Shalom,
from all of us

"I Thought Jews Aren't Allowed to Kill"

One of the great things about Shabbat, we commonly tell our kids, is that nothing from "out there," from the "real world," can bother us on that day. No radio, no TV, no faxes, no e-mail, no internet. We've got each other. Time to take walks, to play, to nap, to sing. What the rabbis called a "glimpse of the world to come." A time when even though the world isn't perfected, we live as if it were.

Of course, hermetic seals aren't quite possible, in Jerusalem, anywhere. But this "disconnect" from the outside world was almost impossible to attain in West Los Angeles. The *Times* would come in the morning. In the middle of lunch, we would hear the thump of mail dropping into the mail slot. And people would come by, of course.

But by and large, it worked. Most of the time.

In the fall of 1995, the days were short, dusk arrived early, and Shabbat ended sooner than at other times of the year. But on November 4th, it didn't end. It was shattered. I heard a knock on the door and Beth went to answer it. My mother-in-law had driven over to spend some time with us. As I came down the stairs to say hi, she and Beth were huddled by the doorway to the family room, speaking almost in whispers. It was Beth who said something first. "Rabin's been killed. Shot. By a Jew."

I'm mostly down the stairs when she says it, my hand running instinctively down the banister just where it curves out at the very bottom of the wide staircase. I don't say anything, but I hold on tighter. I can barely walk and I can't speak. Strangely, a first thought is that now, for all intents and purposes, Shabbat is over. Killed.

For years, until we sell the house, I avoid that little swirl at the bottom of the banister. In some crazy way, it brings back memories. I see the banister, and the whole scene returns. The huddled whisper. Beth's cut-off sentences. And Avi, who's not yet six, overhearing and asking, "But I thought that Jewish people aren't supposed to do that? I thought Jews aren't allowed to kill."

Two Years Earlier:
See What You've Done?
I Hope You're Happy.

Dear Levi:

I'd call you now, but it's the middle of the night for you. I'm here in Baltimore, having just spent most of the day watching the funeral over and over again. The whole thing is just surreal. Not much one can say, really.

Thanks for your e-mail. As always, you wrote with the poignancy and profundity that I've always admired about you. I was particularly moved by your description of how you took Anya to stand in line at the Knesset to walk past Rabin's coffin. It was the right thing to do. I realize that it's probably not easy to take one's young daughter to an event like that, but I suspect that in years to come, she'll remember it, and it will be one of those moments in which you taught her what matters most in the world.

Interestingly, the news reported today that one million people lined up to walk past the coffin. That's pretty hard to believe in a country of five million citizens. There are moments, I guess, when Israel *can* come together.

At the same time, of course, they reported that Yigal Amir has said that he has no regret that he shot Rabin, for Rabin was about to give the country away to the Arabs. What amazes me here in the U.S. is how blind I was to the inner turmoil surrounding the peace process. From this vantage point, fed largely by the American press, Rabin was the fearless warrior turned peacemaker—a veritable dream. But now, even in the last forty-eight hours, it's become obvious to us Americans—or at least more obvious to me than it ever was before—how deep were the divisions inside the country. A friend of mine, someone I don't think you know, e-mailed me earlier today and told me that for the first time in his life, he's not wearing his *kippah* outside the house. He's too ashamed of what a religious person—and the whole religious establishment, which he blames for fostering that foment—has wrought, and he's also uncomfortable. He says that the looks of hatred that he's been getting from secular Jews are actually scary; they think that just because he wears a *kippah,* he probably approves of the assassination.

It's hard for me to say this because anyone else would misunderstand, but I suspect that you'll know what I mean: I can understand some of the fury. Not approve of the murder, of course. It's horrible, immoral, an assault on democracy. And for what it's worth, I happened to think that Rabin was doing the right thing. But still, I can see why some people, even decent people, would hate him and consider him a traitor.

I still remember that campaign speech he gave at Katzrin in the Golan Heights, telling them that they—the settlers on the Golan—were the true spirit of Israel, that the Golan was key to Israel's security, and that Israel could never return it to Syria. Then, of course, he got elected and immediately went and started to negotiate giving it back. Or that comment to the West Bank settlers, who were also encouraged by the government to move to where they did, but were told when they complained that he was selling them out: "I can't be the prime minister of one hundred percent of the people." A dumb, arrogant thing to say, and an attitude that obviously got him killed in the end.

What's going to be now, do you imagine? On the one hand, I see all these people on TV lighting candles all over the streets, and it almost looks as if the country is more united than ever. That would make one think that peace will go on. But there's obviously a large crowd who are not lighting candles, who may not have killed him but probably aren't too sorry to see him gone. What I don't know is how many of *them* are there? Enough to stop the peace process? And even if there aren't that many of them, is there anyone to replace Rabin? Anyone who can survive politically and who's also willing to deal with Arafat?

One little vignette—actually the reason that I'm writing in addition to thanking you for your note—from Danny L. about his flight out of Tel Aviv Saturday night. When he left his apartment in Jerusalem right after Shabbat to go to the airport, they hadn't heard anything. He heard on the radio in the cab that Rabin had been shot, and then, when he got to the airport, they were announcing that he'd died on the operating table in Tel Aviv. Danny was stunned, and called home just to check in. Later he boarded the plane (obviously with his *kippah* on) and sat down next to a man not wearing a *kippah*. Danny put on his earphones to try to see if the plane was broadcasting any news before takeoff, but saw that the person next to him was talking to him. He took off his headphones and told the man that he hadn't heard him. The man said, with obvious disgust, "I said, 'Do you see what you've done? I hope you're happy.'"

It was the most anti-Semitic thing he'd ever had said to him, Danny told me, uttered just because he looked like a religious Jew. And it happened on an El Al plane, spoken by a Jew, a fellow Israeli. He said he had no idea what to say in response. So he said nothing and just tried not to cry. He told me that now, for the first time, he understands the trouble the country is in.

God help us now—we're going to need it.

Let's try to talk in the next couple of days. I'm leaving Baltimore to go back to Los Angeles tomorrow, and hope we can connect.

Love to everyone at home,
D

April 1999: Annata

Dear Elie:

It's after Shabbat here, and I thought I'd drop a line before it gets too late and I run out of energy. Hope things with you guys are OK— we're fine here. The kids are basically enjoying school, Beth and I are having a great time, and in all, it was a good week. Except, perhaps, for yesterday. Everything's all right, in that we're all intact, but I saw things yesterday that you just wouldn't believe. As it's getting late here and I have no one to talk with about this, I'll write it out.

When we were in shul a week or two ago, someone announced that a few people who were part of an organization opposed to the demolition of Arabs' homes by the army were going to a site to meet a family whose home had been destroyed and to begin the process of rebuilding it. This is a big issue around here, as you know, and I figured that going would provide a good opportunity to see a different side of it firsthand.

Yesterday, when I got to the parking lot where we were meeting (the one behind the gas station not far from the LaRomme Hotel), they informed us we wouldn't be able to do the rebuilding because many of the necessary building materials hadn't yet been delivered, but that we were still going to go to Annata—this Palestinian village—to meet with the people anyway. I decided to still go along.

We all got into a small minibus and off we went. Annata—more a refugee camp than a village—is for all intents and purposes inside Jerusalem. Truth be told, I had no real idea where in the world it was. As it turns out, it's right before the turnoff to French Hill, a place we've passed dozens of times without noticing that it's there. You drive up the road towards French Hill, and there's a little marked turnoff to the left that simply says "Annata," and there it is.

Well, almost. To get into the middle of the village, you have to traverse horrible, rocky, unpaved roads that could knock the guts out of any passenger car. We were in a little bus, so we were a bit better off, but the radical difference between the infrastructure of the rest of the city and the squalor of this community immediately hits you. In addition to the unpaved streets (inside what is effectively the city of Jerusalem), there are mounds of garbage piled up and the smell of unprocessed sewage everywhere.

Thankfully, the person leading our little group knew his way around the village well, and helped the driver negotiate the endless turns and narrow alleys to get to where we were going. When we finally arrived, the family and a few others were waiting for us, standing next to the pile of rubble that was their home. Their kids were also there with them, waiting for us to arrive. In what was kind of a brutal wake-up call to what we were about to hear, the first thing I noticed was a twisted and mangled kid's bicycle, crushed under a piece of concrete.

For the next couple of hours, we stood around in a slightly chilly breeze as the owner of the house, Nabil,* told his story. He spoke in a combination of Hebrew and English (the latter for the consumption of a few journalists who were in the area), and wasn't entirely easy to understand. But he was able to make his points sufficiently clearly to be understood. He'd grown up in the area, gotten married, bought the land in what's effectively an ancestral village (Annata, by the way, is apparently Annatot, where the biblical prophet Jeremiah was from), and then began a family. At a certain point, when they needed money, he took his family and went to work in the oil refineries of Saudi Arabia, which they say isn't uncommon for Palestinians who need to earn some serious money. After a few years of saving, he came back to build his family's house on the land that he had bought, and went to apply for a building permit.

That's when the trouble started.

Basically, Israel has a policy of not letting these Palestinians who come from villages in the West Bank build in certain areas. Apparently the unspoken policy applies most to "Area C," the part of the West Bank that is not at all under Palestinian Authority control. You hear differing views of why that is. Some say security; others say that the government is trying to discourage the growth of the Palestinian population in these areas, so that when the time for the final settlement comes and borders have to be drawn, there will be less justification for any Arab claims that these portions should be included within their borders. Who knows? But whatever the motivation is, the ways it's carried out seem absurd.

Nabil is told that he's not eligible for the building permit. Why? Because his land is farming land and no homes can be built there. As we're hearing this story, standing on the rocky and steep hillsides that surround his house, it's rather amusing to think that anyone could tell him with a straight face that this is farming land. Eventually, with the

---

*Not his real name. I've changed the name to ensure that he is not harassed by virtue of my retelling his story.

help of some pro bono Israeli lawyers, he manages to get a document stipulating that it's not farmland, when they begin to come up with other excuses. He's even told that he doesn't own the land. Why? Because a signature is missing on the deed of sale.

"Fine," he says. "Tell me who's missing and I'll get the signature."

"Can't tell you the name of the person," he's told. "It's a closed file."

Talk about Kafka.

Eventually, somehow, he keeps at it with this office until someone tells him unofficially, "Just build your house. Rabin's now in office, there's going to be peace, this will work out. I can't give you an official permit, but you'll be OK."

So he does. He builds this very nice house. Nice, of course, is a relative term. The houses around here are big, as are lots of these Arab homes, but, for example, in the home that I actually visited (and which seemed a lot like what his house had been), there were no bathrooms. Not in the sense that you and I know, at least. There's a room with a sink, with running water, and a hole in the tiled floor. I'm not sure what that's all about. Inadequate sewage? Cost factor? Cultural thing? I don't know, but when I say that it's a nice house, we're not talking the Upper West Side, that's for sure.

Anyway, nice or not, the house is built. And things look fine. But then November 4th comes, Rabin is killed, and it's the beginning of the end. Shortly thereafter, he gets his first *tzav harisah* [notification that his house is going to be destroyed by the army]. Armed with his Israeli pro bono lawyers, he goes back to the office that unofficially told him that he could build: to protest. Why? This time they have a different reason for why he couldn't build: He's built the house on sloping ground (the same ground that previously had been farmland) and it's dangerous. The house will collapse. But the house is standing just fine, he argues, as are all the other houses there built to similar standards. No use. They won't budge, and soon thereafter he gets another *tzav*.

As it turns out, these little notifications have an impact on much more than the actual destruction of the home. For the army doesn't tell you *when* they're going to destroy the house—they just tell you that they will. When a family gets one of these notifications, the father won't go to work anymore, for he's afraid that the army will come when he's away and his family will have to go through this without him. So, for all intents and purposes, this *tzav harisah* also spells economic doom for them. Hand out enough of these to enough families in one village and soon you can bring the economic income of the entire village to a virtual standstill because none of the men are willing to travel any serious distances to go to work, which is what many of them have to do.

So he waits and tries to work a bit here and there for several months, and nothing happens. But life is effectively frozen. The family lives in constant fear that the home will be destroyed, can't plan for the future in any meaningful way, and subsists on whatever he can earn in the immediate vicinity, which isn't much.

But one night, he tells us, he's awakened by the sound of helicopters over the house, flying very low. A searchlight from the helicopter pierces the dark, and at virtually the same time he hears someone with a bullhorn outside telling him that he's got thirty minutes to clear out his house before it's destroyed. Looking outside the window, he sees a few jeeps, the bulldozer he's known would eventually come, and several dozen soldiers ringing the house (to make sure that other villagers don't try to interfere and cause trouble). Again he's called by name: "You've got thirty minutes to take whatever you want out of your house, and then it will be destroyed."

At this point in his narrative, he turns to us and asks, "Now, how much could *you* get out of *your* house in thirty minutes?" I don't know why, but I immediately began to think of those Los Angeles Sundays when we packed up the kids to go to the beach. Coolers with sandwiches and fruit. Beach chairs. Boogie boards. Sand toys. Towels. Umbrella. The works. And never, ever, did we do it in under half an hour. As it turns out, Nabil and his family didn't get very much out of their house. Furniture, some clothes, broken bikes, and more all lay in the crushed rubble that lay in front of us.

Anyway, he wakes up his wife and kids, gives the kids to a neighbor (the entire village is awake by this point and is outside), they take out whatever they can, and then the bulldozer starts. The kids are crying in the arms of neighbors, the wife is shrieking at the top of her lungs and is being restrained by soldiers, and Nabil is shoved to the ground, forced to lie on his stomach, as a soldier puts a booted foot on his neck to make sure that he doesn't move. The bulldozer begins to smash the walls of the house, and for an hour or two, the family watches as the house comes down, chunk by chunk. After the house is destroyed, the commander tells the bulldozer operator to take out all the trees on the property. I look around. There are scattered trees throughout the village, but none here. It's a barren hill, lifeless.

It was pretty damn quiet as he told this story. Almost no sounds at all—just the chilled breeze blowing across the hill, the occasional click of a rock as one of us shuffled our feet uncomfortably, and the hushed whispers of his wife and kids, who were a few meters away, looking like they were trying to figure us out. Jews. Israelis. On our side?

Someone in our group asked him what the rest of the soldiers did while all this was happening. He swallowed and hesitated for a moment, then said in a quiet voice, "They were laughing and singing songs."

That was the last straw. I turned to the guy from our shul who had convinced me to come in the first place, and I said to him, "That's just bullshit. There's no way." To which he responded, "I was here when it happened, and it's true. I was in a unit that did this dozens of times and it often goes down that way."

I didn't know what to say. "Who are these soldiers?" I asked him. "Asshole kids?" "No," he said, "they're basically good kids. But that's the point. They're kids. You can't ask kids to watch this time and time again without having them become callous, even cruel. It's the only way that they can cope."

I thought of Avi and wondered what would happen if he were ordered to do the same thing. I knew that if he were ordered to stand guard while someone's house was destroyed, it would be incredibly painful and horrifying, but if he followed that order, I'd think no less of him. But what if he sang while those parents were crying? What if he laughed as the kids watched their house, their clothes, and all their toys get demolished by a bulldozer? I don't know how I'd look him in the eye. What's happening here? How is this country turning good kids into this?

We said our farewells to Nabil and his family, and promised to come back and rebuild the house. He knew that we meant it, and as he shook each of our hands goodbye and said "*Shalom,*" it was hard to tell if it was a parting greeting, a prayer, or a memory.

On the minibus back to the southern part of town, very few people talked. I kept thinking about the soldiers laughing and singing. And horrible as it is to say, I kept thinking of a different scene. I kept thinking of those stories I've read in which the Nazis gathered the Jews of the shtetls into the train stations and made them sing as they waited for the train that would take them off to the death camps. I tried to tell myself that this is different, and of course it is. It's very different, but it's still too close.

I told Beth the story when I got home, and Avi overheard some of it. He looked at me and asked, "Why would you want to move to a place where people do things like that?"

I told him, at greater length than this, that it's "because it's our home, and we have to make it better." But his question was much better than my answer.

Well, it's late, and I'm going to try to fall asleep. Not always easy these days. I check the kids before I get into bed, look at them sleeping so peacefully, and wonder just what the hell we're doing to them. They sleep so peacefully, and I watched Avi last night after our little exchange, his little boyish face so at ease. He's so little and innocent. He should be playing baseball in the backyard, I thought, not wondering about home demolitions and singing soldiers. I think that part of him thinks that we were nuts to move here. And sometimes, I'm not sure what to tell him. "Why?" It's actually a damn good question.

He loves you—you know that. The e-mail that you wrote him back in January about our decision to stay here and how much you love this place really made a difference for him. I'm thinking we might need you to send him another one soon.

D

Yom Ha-Shoah—When Radio Becomes Liturgy

Yom Ha-Shoah. Holocaust Memorial Day. To be more precise, its official name is "Yom Ha-Shoah Ve-ha-gevurah"—"Memorial Day for the Holocaust and the Bravery" (of those who fought back). But no one calls it that. Everyone calls it Yom Ha-Shoah. This is the day we remember the trains, the mass graves, the gas, the death, the ashes, the smoke. The country has other days, perhaps too many days, for remembering bravery.

What fascinates me, even after all the times I've seen it, is how the country chooses to commemorate this day. With a siren, and with silence.

When the air raid siren went off at ten o'clock in the morning, the entire country came to a standstill. People in the halls at work stopped moving, everyone stood still, silent, at attention. Out the window, on the streets below, cars stopped. They didn't pull over; they just stopped in the middle of the street. The drivers got out, stood at attention. The whole country came to a standstill, remembering. Knowing that in response to some things, silence is the right reaction. The only reaction.

It's like Aaron the High Priest, I thought:

> **10** *Now Aaron's sons Nadab and Abihu each took his fire pan, put fire in it, and laid incense on it; and they offered before the* LORD *alien fire, which He had not enjoined upon them.* *[2]And fire came forth from the* LORD *and consumed them; thus they died at the instance of the* LORD. *[3] . . . And Aaron was silent.*
>
> —BOOK OF LEVITICUS

When nothing you can say will suffice, when no words can even begin to approach what you're trying to convey, silence is the only meaningful response. Aaron knew that. So, too, did the people who created this ritual of the siren and the entire country becoming motionless as it pierces the morning air.

But the silence can't last the whole day. This is a modern country, not a monastery. People need to talk, to move, to do. But somehow, we still need to preserve the unique and painful nature of the day. Enter the radio. The radio, it strikes me, has become the prayer book of modernity.

The rabbis of old didn't have radio, of course. They used liturgy to create moods. On festivals, the prayer book and the liturgy evoke a sense of joy, of having been blessed—and it often works. And on days of mourning, the liturgy sometimes grabs you by the lapel and forces you to confront the enormity of the loss that's being commemorated that day.

They didn't have radio, and we don't have decent enough liturgy for modern events, especially Yom Ha-Shoah. It's probably too soon, even fifty years later, to know how to commemorate a demonic period that wiped out six million Jews, more people than live in this entire country. And here, where there are many, many people who barely escaped that hell, agreement on commemoration is simply not possible, or at least improbable.

Thus the siren and the radio.

I don't think that there's a law about what can be played on the radio on Yom Ha-Shoah, but if there is, I haven't heard of it. But by some tacit agreement, it seems, all the major radio stations played sad music today. Some of it was explicitly about the Shoah, much of it not. But all of it was somber, some of it worse. No matter how many times you pushed the station buttons on the car radio, you couldn't get away from a sense that this was a heavy day, a day in which music, more than words, was the only real response possible after the silence.

. . .

And liturgy also knows how to release us from the grasp of the moment. At the end of Yom Kippur, the sounding of the shofar indicates to one and all that it's over, that the intensity can abate, that it's time to live fully in the new year. At the conclusion of Shabbat, the wine, spices, and candle of Havdalah do something similar, ushering in the new week, signaling that the sanctity of Shabbat has abated.

So, too, with the radio tonight. No announcements on the radio that Yom Ha-Shoah was over, just a change in the music back to the regular playlist. As darkness settled over the city, the change in mood was palpable. People came out of mourning, the usual music started to play, and life returned to normal.

Remembering has a lot to do with what Israel as a country is all about. Remembering how close we've come to extinction, and promising that we'll never allow that to happen. Remembering each year, but then moving beyond. From the mournful music back to regular radio. From the somber tones of Yom Ha-Shoah to the pulsing beat of Israel's usual sound. For it's not only about remembering and mourning. That's only the first part of the equation. We're here to live.

To be alive and to live. That, bottom line, is why we're here.

May 1999:
Lag Ba-Omer—Bonfires and
Teenage Freedom

Dear Elie:

It's too early in the morning (or too late at night, depending on how you look at it) to call you, so I'll just jot a quick note. Wanted to say hi, and figured I'd tell you about last night's festivities. It's Lag Ba-Omer here, not that anyone in the States would have any reason to remember that, which is precisely the point.

Do you remember anything about Lag Ba-Omer from when we were here as kids? I certainly don't. It's obviously not a major Jewish holiday in most of the world, just a relatively minor day about two thirds of the way between Passover and Shavu'ot. There's a little-known story that a plague that had wiped out twenty-four thousand of Rabbi Akiva's students about two thousand years ago ceased on this day—hence the celebration. Here, in Israel, there's nothing to indicate that it's a non-event in most of the Jewish world. For weeks we've been seeing kids collecting wood around town and dragging it home (occasionally, it seems, also stealing some from construction sites!), so I figured that there would be some bonfires or whatever. But I didn't have any clue of how widespread the celebrations here have become.

We were invited to our friends Pinchas and Sandy's apartment in Ramot, and readily agreed. They were planning to build some big fire with their kids on a field not far from home. Tali already had plans with her Bnai Akiva group (or "herd" as I commonly call them), so she begged off. More about her in a minute.

Anyway, we went to Ramot and it was unbelievable. I expected a fire here or there, but the entire city was ablaze. (It's actually amazing that the city doesn't burn down in its entirety, as there are hundreds or thousands of kids lighting huge fires completely without adult supervision. It's a sheer miracle that no one gets killed.) As we looked out from the hill in Ramot towards the city, you could see dozens, maybe hundreds of the fires burning away, the whole city alive with light in celebration of this day. I doubt that most of the children (including many nonreligious kids, for whom this is a kind of Boy Scouts night) had any idea what the real basis of the holiday is, but it didn't matter. It was part of the Jewish calendar, not the secular or Christian calendar, and they were into it. For everyone, for one night, it was clear that this was a Jewish city in a Jewish state, and it was fun. Given all the other things that go on around here, the pure fun and positive Jewish association with no other complications was very welcome. The boys didn't want to leave, even as it got late, but then of course fell asleep in the car so I had to carry them all the way into the apartment, downstairs to bed, and even try to lift Avi high enough to throw him onto the top bunk.

I don't know where Talia went with her Bnai Akiva friends. We knew that she wouldn't be home when we got home, and she wasn't. We went to sleep, and sometime in the middle of the night, I heard the front door open and figured it was her. I glanced at the clock-radio— it was 5:30 A.M.!! I heard her get in the shower, and when I woke up, her smoky clothes were piled outside the bathroom and she was fast asleep in her bed downstairs.

She's really growing up. Just twelve still, but now out until all hours of the morning, and it doesn't seem like a very big deal. But it's amazing how quickly—and safely—it happens here. In L.A. we don't let her cross the street, much less stay out until 10:00 P.M. and walk home. Coming home at 5:30 A.M. would have been so unthinkable that she would never have dared ask. Here, it never even occurred to us not to let her go. There's nothing to be afraid of. It's strange, isn't it? In this little spot of the world that everyone else thinks is so danger-ous, it's actually great—and safe—to be a kid. You own the town. No one touches you. You have nothing to be afraid of.

She's still asleep (God knows how long she'll sleep, since she can sleep until 1:00 P.M. even when she's not out late—the joys of pre-adolescence, I guess), and when I went down to check her, I thought, what a lucky kid. It's not what most people think of when they think of the "good life." Most people probably think that we're taking them away from the "good life." But I don't—I actually think she got a real taste of it last night.

I'll talk to you in the next day or two. Our love to the girls.

L,
D

May 1999: When the Heart Trumps the Mind

In the few months since we decided to stay, we've discovered a new continuum of reactions, one that seems to range from incredulity to support. We were warned about this, mostly by friends who had already made aliyah. One person, who had actually been our rabbi in L.A. and had come on aliyah a few years before we did, said to me before I went back to the States in January, "Be prepared to be surprised by people's reactions. Most will be supportive. But a few, sometimes those whom you most expect to offer support, will surprise you. I guess you're just testing all their own misgivings about their own decisions to stay in the States. Remember not to take it personally."

That actually proved to be very useful advice. I went to see a close friend and colleague—who I thought saw the world much as I did, and

106

who also had deeply Zionist feelings—when I went back to Los Angeles to formally inform the University that I was leaving, and he said, "You know, of course, that Israel's about to head into a recession." I wasn't sure what to say. It sounded so asinine that I wasn't sure I was hearing correctly. After two thousand years of praying for a homeland, after everything that the Jewish people have gone through to get and keep this land, the notion that one shouldn't come because of a possible recession struck me as so absurd as to render me speechless. But that's why our rabbi's advice had been so helpful—it wasn't about me, or us, or even a recession. It was about the person who made that remark; it was his decision not to come, his decision to live his life outside the place that he, too, prays for, that probably led to his comment.

Anyway, to say that it's been a complicated couple of months would be to put it mildly. Many people are asking similar questions in their own ways, and I think that it's fair. I've been struggling with how to put this in words somewhat differently than I did in January in the e-mail that announced that we were staying. Why, people want to know, can't we just work with the "nice place to visit" approach? I'm not sure that I have much more to say than I did in January, but as I was recently asked by *Shm'a* magazine to write a short piece on this very topic, I thought that I'd share it with you. Two birds with one stone. Actually, the *Sh'ma* version was abridged a bit, so for those who read it, this is what it would have said had space permitted:

Not long ago, I wrote a book about why the Jews matter. In one of the last chapters of *Does the World Need the Jews?*, I suggested that to make a difference in the world, Jews needed to live everywhere, not only in one tiny country. For many reasons, I argued, Diaspora Judaism was just as vital as Israeli Jewish life, and Jewish life in North America was no less important for the Jewish people's future than life in the Jewish state.

A year after the book came out, our family came to Israel for a year's sabbatical. We wanted our kids to learn Hebrew, to come to love Israel as we do. Then, we figured, we'd pack up and head back home.

Two months after arriving, Beth and I just knew we didn't want to leave. Since then, we've sold our home, I've resigned my job, and we've decided to stay. "So, what happened?" everyone understandably asks.

There's no simple answer. Yet given everyone's suspicions to the contrary, one thing should be said up front: I still believe what I wrote. I still think that Jewish life in North America is a wonderful and creative experiment. I still believe that American Jews can make profound and unique contributions to the Jewish people and to Israel, and I still don't consider Israel the only place to live a meaningful Jewish existence. So why the move? Sometimes, I guess, the heart can trump the mind.

On the surface, things were great in the States. Professionally, I was building a new rabbinical school, an opportunity important and challenging far beyond anything I'd dreamt might come my way. Jewishly, we had it all. We loved our community, our kids went to great day schools, our neighborhood was filled with people walking home from shul on Shabbat morning. There were dozens of kosher restaurants, bookstores, *mikvot* [ritual baths], day schools of all denominations, Jewish high schools of various sorts, and our kids were growing up surrounded by an entire community that lived just the way they did. In some limited ways, that community was a microcosm of what we've found here in Israel. But despite all that, I now realize, it never really felt like home.

During the Gulf War, I would take my then very young kids to the front porch each morning to put up an American flag in support of the troops who were fighting a war that I thought needed to be fought. But I remember feeling even then that I certainly wouldn't want my kids out there, possibly dying for Kuwait, a country to which I felt absolutely no connection. Yes, America was our country, but that battle wasn't worth my kids' lives. The conflict was unsettling.

Beth didn't experience that conflict. She thought the flag was silly, that there was no use pretending that any place other than Israel was really ours. Ever since she was a kid, she'd wanted to live here.

I was the one who balked, but this year, something about being here got under my skin.

Here in Israel, the days too frequently begin with horrifying newspaper reports that more Israeli soldiers have been killed in Lebanon. At the end of those days, as I tuck my kids into bed, I shudder to think of Avi, my nine-year-old son, going up north in just a few years. I watch his little body in that big bed, gaze at his innocent face, and wonder if we're being fair to him. But at the same time, I never have the feeling that I had during the Gulf War. My gut tells me that this *is* his battle, that somehow he belongs in this complicated business, frightening though it is.

It's about more than battles, of course. It's about destiny. One of the things that we've watched with fascination is the way in which our kids have come to feel that this country, the language of which they don't yet speak fluently, the culture of which they're still figuring out, is theirs. During the Wye River negotiations, analysts on TV noted that without an agreement, Arafat would declare a state in May 1999. Avi simply exclaimed, "That's crazy! How can he declare a state in the middle of our country?"

We explained that this land isn't only ours, that other people have claims to it as well. But what struck me most was that only a couple of months into our stay, our kids already saw Israel as "ours." They, too, I realize, sensed that we'd come home.

As I'm writing this, Yom Ha-Atzma'ut [Israel Independence Day] is only days away. Zionism, rather than the usual cynicism, is in the air again. Songs of the *chalutzim* [early pioneers] are playing in the malls. Israeli flags are hanging from the porches, fluttering from the windows of many cars.

We've got a flag here, too. But this time it was Beth who came home with two flags, which we promptly attached to the windows of our car. And this time, I feel no conflict. After all, the street names are taken from my history, the morning papers are in a language that's distinctly ours. On Friday afternoon, the radio plays Shabbat music. When we got caught in an enormous traffic jam the other week in East Jerusalem and couldn't figure out why, it never even occurred to us that it was because of Easter, with all the pilgrims who had come to town. We didn't even know it was Easter. There are no more of those moments when I'm slightly nervous to be wearing my *kippah,* and yes, even the troubling specter of battles ahead is at least the specter of battles that would be ours. We're home.

As I tucked Avi into bed recently, I again thought of him nine years from now, in the army. I thought of all the articles we read in the press about the excesses of a few Israeli soldiers, about a mean side to this society that sometimes disturbs us to our very core. This time, I worried not for his life, but for his soul. Will he grow up to hate, as those soldiers do? I knew we simply couldn't let that happen. There's got to be a place somewhere in the world, I thought, that Jewish kids will feel is theirs, a place where the songs are theirs, where the history is their history, where the place doesn't just welcome them, but is *for* them. A place where they won't have to fight. And a place where being Jewish will also mean being just.

Can it happen? We're here because we desperately want the answer to be "yes." We're here because as we ask ourselves what we ultimately want to leave our children, having them become part of this crazy, complicated, and wondrous place is the most important gift we can imagine. What, after all, can parents give their kids that's more important than a home?

May 17, 1999:
Giving Peace a Chance

The Israeli Vote: The Overview; Israelis Choose a New Leader and Remake Their Parliament

Israelis overwhelmingly elect Labor Party leader Ehud Barak as new Prime Minister in landslide vote, rejecting tumultuous leadership of Benjamin Netanyahu whose galvanizing character dominated Israel for three years; Barak captures 56 percent of vote, compared with 43.9 for Netanyahu; election of protege of late Yitzhak Rabin is seen as resounding call for revival of languishing peace effort between Israelis and Palestinians; Barak, in victory speech, cites need to strengthen country's security by moving forward to peace agreements; issues call for unity, and vows to be everyone's Prime Minister; Yasir Arafat calls and congratulates Barak.

New York Times: Tuesday, May 18, 1999, page A1

Dear Elie:

This is so amazing! Barak won, as you will obviously know by the time you read this. You wouldn't believe the scene on the streets. Our friends are literally delirious with joy. I think that they didn't believe that they could actually get rid of Bibi. He has an aura of permanence, I guess, and people didn't dare let themselves be that hopeful. But he's

111

out, he'll soon be gone—it's like spring cleaning in the Knesset. Peace has a chance.

I saw our friends from London who live down the street (did you meet them when you were here?). She was one of the ones who told me that if Bibi won, they were going to leave. She was part of a large group that simply couldn't take the feeling that peace would never come, simply because people like Bibi refused to take a chance, did everything they could to antagonize the Palestinians, and had no clear course of action plotted. As this family had come years ago, it was sobering to hear her talk over the last few weeks about the possibility of leaving if he won again. I was never certain whether or not to believe her.

I asked her today if she'd meant it, assuming, of course, that they were staying. She said she didn't know, but at least now, she felt like she was staying in a country that had a chance for a future. I think people believe Barak when he says he's going to bring peace. He seems different, anxious to put the previous period of rudderless foreign policy to an end.

Now at least there's a clear foreign policy question being bandied about: With whom should we make peace first? Syria? Palestinians? Both at the same time? Some sort of regional deal? I assume Barak has some sort of a plan—that's the part that's different, and that has everyone feeling this sense of hope in the air.

On some levels, of course, it's a bit early for euphoria, as Barak's got a lot of work to do to put together his government. The various small parties will all want a bit of his flesh for joining the coalition and for giving him the votes that he needs, but one has to assume that he's figured something out, or that he will. Ultimately he'll get a government together, and then it's off to peace. As they say, it looks like this crazy little place decided to give peace a chance after all.

Well, I'll call in the next day or two. Love to everyone at home.

L,

D

Ellis Island

- - - - - - - - - - - - - - - - - -

It's the summer of 1999. Our sabbatical year is over, but instead of packing up in Israel and heading back to Los Angeles as we'd planned, we're back in the States to pack up everything in California and have it shipped to Jerusalem. We started with a few weeks in L.A., to pack up the house and close the deal, say goodbye to friends, and to give the kids the closure that they didn't have last time we left, since we had told them that we were coming back.

After that, it was off to a family vacation in New York, and the requisite trip to the Statue of Liberty. When we got there, the lines to the statue were ridiculously long, so we got off the boat at Ellis Island and decided to take the kids through the recently reopened museum. I'd never been there before, and found it much more powerful than I'd expected.

My maternal grandmother, or Savta as we knew her, came in through here. As we tour the enormous room where the immigrants were lined up and processed, I'm struck by the fact that I know for a fact that she was in this very room. This was the place where she stood when she disembarked the *Zeeland*, which had set sail from Antwerp, where she stood in line to begin a new life, back in December of 1913, when she was only eleven years old.

She never told us anything about Ellis Island, or much about where she came from. (We only got the dates and the name of the ship many years after she died.) Did she want to convince herself that there was no past, that America was where she belonged? Her English was excellent, with only the barest trace of an accent. And our family followed the traditional path. She had only a rudimentary formal education, though she taught seventh grade and adult continuing education classes her whole life. Her kids (including my mom) became professionals, moved to the suburbs, and lived the good

American life. We grew up, it seemed, as if our family had always been in America, as if we had been the first ones to disembark the *Mayflower*. No one ever mentioned any other way of seeing the world.

Now, with my kids (at just about the age she was when she got to New York) in tow, showing them around the museum, I realize how short the stay here was for us. I'd always thought of our family as a "left Europe and came to America" family. Now, I wonder, are we a "left Europe and went to Israel family," with an "oh, and stopped in America for a couple of generations" added in? What exactly is our story? How would my grandmother have told the story if I'd been mature enough to ask her when she was still alive?

We'd lived in America with a sense that nothing could be more permanent. Now we think of Jerusalem as becoming permanent. Is anything permanent? Or is this constant dream of setting real roots, of being from a place, just that, a dream?

Was that dream part of Savta's story? Will the dream of setting real roots be part of the story our kids will tell about themselves? My grandmother never looked back, seems to have had no regrets about choosing a new land. And why would she? Europe's history proved her right. Will our kids have regrets? What will history say—to us, to them, to their kids—about the choice we're making for them?

December 1999: Citizenship, and Hanukkah Miracles Continue

- - - - - - - - - - - - - - - - -

Two months after we returned from our summer trip to the States—our house in Los Angeles sold, our belongings in storage, and our new apartment in Jerusalem in the early stages of a remodel—we completed the process of applying for Israeli citizenship. As Jews, we're automatically guaranteed the right to citizenship. That law, called the Law of Return, was established by the Knesset in 1950, very early on in Israel's history, as a statement that after all that Nazi Germany had wrought, this country would make sure that Jews were never again trapped with nowhere to go. So the process of becoming citizens is supposed to be pro forma. But this is Israel, and that doesn't mean that it has to be easy. We've been to the Ministry of the Interior five times, each time being told we needed different paperwork.

Before the summer, when we'd started the process, we had been told to bring our *ketubbah* (our traditional Jewish marriage contract) to prove that we're Jewish and married. But our *ketubbah* is calligraphed, large, and framed, and it would be no simple task to get it here. So I pull out a black-and-white photocopy of the *ketubbah* that a friend had told us to prepare for this eventuality, but to no avail. The clerk behind the desk says she can't accept a photocopy—she has to see the original. I try to argue the point, but the conversation goes nowhere. So during the summer in Los Angeles, we tell the movers not to pack the *ketubbah,* and a few weeks later, I bring it back to Israel all wrapped in bubble wrap. It makes for strange hand luggage on the plane, but there's nothing to do. I ignore all the stares and keep it by me.

The next week, I take a cab to the Ministry of the Interior again, to have them register in our file that they've now seen the *ketubbah.* Again I endure the same quizzical stares among the dozens and dozens of people waiting in the lobby. They're all different. There are Russians, Ethiopians, Americans, and Australians doing the same thing I am. There are foreign workers from Thailand, the Philippines, and Eastern Europe waiting to extend their workers' visas. But what they all have in common is a profound curiosity as to why I'm dragging this framed picture around with me.

Finally it's my turn, and I explain to the clerk that I'm there to have them see our *ketubbah*. "Fine, let's see it." I start to unwrap all the bubble paper, and she asks what I'm doing. I tell her that this is the *ketubbah*. Somewhat flabbergasted, she watches (along with the rest of the waiting room) as I unwrap it, and then says, "This is no good. A *ketubbah* can't be in color. It has to be black and white." By this point, I'm not in much of a mood to explain to her that I'm a rabbi, she's not, and believe me, a *ketubbah* does not have to be in black and white. It's not my fault, I want to snap at her, that she's never seen one in color, but really, who is she to be determining matters of Jewish law anyway? But I know that getting into an argument with her is a very bad idea, as she can easily make sure that my file gets lost or delayed, so I take a deep breath and smile.

So, what should we do, I ask her. "Well, I just need a copy in black and white, that's all," she says calmly, also trying to avoid a scene. I happen to have my file of all my paperwork with me, so I take out the photocopy that I'd showed a different clerk before the summer. How about this, I suggest. "This is fine. I don't know why you bothered to bring that other thing with you," she responded.

I'm learning the system, so I said, "Oh, my mistake." She stamped something in the file and told me to return in two weeks with my wife for the final stage. We went back, of course, but then were told that the police investigation of our pasts (routine—they do it for all such applications) is delayed and so is our application. Another visit or two and then finally, after a five-hour wait in the lobby during the last visit, our American passports are stamped with a new visa and our Israeli identification numbers are now inserted. We're official. We're citizens.

. . .

A couple of months later, some friends invited us to go camping with them over Hanukkah vacation. There would be five families, including us, and we were going to spend three days in the desert, on the Israeli-Egyptian border, camping and touring the desert with bona fide Bedouin guides. They'd prepare our (kosher) food; we'd sleep in a Bedouin tent with the other families and tour around during the day on camels. It sounded like a lot of fun, so we readily agreed.

A few days later, before we left for the trip, we learned that one of the families would be the Sharanskys: Natan, Avital, and their two daughters. I remembered the days, when I was in college and graduate school in New York, when we were out parading with "Free Sharansky" signs after he had been arrested by the Soviets for applying to emigrate to Israel, and for his role in leading the refusnik movement. Now he was not only out of jail and living in Israel, but he was Minister of the Interior. It would be interesting, to say the least, to spend a few days of Hanukkah with him and his family in such a small group.

We spent the day exploring the desert on camels, and at one point Sharansky and I were assigned to the same camel. So there we were, he and I, one a former Soviet prisoner and now the Minister of the Interior, and the other a simple American immigrant, clip-clopping around the desert on a camel. We began to chat, and after a while, even though I knew he was on vacation, I regaled him with the story of our attempt to process our citizenship at the ministry. He knew I wasn't complaining, though, and said he knew there was a lot of work to do there. In retrospect, I was sorry that I'd even mentioned it, after all he'd been through. Inconveniences at the Ministry of the Interior seemed like a very petty cost to pay for the gift of being a small player in this drama called the State of Israel.

That night, just after the sun had set, the families instinctively began to gather outside our tents to light Hanukkah candles on the picnic table. Each family had brought a *hanukkiah* (a Hanukkah menorah), and one by one, as they made their way to the table, the families placed candles in their *hanukkiah* and sang the blessings. By chance, the Sharanskys were the last family to do so, so we all happened to be there as Natan gingerly unwrapped a small, plain *hanukkiah*, sang the blessings, and lit the candles. As I looked out at the desert, with this band of Israeli immigrants (one family from Russia, one from England, three from the States) and the Bedouins watching from the side, I was struck by the sheer miraculousness of what was transpiring. It seemed that it couldn't get any better. Then, when it was very quiet, Natan said matter-of-factly, "This reminds me of the *hanukkiah* I used in prison." Silence, again. Fortunately, everyone there was wise enough to know that there's nothing you can say to respond at a moment like that.

Standing around the flames that were struggling to stay alight in the gentle desert wind, we huddled together to try to block the breeze so that the candles would not blow out. This is it, I found myself thinking; this is *kibbutz galuyot*, the "ingathering of the exiles" that the tradition has talked about and dreamt of for two thousand years. With the chill of the desert night getting stronger and stronger, we found ourselves huddled closer and closer together, both for the warmth and to make sure that the candles didn't get blown out. I looked at my kids. For centuries, Jews had been trying to make sure that the lights did not get extinguished, that Jewish life would somehow continue. And here were my kids, living this wonderful moment, part of this small band of people drawn to this one place, just to keep the flame alive.

Hanukkah miracles all over again, I thought. And now, because my kids live here, they not only celebrate them—they're part of the miracle.

July 2000: A Year Later

As it's been more than a year since our most recent "update," it seemed to us that some sort of communiqué was in order. Obviously a lot has happened in the last year, and it's actually a bit difficult to know where to start.

It's been a quiet summer. The big kids are at sleep-away camp near Beit She'an in the Jordan Valley, apparently having a great time despite the heat (it's well over a hundred degrees every day), and Micha's here in Jerusalem with us in day camp. When the kids get home from camp, we hope to take them to Paris for a week or so before school starts. One of the benefits of being here is that Europe is very close and relatively inexpensive, so we go when we can. We realize that we don't have too many more summers for this sort of thing. After this summer, Tali only has three more summers before she gets drafted, and the army's not likely to be particularly flexible about vacation time with her parents. So we'll do Paris this summer, and then see about the future.

Beth is now going by Elisheva, since Israelis can't pronounce "th" and besides, she figured, it *is* her Hebrew name. She took the year to mostly supervise the remodeling of the home we bought last summer, and then to do an advanced *ulpan* (intensive Hebrew language course) in the second half of the year.

We hadn't actually expected to buy property here so quickly, and started looking around last summer just to get an idea of what the market was like. But on the very first day that Elisheva went out with the realtor, she came home and said that she'd found something she liked. We ultimately settled on a different apartment in the same building, and after a few months of negotiations (very different in the Middle East than in the States, and not as pleasant), we bought. In retrospect, I think that though we weren't quite conscious of it when we were looking and negotiating, we were both anxious to feel settled. We had lived in four apartments here in less than two years, and wanted to stop this "wandering Jew" syndrome. The kids were tired of hearing that they couldn't put posters on the walls because the house wasn't ours, and we were tired of living with other people's furniture. If making this move was going to work, I think we realized, we had to have a permanent place.

Unfortunately, Elisheva was in the States when the deal actually closed. I was at the sellers' lawyer's office with our lawyer, the builder, and a few other people, and after we'd signed a large number of documents and shook hands, the builder, with whom we'd had very difficult negotiations for a few weeks, turned to me and said, "*Mazel tov*—you now own a piece of the State of Israel." It was actually a very nice moment. I thought of how absurd a dream this would have been for Jews just a few generations ago, and I found myself wishing that Elisheva had been here to hear that, instead of just getting the documents by FedEx to sign and notarize and return to Israel.

We had hoped to move into the remodeled place by December, but that was (needless to say) overly optimistic, and we ended up moving in at the beginning of February. Elisheva was busy trying to keep the architect, contractor, carpenters, etc., all in sync, which, even though we had done three major renovations in the States, proved to be a Herculean challenge. In the States, we never had to worry that outbreaks of violence would lead to the border being closed and our workers being unable to enter the country! In fact, when we remodeled our house in West L.A., we used to joke about the fact that all the subcontractors were Israelis. Here, of course, they were all Palestinians, and hardly an Israeli ever saw the place. It's an ironic, but also sad, state of affairs.

When the apartment was finally done, we had our lift (everything we owned in the world, basically) delivered. It had been in storage since the summer that we'd gone back to Los Angeles to sell our house, and we timed the delivery to coincide with the completion of the apartment. The truck that arrived with the shipper's container was enormous, and as it pulled up and the movers began to unload everything, Elisheva and I watched from the porch. I'd expected us both to feel elated, thrilled that we were finally settling in. But surprisingly, I found myself feeling sad as I saw all our familiar furniture and belongings being taken out of the truck and carried up the stairs. Suddenly there was something very permanent about this little adventure we were on. We'd arrived in 1998 with just ten duffel bags and a computer in a box. Now, a year and a half later, the commitment was of a wholly different order. Seeing everything we owned land in Jerusalem brought home how big a deal this really was.

I decided not to say anything to Elisheva about this thought, and went to direct the movers as to what went where. Sometime later, I realized that I didn't know where she was, and eventually found her sitting on the edge of our bed, which had just been brought in. She looked upset, so I asked her if she was OK. "I'm fine. But I'm surprised that I'm sad. I guess the enormity of this whole thing is suddenly hitting me." I wondered if that's what happens when you've been married for a long time—you feel the same thing without even talking.

Anyway, now that we're more or less settled, we're beginning to plan for the future. Elisheva's *ulpan* just finished a week or two ago. Now that summer's here, she's beginning to think about what she wants to do professionally for the next phase, and is still mulling it over.

I'm still loving my work at the Mandel Foundation and the Jerusalem Fellows. In addition, now that summer's here and I may have just a bit more flexibility in my schedule, I'm hoping to churn out a major portion of a book on Conservative Judaism in America. Obviously it's a bit more specific than I make it sound, but as the thesis is a bit controversial, I'll leave it at that.

I am also thinking about writing on the Israeli-Palestinian conflict, which is not a topic I ever thought I'd be interested in writing on. I'm not entirely certain why this project is growing on me. I suspect that it has to do with the fact that despite everything we love about Israel, I have a sense that this simmering and unresolved conflict is more nuanced and complex than most people realize. Two peoples both claim this tiny slice of land, but too few American Jews talk about that fact when they speak about this conflict. The miraculous dimensions of Israel will survive, I think, only if that conflict gets resolved, and it's not yet clear exactly how that will happen. So I'm thinking of exploring some of those ideas, but haven't begun the project in any serious way yet.

Back to what's so incredibly wonderful about life here. The miraculous in Israel sometimes happens completely without warning. For instance, in November, several weeks before our Hanukkah camping trip, Tali asked if she could have Shabbat dinner at a friend's house and then sleep over. We agreed, and when she came home the next day, we asked her how it had been. "Fine," she said, adding, "There was somebody at dinner who I think is famous, but I'm not sure who he was." That, obviously, didn't give us much of a lead, but as we pressed her, she said, "I think he's from Russia, and he's not religious, but his wife is." "Sharansky?" I asked. "Yeah, that's it," she replied, not terribly interested in why we thought this was a big deal.

Now, that's miraculous. Maybe not for Tali, but certainly for us. If anyone had told me back then that approximately twenty years later his daughter and my daughter would both be Israeli citizens and would be nonchalantly having Shabbat dinner together and playing Monopoly, I would have said they were crazy. But it does happen, here and there, and it's at moments like that, in the midst of all the craziness, that we feel the momentous nature of the opportunity to be a part of this story.

Simultaneously, there's an ongoing painful side to life here, the sense that we're embroiled in a conflict that has no resolution. We have a couple of Palestinian Israeli students here at Mandel, not in my program, but in one of the others. They are very talented, the cream of the crop of Palestinian society in educational terms. One woman, in her mid-thirties, approached me about a project she was working on and asked if I'd explain to her the nature of the various Jewish universities in the States. She's investigating the ways in which minorities establish their own universities, to see if that has implications for Palestinian Israelis here. I spent some time with her explaining the differences between places like Yeshiva University, Brandeis, JTS, the various Hebrew colleges, the University of Judaism, etc., and we struck up a nice relationship. We continued to meet about a variety of issues, and as we concluded a meeting at the end of April, we opened our calendars and scheduled a meeting for May 15th.

On May 14th, the internationally recognized date of Israel's independence (Israel celebrates it according to the Hebrew calendar), huge riots broke out in the "territories." Shots were fired in several places, and there were casualties on both sides. Several of our students who live in the territories couldn't get to school that day because the mobs had closed the roads, and in general it was a tense day. Here in Jerusalem, you couldn't sense anything different, but from the radio, it was clear that things were wild just a few moments' drive away.

When this woman and I met the next day, it seemed to me unrealistic to expect that we could simply have a normal conversation without mentioning the previous day's events. So I simply said, "Yesterday was a difficult day." "Yes," she responded, "we call it 'El Naqba,'" alluding to the Palestinian name for Israel's independence day. "That means 'catastrophe,' doesn't it," I asked her. To which she responded, "Yes, but that doesn't capture the full meaning. You have to understand that Israel's independence is basically our Holocaust."

Although I have a good poker face, I must have looked aghast, because her demeanor changed after that. I was aghast not only at what struck me as a nonsensical analogy (after all, say what one might about Israeli misconduct over the past fifty years, and there has been plenty of it, no one can claim that we've tried to annihilate their entire people, or engaged in genocide or anything of the sort), but also at the fact that she's a moderate Palestinian, someone who lives in Israel with Israelis, speaks Hebrew fluently, and studies in an Israeli institution. At that moment, only a couple of months ago, I was confronted by the very real possibility that there's no one to talk to even among Israeli Arabs, no way that this thing is ever going to be resolved. If *she*, of all people, sees people like *me* as Nazis, where do we go from here?

Not long ago, I cut out an article from the front page of *Ha-Aretz* (the closest thing we have to the *New York Times* here) on the day before Independence Day, when Israel observes a Memorial Day for soldiers who have been killed in the conflict. The second paragraph of the article read, "The number of fallen soldiers since Israel's establishment is 19,105. . . . According to Defense Ministry statistics, these soldiers have left 17,812 bereaved families behind." Implicit in that obtuse statement, I later realized, is that 1,293 families have lost more than one person, often a father and a son. What more need one say?

That day, one of the television stations listed each and every one of the names on the screen. The name and the date of their death appeared for a second or two, and then the next name appeared. It took the entire twenty-four hours to go through the whole list, which began in 1948 and ended only a few weeks ago. We left the TV on that channel the entire night without turning it off. When the kids woke up the next morning and the names were still flashing on the screen with soft music in the background, Avi couldn't believe it. When we explained that there were more than twelve hours left to go, he began to understand for the first time the enormity of the price that has been paid. For large parts of the day, the kids just sat on the sofa and watched the names go by, one by one, without saying very much at all. I wondered what they must be thinking about their parents' decision to move them to a place where this was part of life.

A couple of weeks ago, Micha asked Elisheva, "When I get older, am I going to go to a war?" She said to him, rather shocked, "Well, you're going to go to the army, but I hope that by then there will be peace, and you won't have to go to war." "That's good," he replied, "because I know that if I go to a war, I'm going to die."

My brother and his family are here for a spell, and the other day, as we were out with my nieces, Tamar, the four-year-old, saw a soldier and said, "Look, a hunter!" I was struck by the different states of realities our kids lived in. One knows about guns only from *Bambi*, and one is worried about getting killed in a war.

Which is why peace is so critical, and why, if I read it correctly, the country is basically despondent. This is the moment of truth. I think that most people are afraid that Camp David 2000 is going to fail, and that the entire notion of us ever living in peace is pure fiction. If there's no agreement, the Palestinians are going to run out of patience. Arafat will declare a state at some point, and Israel is not likely stand by and watch (for reasons I don't personally understand). But more important, the Palestinian populace is (understandably) out of patience, and they're likely to return to the streets. But unlike the situation in the Intifada in the 1980s, this time they're armed with a lot more than stones, and there's little reason to assume that they'll take only to *their* streets. After all, their streets and our streets are more or less adjacent. We've been fortunate enough to live here during two years of relative calm, with scarcely a terrorist incident or any reason to have to fear for our children's safety. Many of us sense that in the absence of a major reason to celebrate in the days to come, things are going to get a lot worse before they get better.

At Shabbat lunch a few days ago, we had another family over (Israeli born) and the conversation turned to this. The wife said she thinks nothing will come of these negotiations, for the Palestinians have no interest in a permanent settlement. "They hate us, plain and simple," she said. To which her husband responded, "And probably with good reason."

It occurred to me later that this very conversation had taken place in what we think is our home, but which is really part of a building abandoned by Palestinians when they fled in 1948. So much for the simple life. The coming weeks will probably tell us all a great deal about what the future will look like. Maybe there's hope for an end, or at least the beginning of an end, to this conflict.

Let's hope. In the meantime, have a great and productive summer, and let's keep in touch.

July 25, 2000: *Crash and Burn*

Our vigil around CNN has become constant. The tension in the country is palpable and Israelis from all walks of life are huddled around radios, watching television, scanning each new newspaper for some suggestion of whether Camp David, on which Clinton has staked the entire Mideast peace process, will really provide the long-hoped-for deal. But it's a roller-coaster, and virtually everyone here is agitated. One day, the parties announce that there's nothing to discuss and that they are preparing to pack up and go home. The next, the newspapers report that Arafat and Barak have decided to stay on, with reports abounding that Barak is offering more than anyone imagined possible.

There are rumors that he's offered almost the entire West Bank. Someone leaks a story that he's offered East Jerusalem, which he promised in his campaign that he'd never do. Arguments rage. One view says that he's a visionary, and even if the compromise on our part involves Jerusalem, peace will be worth it. Besides, the argument goes, he's just doing now what we'll be forced to do later. Why should more kids have to die defending what we all know we're going to give away?

The other side says that Barak specifically promised in his campaign not to divide Jerusalem and that he's a traitor. That he wants the Nobel Peace Prize and will give away the country to get it. And look, even with everything on the table, Arafat can't just say "deal." Nothing will ever be enough for him, and if Barak doesn't figure this out soon, it's going to be a disaster. Let's hope the talks crumble before we have a real catastrophe on our hands.

. . .

July 25th. There's a sense that some announcement is imminent. CNN is on in the background, and suddenly "breaking news." An Air France Concorde plane has crashed, killing all 113 persons on board, and the Camp David peace talks have collapsed. Two "crash and burns" in the very same day. What a sickening coincidence.

Something about plane crashes attracts kids to TV, it seems. The video of the crash site, discussions with experts, eyewitness reports. The standard works, and tragic. The kids are glued.

Then, a comment or two about the Middle East. The talks are over, with no agreement. Barak is headed back to Israel, no agreement in hand. Clinton does everything but actually say that it was Arafat's fault. He says he hopes that the two sides will continue talking soon. The public endorsement of Barak feels good, but weeks of anticipation and hope are now dead.

I'm still watching the news, but my mind is already wandering, contemplating the future. Barak is going to be a wounded animal—and thus easy prey—in the Knesset; having put all that territory on the table and having come back with nothing, he's in big trouble. The right will think he's a traitor and will say that it's clear that nothing we offer will be enough; the left will think he didn't offer enough or offer it in the right spirit. It's very possible he won't survive this. He'd staked his entire premiership on getting peace. First it failed with Syria, and now this. Clinton's days in office are numbered; could the same be true of Barak? How far we've come from those euphoric days when he was first elected.

The TV prattles on, and one of the kids asks, "So what's going to happen now?"

"It'll probably take a bit of time until they start to talk again," I assure them, "but don't worry—this was a good start. It's going to be fine."

After

Muhammad Jamal Al Dura

- - - - - - - - - - - - - - - - -

There are certain photographs that just won't go away. Images that are engraved not only in our memory, but in our consciousness, that come to symbolize epochs, eras, opportunities missed. The *Hindenburg* exploding. Iwo Jima and the flag raising. C.P.O. Graham Jackson playing "Goin' Home" on his accordion, his face streaked with tears, as FDR's body is carried to the train the day after his death. The little Jewish boy in his finest coat, looking up at the Nazi storm trooper and raising his hands high in surrender.

Skirmishes have broken out between Palestinians, frustrated by the lack of progress in the peace process, and Israeli soldiers trying to maintain security at critical checkpoints. This past Shabbat, September 30, 2000, Muhammad Jamal Al Dura, twelve years old, was killed—apparently by an Israeli bullet, though the army says that further study is needed—as he huddled for protection with his father behind a metal barrel. The image of the two of them hiding from the gunfire was captured by a photographer, and it is all anyone seems to be able to think or talk about.

It's clear that we didn't start this little round of violence, but the picture has pervaded all the nooks and crannies of reality. It's been in one paper or another virtually every day. TV is no escape. CNN obviously has the picture too, and seems to be unable to show anything else, the image of his terror-stricken face flashing over and over across our TV screen. England's SkyNews is no escape. Surf enough cable channels, and you see that it's everywhere. World opinion is already formed. In July, Clinton made it clear that when the talks collapsed, we were the good guys. Seems everything's different now.

Even the Israeli press is completely preoccupied by what happened. No one likes when a child gets killed, especially when it's us doing the killing. The left and the right are lining up, and the old conversations about occupation, excessive use of violence, the decaying Israeli sense of right and wrong, are all reignited.

In hushed, staccato discussions, our friends are chatting and wondering. Why was he shot? What was he doing there? Do we really believe that they were on their way back from trying to buy a car? Who buys cars in the middle of a riot?

It couldn't have been intentional, could it? We don't do these things on purpose, do we?

October 2000: Surgery and Shooting on Rosh Ha-Shannah

Violence Spreads to Israeli Towns; Arab Toll at 28

Israeli-Palestinian agreement to restrain fighting in West Bank and Gaza disintegrates as violence continues for fourth consecutive day, spreading to Arab towns inside Israel's borders; Palestinian death toll rises to 28; rioting stuns Israeli police officials, who are shocked by size and intensity; claims first Israeli victim as border policeman is fatally wounded in gun battle in Nablus; Israelis blame Palestinians for failing to control streets; accuse them of orchestrating clashes, which followed visit of right-wing political leader Ariel Sharon to steps of ancient mosque in Old City of Jerusalem; Palestinians accuse Israelis of using excessive force.

New York Times: Monday, October 2, 2000, page A1

A quick note, before Yom Kippur begins in the "City of Peace." Things are very tense, but physically West Jerusalem is at peace. People are out on the streets, buying groceries for tonight's pre-fast meal, kids are playing on their scooters, and all seems normal. The soldiers and heavily armed police who had filtered through our neighborhood on Friday in anticipation of riots worse than the ones we had have now gone, and it's now a matter of waiting.

Israel Radio, which normally goes silent on all stations on Yom Kippur, is going to a wartime mode tonight. There will be one station broadcasting news on the hour, and one that will be silent but "on" so that if there is an emergency, people who've left their radios on will hear nothing but emergency news. We'll probably leave one radio on, tuned to one of those stations.

The long-term picture is less reassuring. All the liberal assumptions with which we so confidently arrived here—the Arabs want peace, we *can* get out of Lebanon and have a quiet border there, the world understands our predicament, our neighborhoods are safe for our children, at least—have all been blown pretty much to pieces, and it will take us all a while to get our bearings. Clearly, there's no area that's completely safe, and in many respects, we're back to the neighborhood rioting of the 1920s and 1930s that preceded the formation of the state. Where this will go, with whom one can negotiate, with whom one can genuinely hope to live in peace, are all real questions. My hunch is that Arafat missed his chance, and that the good deal he might have gotten just a few days ago will now be hard to resurrect. But who knows—he somehow seems to play his hand much more cleverly than we do ours.

That, in many respects, is the fundamental dilemma that faces Israelis: figuring out who Arafat is. There are those who believe that he is still the cold-blooded terrorist he always was, having changed only his public persona. They point to the fact that Arafat has never said—in Arabic, on Palestinian TV, or in the Palestinian press, directly to his population—that Israel has a right to exist. He's said it to the world press in not so many words, but not to the people who need to hear it most. Right-wing Israelis are convinced that that's because he knows what the world wants to hear, but he wants his own people to hear something very different. If they're right, there's probably no deal to be had with him, and in the meantime, of course, we've armed him and made him legitimate, facts that he's using now to kill us.

Left-wing Israelis see things entirely differently. They think—or want to believe—that Arafat has genuinely changed, that giving him the Nobel Peace Prize was not an absurd joke, that he does want to make a deal. They explain his silence about Israel's right to exist by reminding each other that Muslim culture is different from the West, and that the kind of expectations we have about what he should say simply do not work in his world. Besides, they argue, there is absolutely no one else with whom we can negotiate, so if we assume that Arafat is unreformed and unrepentant, then we have to admit that we're going to be at war for the long haul. And the left, particularly, has been predicated on the assumption that peace can be had for the right price.

Truth be told, I don't know what to believe. What I do know is that things here are very unsteady. Indeed, they change hour by hour, and by tomorrow night, at the end of the fast, they'll undoubtedly be different. How, of course, remains to be seen. Most important on the home front, the kids are OK and seem to be coping with the tension. Tali and Avi listen to the news and read the paper. Tali doesn't say much, but is clearly processing. Avi asks a lot about the army, undoubtedly concluding that in a few years, *he'll* be the one getting mobilized. Micha is the one who understands the least and seems to be the most scared. We were watching CNN yesterday where they showed some footage of the revolution in Yugoslavia, including a burning building. We just watched, and he said, "Great, next they're going to burn down our house." When he saw some footage of Israeli soldiers being shot at by Palestinian policemen, he said, "We had better get back to America fast." It hurts to see him scared, but all we can try to do is make life as normal as possible for him.

Needless to say, we're not going "back to America fast." We did assume that the Israel we'd come to would more or less be at peace, and we now realize that we may be in for some rough days, weeks, or even a few months. But even with all the tension, we're not ambivalent about being here. We're here because we believe that Jews need a country of their own. We also know that if Jews had run away from here whenever it got dangerous or unpleasant, there would simply be no Jewish state at all. We're safe, and frankly, I'd much rather be here during this time than watching it from afar.

In the meantime, my thanks to all who called about my surgery.

Just to set the record straight: I didn't feel great the night before Rosh Ha-Shannah, but didn't think much of it. When I went to sleep, I had some pretty severe abdominal pain, but took some Advil and slept fine through the night. Woke up early to review my Torah reading for shul, and noticed that the pain had moved to the lower right side of my abdomen. I took out our copy of the *Columbia University Complete Home Medical Guide* (or whatever it's called) and looked up appendicitis. It said that often the pain begins in the upper abdomen and then several hours later moves to the lower right quadrant. Uh-oh. I began to be suspicious but still went to shul. Didn't feel great, but read Torah, but during the last aliyah, really began to feel bad. Finished up, and consulted with a few M.D.'s in shul who said that if it didn't go away in a few hours, I should probably go to the emergency room.

To make a long story short, I lasted only about another half hour, and then decided to go home and rest. It was weird leaving Rosh Ha-Shannah services in the middle, but after resting at home for a while and still not feeling well, I just knew something was up and went to the hospital. There, they examined me and concluded that I needed an emergency appendectomy.

As they prepped me for surgery, they told me to take off my wedding ring. I knew that it wouldn't come off, because I'd moved it to my right hand when I jammed my left hand playing basketball a few weeks ago and wanted to get the ring off before the finger swelled. Not having a pocket in my gym shorts, I just forced the ring onto my right hand and figured I'd eventually worry about how to get it off. Now they said it had to come off or they'd cut it off. They gave me Vaseline and another kind of skin lubricant, but I just couldn't get it off. By now I was sufficiently in pain from the appendix, their probing, the shots, and the IV's that I didn't care very much about the ring. "So cut it off," I said, figuring that I'd get it fixed somehow. The nurse nearby overheard this, ordered everyone away from my bed, and said, "Give me five minutes. It's Rosh Ha-Shannah, and I'm not going to let his year start with his wedding ring getting cut off." Everyone moved away, and in a few moments of patient maneuvering, she had it off. Even just outside the operating room, the Jewishness of modern Israel is at times simply moving beyond my expectations.

The surgery went fine. The first morning I was in the hospital, the second day of Rosh Ha-Shannah, one of the orderlies came around and asked if I wanted to go to the synagogue downstairs for services. The nurses wouldn't allow it, for they didn't want me walking yet. He offered to wheel my bed down, but it proved too complicated. Finally, he made it his mission in life to get someone to blow the Shofar for me. He came back several times during the day to see if I'd heard the Shofar, and didn't relent until someone came to my ward to blow the Shofar for me.

On the second or third morning I was in the hospital, the nurse came in to refill my IV, and I could tell she was crying. I asked her if she was OK, and she said, "I'm the one who's supposed to ask *you* that!" But I pressed, and she told me about the soldier at Joseph's Tomb who'd been shot and who the IDF couldn't evacuate and who subsequently bled to death. "Did you know him?" I asked, still curious that she was crying. "No," she said, "but they always bring those boys to our unit, and we always save them. I know we could have saved him, too." She adjusted my IV, wiped her face, and walked on to the next patient.

I didn't understand what in the world she was talking about, to tell you the truth. I couldn't understand why there would be shooting at Joseph's Tomb, or who, for that matter, would be shooting at whom. When Rosh Ha-Shannah had begun, things were tense but certainly not violent. Then, during the holiday, as we do not use radios or televisions, and there are no newspapers printed, we were basically completely out of touch with the rest of the world. That was even more true during my hospital stay. So I was pretty much oblivious to what had been going on while I was out of circulation, completely unaware that while I was lying in that bed, the "war" had basically started, that soldiers had died, or that one, at least, might have been saved.

Hard to know who and what could have been saved, I guess. It struck me that it's ironic that the last thing I did before driving off to the hospital was to read the Torah's story of Sarah's jealousy over Ishmael, and the beginning of the conflict between the children of Isaac and those of his half-brother, Ishmael. Sarah, childless for so many years but now blessed with a child, instructs Abraham to take Ishmael, his other son by Hagar [his concubine], and to send him out into the desert, presumably to die. Abraham resists, but in the end does exactly that. It's a story about these two peoples, the Children of Isaac and the Children of Ishmael, constantly at odds because of the sense that there's not enough of something to go around—land, water, love. And when you think about it, thousands of years later, nothing much has changed.

It's a conflict that's been going on a long time, and one some of us thought was just about to be over. I guess that was premature. Will our children know peace? Our grandchildren? It's not an optimistic day in this part of the world, but neither can we lose hope. We'll see.

As we were finishing up *Birkat HaMazon* [The Grace After Meals] at lunch yesterday, I paid attention to words that I don't often think about as we say them:

> *Ha-Shem Oz Le-Amo yitein,*
> *Ha-Shem yevarekh et amo ba-Shalom.*

> May God grant His people strength,
> and may He bless His people with peace.

We need the two, together, no less than ever. *Shannah tovah* and *g'mar chatimah* to all.

December 2000:
Life in the "Matzav"

It's been a long time since we've written, so it's time to fill you in on what's going on, and to send wishes for a joyous Hanukkah or Merry Christmas. The past couple of months have been tumultuous, to say the least, which is part of the reason that we haven't written in a while. Life here has been not only complex, but relatively indescribable.

Before turning to the *"matzav"* (the Hebrew word for "situation," which is the euphemism by which the entire country refers to the catastrophe in which we find ourselves), a few words about us and the kids. Basically, I think that we've finally turned the corner in terms of

139

the kids' acclimation and our general sense that we're settled. First the kids.

Tali, as I reported a while back, is at Pelekh, a rigorous high school about a four-minute walk from our house, and thriving. They work the kids incredibly hard, and she's usually awake doing homework long after we're asleep, but she seems to love it. They're studying French, Greek mythology, trigonometry, etc., plus a very heavy load of Judaica, including Talmud, biblical commentaries, philosophy, and Israeli history. As she was finishing a paper last night, I noticed that (since all her papers have to be turned in typed, and in Hebrew of course) she's now become by far the fastest Hebrew typist in the family.

More important than all that, I think she's genuinely happy. Of our three kids, she's the only one who never really pined for the States, and whatever minimal sense of being out of place she once had seems to have disappeared. She's very involved in her youth group, Bnai Akiva, which keeps her out until early in the morning on Friday nights and with friends a couple more times a week, and she loves it. What is interesting for me is watching the youth group's reaction to the latest *"matzav."* She occasionally comes home with photocopied sheets from the works of various Zionist thinkers that they've discussed during their youth group meetings. The counselors' response to the events surrounding these kids is to delve deep into Zionist ideology, to give them a sense of what this whole conflict is about. In an era in which ideology is either not terribly important for most people (the United States) or in which ideologies are crumbling (Israel), I actually find the insistence on the importance of forging a personal ideology an appropriate way to get teenagers to respond to the current situation.

Of course, the "teenager" I allude to is the other side of her personality, which we'll mostly leave to your imagination. But suffice it to say that we're in the throes of that wonderful difficult stage.

Avi is also doing well. His school (Micha also goes to the same school) is in the Old City, which has meant that life has changed rather dramatically for him in the last few months. This year he begged to be allowed to walk to school, which we finally permitted. But as soon as the situation broke out, we obviously had to stop that, as his school is about 250 yards from the Temple Mount and there have been serious confrontations between police and Palestinians there. They've even canceled school on Fridays this month since they felt that they could not guarantee the kids' safety with the enormous crowds there during Ramadan, so Avi's turned into a major fan of this Muslim holiday!

He's actually not aware how much he's enjoying school, but he is (we think). Avi and I often get up at six in the morning to study for an hour or so before school, and he regularly has exams three or four times a week. When you add to a busy load the fact that his Hebrew, while quite good, is not as well developed vocabulary-wise as other kids in his grade, he's got even more work. He's working like a mule, and doing nicely.

Thankfully, school's not all he's doing. He's back to studying cello very seriously, and is making great progress. Between school, his cello, his scooter (of course), and being a relatively voracious reader in both languages (which we owe directly to Harry Potter, before which he never read anything), he's busy, and happy.

Micha, always last and usually with the shortest paragraph, has made the most dramatic leaps forward in the last few months. He loves math and is a grade ahead, racing through and rapidly reaching the edge of our ability to help him! He's incredibly artistic, and he and Tali both take serious classes at the Israel Museum once a week. Most important, as with Avi, he's got that one special friend who makes life as a kid fun and secure, and in general he's doing wonderfully.

Interestingly, he was our major America-phile, and he's also stopped asking about going for a visit. He still speaks periodically of his friends in the States, and we still have pictures of them up in the kitchen, but he's also feeling more situated and settled here, and seems happy. All this might sound a bit mundane, but believe me, after the last two years, it feels like something midway between a major accomplishment and a minor miracle!

Elisheva (my second wife, as she sometimes jokes) is doing well, but I would say that this latest insanity has been hardest on her. The kids have pretty good coping mechanisms, and I've been out of the country quite a bit (four trips to New York in the last seven weeks, for example), but she's basically been stuck in Jerusalem since it began. Our vacation to Tzippori in the Galilee for Sukkot, which we've done every year and which she loves, got canceled (it was too dangerous to get there at the time), and with all that's going on, we haven't felt that we could leave the kids for a night or two to get away. So this has been hardest on her. She hopes to start looking for work very shortly, a bit later than she'd originally planned. For her, like everyone else here, life has been put on hold for the last two months as people have been more or less glued to the television and newspapers. But we're all coming out of it now; not, by the way, because the situation is much better, but because we're resigned to its continuing.

Despite the *"matzav,"* she's extremely happy to be living here. She's the one who always wanted to live in Israel, and in some ways is the most passionate about staying. At the height of the crisis a little more than a month ago, when things were seriously out of control, I told her that if she wanted to take the kids back to the States for a while, I'd be supportive of that. She looked at me like I was completely nuts. (Not an unusual way for her to look at me, to be sure.) Of course, with my work schedule being as heavy as it is, she's the one who's put in the most time with Micha and Avi over the past months, and as we don't let them take buses anywhere now, is also schlepping them to art lessons, music lessons, dentist appointments, shopping for shoes, and the like. She's become an avid runner, and runs (inside on our treadmill, watching the CNN daily reporting for the umpteenth time) virtually every morning.

As for me, I'm enjoying work immensely. The pace is fierce, but I like working that way, and the Fellows are great. Occasionally, being around them provides a literally riveting moment.

Each of the Fellows does an independent project on which s/he works for the two years, and periodically the Fellows present their work to the rest of the group for feedback. Today an Israeli woman talked about her desire to reform the curriculum of the government's religious school system (there are two public school systems here: secular and religious) to allow for greater equality for women in religious society in general. It was more subtle than that, but that's the basic idea. Anyway, during the discussion of whether this could work, and how, a Muslim Fellow from another one of our programs piped in. His project has to do with opening up the religious establishment in the Israeli Arab community, and combating the role that Israeli governmental influence has in stymieing that effort. She and he got into a fascinating discussion, he arguing that she was being too radical, too disregarding of halakhic authorities, and that it wouldn't work. In many dimensions of his existence as an Israeli Arab, she, as an Orthodox Israeli woman, is his problem—some would say his enemy. But here, he was trying to get her to learn from his experience in the Muslim community, and she was genuinely receptive. Fascinating, the kind of thing that one rarely sees and that I'm genuinely fortunate to be around on a day-to-day basis.

Obviously, though, the most pressing part of life here over the last two months has been the *"matzav."* I'll skip all the "we did this and they did that" stuff, as it's being covered—sometimes well, usually not—in the media, and is frankly quite irrelevant. We get a lot of e-mail from various groups in the U.S. who forward daily updates of what shooting took place where; while sometimes interesting, it strikes us, as it does most Israelis, as utterly irrelevant. It's not, of course, that the shooting is not important. What bothers most of us is what the whole uprising has done to Israeli society and, most particularly, to our dreams of the life to which we'd thought we brought our kids.

I remember just this summer, as we'd talk with our kids about Israel, we'd wonder aloud whether they'd have to go to the army. With Tali, it's just a question of two years out of her life, but not a time of real danger. But as the past twelve weeks have reminded everyone, sending your boys to the army here is no joke. We had simply imagined that either they wouldn't go or it would be some pro forma kind of service, since peace seemed around the corner.

This notion of life having been turned upside down is the part that has all Israelis (particularly the intellectuals, and especially the left-leaning ones with whom I work) most distraught. For what's happened here is that the ideologies of both the right and the left have crumbled. The right, which had advocated a "complete Land of Israel" ideology, knew as soon as Camp David was over that they were finished. True, nothing (good) came of Camp David, but the mere fact that Barak had put all that on the table (and as I write this, is apparently OK'ing putting even more on the table in Washington today) signaled to them that their dream was over. We were clearly going back to something like the pre–June 1967 borders, and they're devastated.

But interestingly, so is the left devastated. The left was convinced that if we just gave back what we captured in 1967, perhaps holding on to small pieces here and there, we could and would get peace. We want peace, they want peace, went the saying. But now, virtually no one here believes that. Peres and Beilin still talk the talk, but most intellectual leftists that I know simply say that on this count "the right was right"—the Palestinians simply hate us, and want us out. Not just from the territories captured in '67, but from the whole place. And nothing shy of that will satisfy them. Painful as it is to say, I've begun to suspect that it's true. I tried to convince myself for twenty years that that was wrong, but now I'm not sure.

About two weeks ago, the Jerusalem Fellows went to Ein Harod in the Galilee to meet some *Israeli* Arabs to hear about their perspective. We went to the Galilee because it is more neutral territory than Jerusalem, which, after all, is the capital of the Jewish state, though we met on a kibbutz and not in their Arab village for security reasons.

We first met with the principal of an Arab school, funded by the Israeli government and governed by the ministry of education, as are all Israeli schools whether they're Jewish or Arab (only two or three schools in the entire country are mixed). This principal, who proved to be a politically moderate Israeli Arab, told us the following. His high school students, all Muslim, have to take at least two units of Hebrew Bible and pass the *bagrut* (Regents-like exam) on the material, but are not permitted to study the Koran as part of the regular school day. They are required to study Bialik, Tchernechovsky, and the rest of the classic Zionist poets, but Darwish, the Palestinian national poet, is not allowed. When the principal himself was in high school, he told us, Darwish's love poetry was permitted, but not his political poetry. Now, he said, the ministry of education doesn't allow any of it. He told us that when he took his students to a Jewish high school in Haifa for a day of interaction, the Jewish students wanted to talk about the Palestinian Charter, which they'd studied in social studies (called "citizenship" here). His students, the Arabs, were dumbfounded because their school was not allowed to teach the Charter, and they didn't know anything about it other than the fact that it existed.

I could go on, as he did, but the point is clear. On one level, it's true that the occupation was initially forced on us because we were attacked in 1967, and we won. But on the other hand, the occupation, and the ridiculously small-minded way in which both the occupation and our treatment of Israeli Arabs are carried out (don't forget—this principal is an Israeli citizen, and so are his students; they don't live in the occupied territories, but inside the green line) just sows generations of seeds of hatred, and for good reason, even Israeli Arabs detest what the Jewish state has done to them. As we sat and listened to this man, who clearly said that he wants peace and coexistence, the right-wingers among the Fellows were noticeably silent. The absurdity of much of what we've done was simply undeniable.

Yeshayahu Leibowitz, the Orthodox Israeli philosopher (1903–1994) who argued in July 1967 that we should retreat right away and give back everything we'd captured the previous month because an extended occupation would rot the soul of the country, was clearly right. In a faculty meeting a week or two ago (no meeting, no matter where or when, takes place without politics entering the discussion), a well-known contemporary Israeli philosopher—Orthodox, too, and by no means a left-winger—who teaches for us said, "The first thing this country should do is to go en masse to Leibowitz's grave and beg his forgiveness that we didn't listen to him." Silence there, too.

But the leftists were in for more of a shock later in the afternoon of our trip to the Galilee. We met with three representatives of Arab Israeli political parties, the three largest and most mainstream such parties. Despite minor differences among them, they all shared the following: (a) They do not acknowledge any difference between themselves and the Palestinians, and now want to be called Israeli Palestinians, not Israeli Arabs; (b) they insist that their "brothers" be given a state with East Jerusalem as its capital; (c) they insist on the right of return for the refugees (this is a huge political issue here, which gets little play in the West, probably because everyone knows that it will never happen); and (d) they insist that if the state genuinely wants to respect them as citizens, then the national anthem and its references to two thousand years of Jewish yearning for Zion has to go. So far, no real surprises.

At a certain point in the conversation, one of the Fellows raised his hand and asked, "What you're demanding actually makes perfect sense from your point of view. But from our perspective, from the perspective of people whose parents or grandparents came here from across the world to build the one place on earth where Jews would be able to live in a Jewish state with Jewish content and Jewish values at its core, what can you say to reassure us that the Jewishness of the state won't disappear if you're given what you want?"

The most articulate of the three speakers responded more or less as follows: "I don't understand the question. Your question shows that you don't really understand the Middle East. The Middle East is a Muslim part of the world, and this country will ultimately be Muslim, too. It may happen next year, or in fifty years, or in a hundred years. But it's going to happen. And there's no reason for you to be worried about that. Maimonides thrived under Islam, and so did Sa'adya Ga'on. Relax. The sooner you accept the inevitable, the sooner the region will know peace, and then we can all get on with life."

That was the gist. And remember, he's an Israeli citizen, the leader of a major party represented in the Knesset. The silence in the room was astonishing. Here were several dozen rabidly left-wing Israeli intellectuals, confronted for the first time with the realization that even these Israeli *citizens* want something radically different not only from what is, but from what these left-wing Jews are willing to contemplate. Coupled with that, they were stumped by the fact that even though they've grown up here, they've given very little thought to what they want the "Jewish state" to be. Their whole intellectual arsenal has been crafted to fight the rabbinate, to battle against the stranglehold that they believe Orthodoxy has on private life; however, while they know what they want to change, they have no idea what they want to preserve. What should be Jewish about Israel? Its language only? A majority of Jews in the population? Or something more core to the country's culture and ethos? And if so, what should *that* be?

Thus, confronted with this speaker, they had nothing to say. It was a sad, pathetic, devastating moment. It's the sort of thing that's being replayed in hundreds of venues each day, and that's what's making the country not so much nervous as profoundly depressed and sad. It's the sort of issue, of course, that the "who shot whom today" e-mails completely miss, but it's also the issue that will ultimately determine the future of the country.

So where we're left, I think, is with an emerging consensus that we have to at least begin to redress the Israeli Arabs' mistreatment and end the occupation soon (probably except for certain areas with serious Jewish populations), because it has become intolerable not only for them but for us as well. But the question is how, when, and how much to give back. About that there are deep divisions, with no solutions in sight.

The other consensus, shared by more people than I imagined possible, is the belief that "they" just want us out of here. Remember that Arafat, the winner of the Nobel Peace Prize, is the one who used to speak of "driving the Jews into the sea." He got the Palestinian Charter calling for Israel's destruction changed only under intense pressure from Clinton and, according to some Israelis, never took the steps to make those changes fully validated by the Palestinian "parliament." Now, it seems, it may be that not only does Arafat still hope to "drive the Jews into the sea," Israeli Arabs may want the same thing. Since we're not going to go voluntarily, some form of conflict is probably going to continue forever. No need to comment on how depressing that is.

My sense is that somehow we're going to retreat. We have to. The vast majority of Israelis are no longer willing for their sons to die defending Kfar Darom in Gaza or Hebron for a few dozen entrenched families. Here Elisheva and I completely disagree. She's opposed to leaving those places; she says that first we'll retreat from Kfar Darom, and then it will be the outskirts of Jerusalem, then it will be East Jerusalem, and Jerusalem and Tel Aviv will still be on the Palestinians' list, so why even start? I think we'll keep retreating until we get to a line where people say, "This is worth defending, even if my kid dies for it." Where that line is, I have no idea. I don't think anyone does.

The other factor that will determine where we stop retreating will be a sense of justice. People here know, deep down, no matter how right-wing they are in other ways, that we've screwed up this occupation badly. Schooling is the least of it. There's a constant military presence, land expropriation, home demolition, and arrest without due process. True, much of it is for reasons of security. But it has been mishandled in almost every way possible. Most people here simply don't have the stomach to fight for what's not just. Without a sense that justice is on our side, too many people here have no desire to do battle. A sense of justice, for better or worse but probably for better, is too deeply ingrained in the Jewish consciousness to be able to avoid it. But since we're going to have to battle, we need to feel that we're battling for a just cause. And I suspect that we'll keep retreating until we've got the bare minimum of space to restore that sense that we're fighting for life, not land, and that simple human justice is on our side. But none of this is going to happen tomorrow, and none of it will happen without huge fights—hopefully only rhetorical, but one fears it could be more—inside Israeli society. And outside as well. That's what the future holds, I suspect. Not that I like it; it's just what I think will happen.

And all of this discussion, of course, takes place under fire, fire that we didn't start and to which, no matter what the media may say, we've responded relatively lightly, despite massive public pressure to "just wipe them out"—a phrase that one occasionally hears, even from intelligent people, as a response to incredible frustration. We were so close at Camp David, it seemed. So in addition to everything else, there's profound disappointment, fury at Arafat, mistrust of the Palestinians, all justified. Now fit all that together into a coherent policy!

I realize that much of what I've just said may not be coherent, but that's precisely the point. None of this *is* coherent. We're part of a society being rocked and shocked to its very core, coming to terms with the fact that its founding ideologies have all died, and that none have arisen to replace them. The right wing thought that by moving to the territories and building settlements, it could guarantee that that land would never be returned. But the territories, and the settlements in which these people live, were clearly on the table in Camp David, and these people feel completely betrayed. The left always said that the Arabs were just like us—that given a fair settlement, they too wanted to end the conflict and live in peace. The last few months have made that very difficult to believe. So no one is able anymore to believe in what they used to. But when you live in a place where you have to fight to stay, you can't manage without a governing ideology. And that's why we're barely holding on in any way except militarily.

That is what paralyzes us. You see people at work literally sitting at their desks and staring at their computers, doing absolutely nothing. And you don't say anything, because you know what's going on. They're mourning. Devastated by a dream that's gone up in flames in the last two months, e-mails or budgets or the next iterations of some document don't seem that pressing. You can come here and tour around in one of those air-conditioned tour buses with the video screen in the front and the charming, handsome tour guide with the microphone standing by the driver, and everything seems normal. And yet in reality, in the real Israel, nothing is. And nothing will be for a long time.

For us, in our family, I think that the most painful thing is contemplating what we've done to our children. Our kids have become news junkies, just like us, and watch and hear things that I don't know how they internalize. What do they do with the fact that on Fridays the bagel store just two blocks from our house is patrolled by a dozen fully armed soldiers in complete battle gear who stand guard to make sure that the masses in the Old City don't make it into Jewish residential neighborhoods? Do they think that we were crazy to come here? I don't know what to say when Avi comes downstairs at night and says that he can't fall asleep because of the shooting in Gilo, which we hear. Or when I'm in the States on business and Elisheva tells me that she and the children were up all night because helicopter gunships were hovering over our house before they finally dove and fired missiles on Bethlehem, causing our whole building to shake. How do your kids make sense of the fact that you took them from a quiet Los Angeles neighborhood with tree-lined streets, where nothing dangerous ever happened, to a place where they know that there are people out there who would like them dead? They don't say anything about it at all, but at night sometimes, as I watch them sleeping, I wonder just what they think about all this and what they're dreaming.

Avi told us a couple of weeks ago about a drill that they did at school, kind of like our nuclear attack drills in the '60s, or the earthquake drills that they did in California. But this was a terrorist drill. As the oldest kids in the school, Avi's class, the sixth grade, got different roles. Avi's is to crawl on his stomach (staying below window level to avoid bullets) to the principal's office, and bring some equipment and first aid back to the classroom. They actually practiced this nonsense, and when I asked him why they just don't keep the equipment in the classroom all the time, he laughed and said, "Abba, don't you understand? The whole thing's ridiculous. Eleven-year-old kids are going to fend off terrorists? If they come, we're going to die. The school's just doing this to make the parents feel better."

That's life in Israel. Wonderful, pathetic. Exciting, devastating. Not too long ago, Elisheva and I were hanging out one evening. We were reading the paper, and suddenly, it was very calm. I looked up. Tali was lying on the sofa reading a book. Micha was building a Lego model on the floor, and Avi was playing the cello. Incredibly nice, wonderfully civilized. And in the distance, barely audible but audible nonetheless, the firing continued, and I realized that we'd kind of grown used to it. It's not a way to bring up your kids, and yet we still don't want to be anywhere but here.

So, here's wishing you a Hanukkah filled with light and joy. I guess this year more than ever, we need to add some light to the dark, and to recall that we've gotten through tough times before, right here, in this very city, for centuries. So we can probably get through this one, too. At the same time, we could use some more miracles. It would be nice, though, to be able to believe that they still happen.

Happy Hanukkah.

February 2001:
The Calm Before the Storm

As Israelis Vote, Dreams of Peace Seem to Be Fading

Israel that will vote in February 6 election is markedly different from hopeful nation that overwhelmingly elected Prime Minister Ehud Barak in 1999 with confidence that he could secure peace with Arab neighbors; after four months of violent conflict with Palestinians, many Israelis have lost faith not only in Barak, but in peace effort itself and Palestinian peace partners; poll after Barak's election showed 67 percent of Israelis believed real peace was possible, compared with current one-fifth of population, which believes agreement will solve and end bitter conflict.

New York Times: Tuesday, February 6, 2001, page A1

It's Monday morning, the day before the Barak versus Sharon elections, and a kind of eerie calm prevails. By and large, Israeli neighborhoods are quiet, although it's easy to forget that just over three days ago, on Thursday evening, two Israelis were murdered, one of them a Hadassah Hospital hematologist who was shot driving home from work just outside Efrat, which is just a few minutes away from here. The press has long since stopped reporting on shooting in the territories, so one lives with a sense that a new sort of normalcy has taken hold.

Tomorrow at this time, the polls will open, and the big question is whether Ehud Barak will get so trounced that he'll lose control of the Labor Party and thus conclude his political career. Or will he manage to eke out a "respectable" loss that will enable him to remain head of his party and return to a leadership position once Ariel Sharon crashes and burns? Great, no? Just the kind of choice one needs when a country is in crisis.

Seeking to gain some relief from the crisis, and wanting to watch something that reflected a well-entrenched democratic tradition, we decided to watch the Bush inauguration. We had CNN on for the pregame festivities, and gradually the kids filtered in until we were all watching TV together. As CNN showed Clinton and Bush chatting in the White House together, Tali remarked, "That's pretty amazing—here they wouldn't even shake hands." The kids have come to see how uncivil Israeli civil society is, and (thankfully) they don't like it.

The kids actually liked the pomp and circumstance of the inauguration. But watching, Elisheva and I both found the opening prayer and the benediction incredibly Christian. Now, I don't remember other inaugurations well enough to know if this was a change or just a side of the U.S. that I'd forgotten, but both of us were immediately reminded why we came here. The U.S., as great a place as it is to live (and by virtually all measurable standards, it's a much better place to live than Israel), is simply a Christian country. Many of our friends here and back in the U.S. wrote in the days following that they were appalled by the blatantly Christian character of the ceremony. I wasn't appalled at all. After all, it's a Christian country, and the vast majority of Americans are Christian. Why shouldn't they be allowed to mention Jesus? No, I didn't see anything wrong with it, but had I lived in the States, I would have felt very excluded by it. The truth is, I now realize more and more, that the inauguration encapsulated for me why we're here in the first place.

And that's exactly what makes the upcoming elections so critical. For when we go to the polls tomorrow, we effectively have to give up on one of two dreams that almost all of us have had for the country:

peace, or physical security coupled with a profound sense of the Jewishness of the country. However you vote, you're giving up on one of them. What are the choices? There are essentially four alternatives: (1) Don't vote, (2) a *petek lavan*, which means "white slip of paper" (even though it's actually yellow), which is an official abstention, (3) Sharon, (4) Barak. Nothing else is possible. And none of them is tenable either.

The "don't vote" option seems to me to be completely unacceptable. Part of living in a democracy, I think, means taking seriously the right—and responsibility—to vote. Staying away entirely because the two candidates are revolting is no way to strengthen the democratic tradition of a fledgling democracy. For that reason, the "abstention" ballot is also useless. Election officials have announced that they're not going to reveal the numbers or percentages of people who "abstained" (there was a big Supreme Court ruling last week upholding their right not to release this information), so that vote, too, counts for nothing. Which leaves a choice between two failed ex-generals.

Sharon is running under the campaign slogan *"rak Sharon yavi shalom"*—"Only Sharon Will Bring Peace." That's rather ironic, considering the fact that some people used to hold him responsible for all this violence in the first place. In September 2000, shortly before the outbreak of violence, Sharon decided to visit the Temple Mount, nominally under Israeli jurisdiction. But as it's a sacred site for Muslims, one that we've allowed them to manage and patrol for years, they basically control it, and there's an unspoken rule that Jews don't go up there. Technically, of course, as it's territory under Israeli control, Sharon had every legal right to visit the Temple Mount. Nonetheless, many people felt it was unnecessarily provocative.

It's still not entirely clear why Sharon chose to go there, accompanied by dozens upon dozens of security personnel. Some argue that he was trying to sandbag Barak's peace negotiations by doing something that he knew would lead to a violent outbreak. His supporters suggest that he was simply trying to show Barak and the rest of Israel the true nature of the people with whom we were negotiating, and to

whom we were about to make serious territorial and security concessions. "Watch what they'll do if I just walk on the Temple Mount," his
supporters suggest he was saying. And, of course, the horrible violence
since then has—at least in their own eyes—proven them right.

But Sharon's reputation as a warmonger has little to do with this
latest episode. He's had a long past of violent confrontations with
Arabs. As a general who fought in 1948 and beyond, some of that is to
be expected. And no one here has forgotten that he won several key
battles in Israel's history. At the same time, for the leader of Com-
mando Unit 101 (responsible for the unnecessary deaths of dozens of
Palestinian women and children in an anti-terrorist raid in the early
1950s), the general who allowed the Sabra and Shatilla massacres to
take place, the man who was then declared by the Knesset's investigating commission to be unfit to ever serve as defense minister, and the
architect of the eighteen-year-long Lebanon war to now run for prime
minister under the slogan "Only Sharon Will Bring Peace" is like Bill
Clinton running for a third term under the slogan "Only Bill Clinton
Can Restore Moral Integrity to the White House." One has to wonder
what kind of a laugh Sharon's campaign managers had when they came
up with *"rak Sharon yavi shalom."*

Barak's people know how absurd it is, and every night on TV, the
Barak ads show Sharon saying "I believe that the Lebanon war was
among the most justified of all Israel's wars." They play it on a continuous loop, with a haunting echo in the back, portraying Sharon as
a trigger-happy, violence-prone general who just hates Arabs, treats
Israeli soldiers' blood as cheap, and is completely unrepentant about a
war that cost thousands of lives and got us virtually nothing. It's actually a very unsettling ad.

And yet the vast majority of people we know are voting for
Sharon. With disgust, they add, but yes, they'll vote for him. They'll
vote for him because the other option, Barak, is completely unthinkable. Barak, they say, has completely failed as prime minister, and he
simply must go.

Very few people here hold Barak responsible for the outbreak of violence in October. (Nor do they hold Sharon responsible, arguing that a simple visit to the Temple Mount, no matter how provocative, couldn't justify machine-gun fire on civilians. Arafat was looking for an excuse, they say.) If anything, they say, Barak called Arafat's bluff by offering a decent deal at Camp David. Although it may not have been fully palatable to Arafat, it was certainly a valid opening gambit. When Arafat realized that the game was up and that the Israelis were willing to deal, his only choice was to unleash the Intifada. That, everyone acknowledges, is hardly Barak's fault.

But people do hold Barak accountable for not hitting back harder. Presumably it was because he feared destroying the infrastructure of the very entity he wanted to have as a partner. But Israelis couldn't abide his continuing to negotiate while we were (and are) being fired upon, and for making such extraordinary concessions to a regime that it's now clear envisions not two states, one Jewish and one Palestinian (as called for in the U.N. resolution), but two states, one Palestinian now and one Palestinian later on. There are very few people left here, even those on the political left, who believe that Arafat has any other intentions. Given that, most people ask, why give up the Jordan Valley to a regime that unleashes fire and kills innocent adults and children when it doesn't get what it wants in the first stage of negotiations; why give up East Jerusalem to a regime that we cannot trust to let West Jerusalem live in peace; and why give up the Temple Mount to a "government" that says publicly that the Jewish claim to having had a temple there is completely baseless and fabricated only for political purposes?

That's the question people would ask Barak. Why? Why didn't you stop negotiating? Why did you offer so much, especially in the Middle East when that's not how it's done, and when Arafat didn't concede anything at all? How could you run on the explicit campaign promise (which Sharon's campaign now replays on TV nightly) that you'd never split Jerusalem, and then do it without so much as a public explanation? How can anyone take you seriously, when you offer ultimatum after ultimatum and then back off and do nothing?

Why should anyone believe anything you say, no matter how sincere you look?

I think that even our seven-and-a-half-year-old has begun to sense (or more probably, hear) how crazy this policy has been. He's now at that stage when he reads everything in sight, including billboards, ads, and bumper stickers. Yesterday, Elisheva told me, they were driving around town when Micha saw a bumper sticker that read *"ha-am im ha-golan"*—"The People [Is] with the Golan." It's a ubiquitous sticker in this country, a "jingle" that's been around for years. Micha sounded out the words, and then said, *"Ani maskim"*—"I agree with that." Elisheva asked him why, to which he said, "Well, I don't think we should give it back. That's all. Ema, did you know that we gave them all the guns that they're using to shoot at us?"

He's right, of course. We did. Perhaps not all, but a lot. How do you explain that to your kid? It's hard enough to explain why anyone is shooting at you at all. But with guns that *you* gave them? I think our kids must think that grown-ups are just insane. Nor is Micha the only one. The other night, Avi and I were watching the news on CNN, and they showed a map of the Middle East. I didn't notice anything too strange about the map, but Avi immediately asked, "Abba, what's the line in the middle of Israel?" I looked and realized that he'd never seen a map with the green line (the pre-1967 border) on it. Israeli maps, of course, don't show it. I explained what the green line was, and told him that that was the area about which we were negotiating with the Palestinians. He looked completely aghast. "Abba, but that's right in the middle of the country! That's crazy. I'm telling you, Abba, you're nuts if you don't vote for Sharon." You can raise a kid in this country and teach him to see both sides of the conflict, and still have him look at the map and tell you straight—you're just nuts to give that back.

But there are more subtle costs of not giving it back that kids just can't see. And those costs are what lead many people to feel that, distasteful though it may be, we simply have to keep talking to Arafat and his gang, and probably even give them a lot to get to a settlement. Last week, I was walking home from work at the end of the day and waited for a pedestrian sign to turn green. Stopped at the light, in front of me in the middle lane, was a car with four young Palestinian women in it. I barely noticed them, but they seemed to be in their late twenties, well dressed, minding their own business. In keeping with unspoken Israeli etiquette, they didn't look at me, and I didn't pay them much attention, either. While they were still at the light, another car pulled up next to them in the left lane. This car had four Jewish kids in it, all in their late teens or early twenties, two men and two women. All four were wearing army uniforms. Suddenly, something apparently rolled under one of the seats of their car, and laughing hysterically, they were trying to pull it out but couldn't. So, still at the red light, they all opened their doors and stood outside the car, presumably to bend down and find whatever it was. As they got out, their M-16's slung over their shoulders, laughing good-naturedly and just having wholesome fun, I noticed the four Palestinian women, who were terror-stricken to see four armed soldiers suddenly standing next to their car. *I* saw four kids, barely older than my daughter, having a grand old time about some joke, while these women saw the enemy, the occupying soldiers, unpredictable danger.

Walking home, I realized the mess we're in, how impossible the current situation is and how desperate we all are to disentangle, to separate from each other. That's what's tempting about Barak. That's why even (many) people who will vote for Sharon will regret that they couldn't vote for Barak.

Israelis want peace, at best, and a bloodless separation if peace isn't possible. But bottom line, they think that Barak is so intoxicated with the idea of his having brought peace with the Palestinians to Israel that he's blinded himself to the fact that there is simply no "partner," no one with whom to make a deal. Arafat is seen as a scoundrel, a leader who's promised his people for so long that they're going "home" (home being our apartment building, for example) while knowing that it was never going to happen, that he now can't bring them a deal in which he doesn't come through. Not all his people share that perspective—the Palestinians being no more monolithic than the Israelis, of course—but in the absence of a democracy there, there's little way for the person on the street to bring about a change in Palestinian policy.

So that's where we are: Either Barak and more of the shooting, more endless negotiations with a "peace partner" who has no apparent intention to make peace, continuous concessions that, even if he did get a deal, would *never* pass the Knesset, and the gradual erosion of any sense of Jewish purpose for the state. To be the first Jews in the history of the planet to willingly give up the Temple Mount will, I think, do something irreversible to the Jewish sense of self of this country. Or Sharon, whose hatred of Arabs is palpable, whose lust for a quick military "solution" to this mess is obvious, and who will undoubtedly destroy the last remaining shred of standing that Israel has in the international community. Quite a choice for tomorrow morning.

I asked Tali the other day for whom she would vote if she could. "I'm just glad I can't vote" was her response. "But let's say you could," I pressured her. To which she responded, "I don't think it matters. Either way, we're going to have a war. Barak will get us there later, Sharon sooner. I guess we should just get it over with and have it now."

Even accounting for pouty adolescence, it was a sobering remark from a generally upbeat kid. But she's right. The Barak camp sent out a campaign "note" to hundreds of thousands of homes, disguised as a *Tzav Shemoneh*—Order to Report #8. It's apparently what you get when you're called up to war (I say apparently only because I've never seen a real one—yet). It was actually shocking to come home from work and find a note telling you to report to the front, only to then realize that it was an election ploy with the words inside, "You can avoid this. Vote . . ." Many people thought it was a bit inappropriate, but few disputed the notion that the real thing may well get distributed in the near future. But most also know that it won't be Sharon's doing—even if Barak were to stay in power, we've reached the end of the road. The violence has to resume, with greater intensity, relatively soon. Or so it would seem.

There's something about this cycle that seems never-ending. Last week, Egyptian president Hosni Mubarak announced that he's never seen eye to eye with Sharon. Sharon responded the next day, "Don't worry, I wasn't about to call you, anyway." Then, in shul on Shabbat, as we were reading the Torah, I couldn't help but notice a similar conversation that tradition says took place thousands of years ago (Ex. 28:10 ff): "Pharaoh said to Moses, 'Be gone from me! Take care not to see me again, for the moment that you look upon my face, you shall die.' And Moses replied, 'You have spoken rightly. I shall not see your face again.'"

It's the story we've been telling for generations, a story that is no less apt today than it ever was. Centuries have passed, but nothing much has changed. True, we're not slaves now, and we've got our own country, but barely, and the dream is hanging by a thread. Tomorrow we have to decide whether to be the first Jews in history to willingly give up the Temple Mount, or the first generation of Israelis to say "no" to peace. When you come down to it, when we walk into the polls tomorrow, the question is which dream we're willing to betray.

So Elisheva and I are going to vote, and then, as schools and businesses are closed, we're taking the kids to Tel Aviv, a place they rarely get to visit. We'll take them first to the memorial at the spot where Rabin was murdered, the place where the whole thing began to unravel. Then, we thought, we'll take them to Hayim Nachman Bialik's house and Ben Gurion's house. The old, noble, aristocratic Tel Aviv. The Tel Aviv of art and poetry, Bialik's gorgeously appointed apartment, Ben Gurion's library with its Herodotus in Greek and its well-worn Bible in Hebrew. The Tel Aviv that represents the dream of what this place could have been, the place that somehow represents the memory of what it was we thought we were bringing our kids to. Then we'll probably take them out to a quick dinner and, at the end of the day, drive up the hills back to Jerusalem. Back to Jerusalem, back to reality, back to the election results, and to the storm that will almost certainly follow the calm.

Anything's possible, but much seems likely. Sharon is going to win. Arafat will have missed his chance. He'll resort to violence, sooner or later, and Sharon will slam him much harder than Barak did. And then, who knows? It's not likely to be pretty. Which is why I think that our little family trip tomorrow is important. Maybe this way, at least, in the midst of the storm, our kids will remember the dream that was once at the core of it all.

Election Morning—
This One Makes a Difference

- - - - - - - - - - - - - - - - - -

Election morning arrives, a gorgeous day. It's the first time we can vote here; when Barak was elected, we weren't citizens yet. Now we're real Israelis, with shiny new passports and national identity cards to boot, and this business is our business too.

Interior Minister Natan Sharansky has generously sent us a mass-produced postcard to inform us that we're to vote at the local public school, about fifty yards from our house. We're to bring this postcard, our national identity cards, and leave all guns and other weapons at home. Check, check, check.

Off we go. Here, Election Day is a national holiday, so schools are out and work is closed. We've never voted together before. We've always voted separately, in New York and in Los Angeles on the way to work or on the way home. And it strikes me as we walk the two blocks to the school, hand in hand as in days of old, that we've never talked about—or disagreed about—whom to vote for as much as we have in the past few weeks.

For in reality, what was there to discuss in the past? We generally opted for the same candidates, and voted mostly because it was what you were supposed to do if you lived in a democracy, not because it made that much difference. In the day-to-day living of our lives, did it honestly make a difference whether Bush or Clinton won? Or Bush-the-second or Gore? We had our preferences, to be sure, but really, when you woke up in the morning, was anything really that different—for us middle-class Americans—because one won and the other lost? Never seemed that it was.

But here that's not true. This election matters. They all do. When Barak was elected, it was a choice to abandon the Netanyahu "we'll just wait it out until the Arabs grow up and give up" policy, which had gotten us nothing except the world's opprobrium. The country abandoned that, tossed Netanyahu out, and brought in the shiny general, "Mr. Security" they called him then. Because he promised us peace, aggressively sought. So Barak pursued them, Syrians first and then Palestinians, as if they were the last girl in high school without a prom date. And that, too, got us nothing. Actually, worse. It got us this.

So now we have to choose between more of this (no matter what Barak says) and a "hit 'em back much harder so they cut this crap out" policy, which will either work or completely backfire. It really does matter.

We've argued about whom to vote for, for weeks. Truth is, neither of us loves our choice, and we've both flip-flopped twice during the campaign. But now we're set.

. . .

"I know you think I'm nuts, but I just can't vote for Sharon. I'll throw up."

"Fine, why don't you go to the local Hallmark store, buy a huge ribbon, put it on the country, and give the Palestinians the whole damn place as a gift-wrapped present. Because that's what Barak's doing, you know."

"I know, but I'm not voting for a racist murderer disguised in his TV ads as a pudgy grandpa."

. . .

Or the next night, as the news shows more shooting here, more shooting there, but Barak's team is still in Taba, still negotiating until the last minute, when he has no majority in the Knesset, has resigned, and has virtually no public support for this marathon "please talk to me when you're not shooting at me" negotiation session.

"That's it, I've decided. I'm voting Sharon."

"Last night you said Barak."

"I changed my mind."

"You switch so often I'm beginning to wonder if you even have a mind."

"Well, this time I'm not switching. This negotiation stuff is inexcusable. It's entirely anti-democratic. He has no right."

"He wants peace."

"I want peace too, but I'm not an idiot."

"Go ahead. Vote Sharon. We'll have a war and spend some nice time together. We'll get to go to a lot of kids' funerals together."

. . .

We've made up our minds, and we're splitting. Sharon's getting one vote, Barak the other. After weeks of soul-searching, thinking, and arguing—with friends, with each other, and with ourselves—we've decided. It feels momentous. What happens today will change things. People will literally live and die based on the count. It's no exaggeration to say that the future of the country will be determined in part by this election. This, I think, is what voting should be all about.

Elisheva keeps harping on the fact that we're going to cancel each other's vote out, and thinks it's some metaphor for how stuck the whole place is. But I don't see it that way. I think this is amazing. Jews, back home, after all these centuries. Walking to the polls peacefully, no threat of riots, no question that the election will be fair, whatever the outcome. And we'll be the ones to decide for ourselves how to live, without waiting for the Czar, or the Turks, or the British to determine what will be. The choices may not be great, but it's our choice.

And that, this morning, is really all that matters.

February 6, 2001:
Landslide

Dear Elie:

Tried calling you a few minutes ago, but you're out. Nothing urgent, just wanted to say hi. Thought about you in the car ride today on the way back from Tel Aviv. We had a great time with the kids, and

165

of course monitored the news during the day. On the radio home, it was clear that Sharon had won—actually crushed Barak to a degree far greater than anything anyone had anticipated. Tonight they're saying that it was 62.6 percent to 37.2 percent, even more of a gap than the initial exit polls had suggested. It looks like not only is Barak finished, but the Labor Party itself is in tatters.

So, the first stage of waiting is over. Now we have to wait to see what he'll do. Hard to know whether to be hopeful or filled with dread.

I thought of you because I remember calling you and then writing you after Barak won and beat Netanyahu not that long ago. Remember how excited we all were, how it seemed that finally we'd elected a sane person and peace was just around the corner? A lot of water under the bridge in a very short period, no?

Anyway, we'll catch up. Just didn't want to let a day like this go by without at least touching base. Give a call.

D

The Indian Cemetery in Talpiyot

- - - - - - - - - - - - - - - - -

Not too far from our house, in the next neighborhood over, there's a small park in the middle of the block. There's nothing particularly unusual about a park in Jerusalem, for the city's full of them. A fifteen-minute walk from our house, and maybe a ten-minute stroll from my office, I've passed this one dozens of times, but until recently paid it no attention.

A couple of months ago, though, walking by that park for the umpteenth time, I noticed two stone monuments. Almost hidden behind the oleanders that line the street for the length of the park, on the other side of the grass along the rosebushes, they stand there unadorned, looking just like gigantic gravestones, only they can't be, I figure. This is a residential neighborhood; there's no cemetery here.

I mention the park to a friend who knows Jerusalem like the back of his hand, tell him there's this park on Koreh Ha-Dorot Street (it means "He who announced the generations" and is a quote from Isaiah 41:4)—right where Klausner Street (named for Joseph Klausner, the Zionist historian and literary critic) runs into it. Sure, he tells me, it's the Indian cemetery.

The Indian cemetery? At home I check it out in one of those detailed tour books, and turns out he's right. There are two mass graves there, dug sometime between July 1918 and June 1920, during the First World War. One of the graves contains the remains of 290 Turkish soldiers. The other one has Indian soldiers from the British army, thirty-one of them Muslim Indians and forty-seven of them Hindus, Sikhs, and Gurkhas.

As I walk by now, I usually pause and stare for a minute. For some reason, it's the Indian grave that fascinates me. These young kids, so far from home, fighting for an army that wasn't theirs, for a land they didn't need, had no reason to see. They died for that land; the land consumed them and they didn't even make it home. Ever.

I think about the parents of those soldiers, also long gone now of course. I try to imagine how they lived with having said goodbye as their sons went off to war, and then never even having had a funeral for them. Did they think those lives had been totally wasted? Did they forgive? Whom would they have forgiven? Did they even know what happened?

Some days, often when it's been a week of this bombing or that explosion, this soldier killed or that one maimed, I think of the strange little Indian cemetery in Talpiyot, with its two marked but scarcely remembered mass graves. They died more than three quarters of a century ago, and now lie virtually hidden by the oleanders and the roses in a quiet residential neighborhood. They weren't the first, of course. The Romans, the Crusaders, the Mamluks, and others—they came here and died, and they, too, are gone. And they weren't the last, these dead Indian soldiers. They're gone, the war's over, and the British have long since been booted out of here, but in their wake, thousands upon thousands of other kids have died capturing and losing and then winning again the very same hills, the same neighborhoods, the same cities that seem to refuse to rest in quiet.

Perhaps the Ten Spies whom Moses sent to scout out the land were right. They took a look, and said not to go there. They sized the place up pretty pithily:

> 13 31But the men who had gone up with him said, "We cannot attack that people, for it is stronger than we." 32Thus they spread calumnies among the Israelites about the land they had scouted, saying, "The country that we traversed and scouted is one that devours its inhabitants."
>
> —BOOK OF NUMBERS

Who will be the next to be devoured? The Romans, Crusaders, Mamluks, Turks, and British all came and went. They left some ruins, some buildings, and lots of dead people. We want to be different, don't we? We tell our kids that this isn't any old land, some battle we're fighting by chance. We tell them that we're building something permanent for the Jews, that after two thousand years we've come home, and we're here to stay.

Or are we?

It's possible, it suddenly occurs to me when I see those graves, that the spies were right, and in the end, it will be no different with us.

March 2001:
Of Pistols, Palm Pilots, Political Philosophy, and Purim

Arab Drives Bus into Crowd, Killing 8 Israelis

Palestinian bus driver with strict Israeli security clearance veers wildly off course in Azur, Israel, plowing into crowd of soldiers and commuters, killing eight Israelis, then leading police on 10-mile chase before crashing and being apprehended; hit-and-run assault by driver, Khalil Abu Elba, is presumed to be unorthodox terror attack by unlikely terrorist; deaths of seven Israeli soldiers and one civilian is highest single-day Israeli death toll since Palestinian uprising erupted early last fall; 17 people are injured; Abu Elba, father of five, has long held Israeli work permit, driving Palestinian laborers from Erez checkpoint to their jobs inside Israel; Israeli authorities say he either snapped or proceeded to carry out homicidal mission at direction of terror group; they discount mechanical failure of bus because of way he maneuvered bus from scene and led police on chase; Ehud Barak, caretaker prime minister, seals off West Bank and Gaza, as anxiety level inside Israel rises palpably.

New York Times: Thursday, February 15, 2001, page A1

There's not much to report in the last few weeks, at least in terms of what's being reported in the media. Somehow, though, things have profoundly changed. In a word, life is now surreal. The tension is virtually indescribable, the sense of imminent explosion palpable. And no one—at least no one sane—has any idea what to do about it.

We were at a Bat Mitzvah party about two weeks ago, for the daughter of friends who live in Efrat. Though they'd planned to have the party in Efrat, the road to the "Gush" has become so dangerous of late that they moved the party to Jerusalem and hired a bulletproof bus to bring all their friends into the city. Quite a setting for a party. Early in the evening, a few people decided to organize a minyan for a quick *ma'ariv* at the side of the hotel lobby. I joined them. No one had siddurim, but most of us knew it by heart so it was no big deal. Halfway through, though, I noticed that a good number of the men were davening off their Palm Pilots, on which they'd saved the texts of *ma'ariv*. It seemed that I was one of the few without my Palm Pilot in hand (for the record, I've got *ma'ariv* on mine, too, but it was in the car), and, I noticed, I was one of the *very* few without a pistol stuck into the back of his belt. New dress code for Israeli Bat Mitzvah parties, it seems: dark pants, white shirt, Palm V, and a pistol in the back. Thank God it's still no ties.

That's Israeli life today: part Europe, with academic, cultural, and technological sophistication; part Middle East and Africa, with everyone armed and either willing or eager to fight. Last week, late one evening, the house was very quiet, and we were both just about asleep, when we suddenly heard a relatively brief burst of gunfire from Beit Jala. Now completely awake, Elisheva said to me, "You know, don't you, that if *this* was our sabbatical year, there's no way we would have stayed." It was obviously true, but the implications were so far-reaching that I didn't know what to say. I was in the States last week for a few days, and mentioned to Elisheva that some friends I'd seen who were once talking seriously about moving here, are now staying put. "Listen," she said, "no one in their right mind is going to do what we did for a few years." Also true, for the most part, and to say that it's sobering is to put things mildly.

Looking back on the last few weeks, I think that the real turning point in how people feel about this situation was the bus murder at the soldiers' bus stop near Holon, not far from Tel Aviv. Khalil Mohammed Abu Ulpah, a thirty-six-year-old Palestinian who was a licensed driver for an Israeli bus company, purposely plowed his bus into a crowd of people waiting at a bus stop, killing eight and wounding twenty-three. A day later, Arafat said he was certain that the incident was a simple traffic accident. This event changed a great deal of sentiment, I believe, not only because more people died in that incident than in any other of recent memory, or because the eulogies—offered mostly by siblings and by a few fathers—were all reprinted in the papers and had people literally in tears at newspaper stands, but because it destroyed many of the assumptions people here had taken for granted.

The first assumption that died in this attack was the sense that the many security forces that patrol Israel (and are responsible for who can and cannot get into the country) know what they're doing, and if they let a Palestinian in to work, they've got good reason. But the reality is different: The driver had had his security clearance renewed two weeks earlier, and no one suspected anything. Bottom line: Anyone is now a potential terrorist, and we've got no way to weed them out.

A second assumption has long been that having your kid in the army these days is no fun, but if she or he is serving inside the green line, it will be OK. Even the terrorists know the unwritten rule that you don't "do stuff" inside the green line. But now we know that things are different: Forget the green line. Jerusalem, Netanya, the Tel Aviv road, all are game. The old rules are no longer.

And the third assumption has been that though some girls don't like being in the army, at least they know they're safe. The work may be boring or tedious, and the army may be (i.e., is) sexist, but you can't get killed if you're a girl. Reality: Six of the eight people killed were young women in uniform, all where they were because they were going back to their bases.

And one could go on, but the point is clear. All bets are off, all the rules are changing. And the most powerful armed force in the Middle East has absolutely no idea what to do. The frustration, even rage, is becoming palpable. We'd thought—all of us—that we were beyond this. Camp David didn't work, OK, but how far apart could the two sides really be? Very.

The other thing that's new is that for the first time since we got here, people are talking about leaving. Actually, it's not the first time. When Barak ran against Netanyahu in 1996, the sense of frustration with Netanyahu and his (seemingly) utter incompetence led many of our friends on the left who'd been here for years to say that if Bibi were reelected, they were packing up. I have no idea if they meant it, but he lost, everyone was euphoric, and they stayed. This year, if Bibi had run against Barak, he'd have won by an even larger margin than Sharon did.

But now people are beginning to talk about getting out. The father of one of Talia's closest friends is being "transferred" to a European post. They've been here for fifteen years, and now they're leaving. Of course there are always many factors at play in these kinds of familial decisions, but our poor kid now has to deal not only with the ongoing process of making a life for herself here, but also with the sense of abandonment at the hands of friends whose parents are moving in the opposite direction. As if adolescence in a new country weren't tough enough. Other friends of ours who came on aliyah in August are still buying their apartment, but have decided to let their kids finish high school in the States. And today I asked one of our Fellows (who had reluctantly agreed last year to sign the contract that obligates her to serve a Jewish community in the Diaspora for five years) how she was doing, and she said, "Fine, but boy, I'll tell you, whatever frustration I felt about making that commitment, you're forgiven! I can't wait to get out of here." And by the way, she'd call herself to this day a passionate Zionist.

Thus, those of us planning to stick it out are conflicted. It's not the country we thought we were coming to, people are beginning to pack it in, and if you read the international press, you feel even more abandoned. Today's *New York Times* (at least on the web) had a headline that read "Suicide Bomber Kills Three Israelis After Deaths of Six Palestinians." The implied cause and effect was nauseating. A recent

Los Angeles Times headline asked, "Is Ariel Sharon Israel's Milosevic?" And the *London Independent*'s Review section led with a piece saying that Sharon's "name is synonymous with butchery; with bloated corpses and disemboweled women and dead babies, with rape and pillage and murder." To be sure, Sharon's not the guy you want your daughter to come home with (though he does have a nice ranch in the Negev, so maybe . . .), but this?

Perhaps the icing on the cake in terms of the desperation that many of us feel is that none of this is one-sided. We're grateful that the terrorist with the bomb in Netanya wasn't let onto the bus, but along with that come dozens, perhaps hundreds, of incidents each day in which Arabs aren't let on buses (no policy, just the driver's discretion) just because they're Arabs. Those of us liberals from the States have to fit that into our set of civil rights commitments.

And the closure of the territories, which virtually everyone supports, comes at a huge human cost. We know that. People are hungry, and the PA is on the verge of economic collapse, with all that that means; babies are (literally) being born at roadblocks because young women in labor aren't being let through, and *Ha-Aretz* has reported on countless cases of Palestinians who died for lack of medical care because soldiers let absolutely no one through. But what are we to do? Again, no one knows.

This week, B'tzelem, Israeli's equivalent of Amnesty International (and a very, very reputable outfit) published the following on their web site:

> On Saturday a nine-year-old Palestinian boy was killed by
> Israeli security forces gunfire north of Al Bira. A week prior,
> IDF soldiers shot and killed 15-year-old Husam a-Disi from
> Qalandya Refugee Camp. According to testimonies collected by
> B'Tselem, Husam a-Disi was hit by four live bullets, three of
> which entered his back. The boy was shot while throwing
> stones at IDF soldiers from a distance of about 100 meters.
> Since the eruption of violence in the Occupied Territories on

September 29, 2000, Israeli security forces have killed 88 Palestinian children. Some 4000 children have been injured.

For some of us, if what's being done to us isn't bad enough, this "other side" of the picture makes life completely incomprehensible and morally much too murky. Many of us don't understand the logistics of how so many kids are being shot, but when bombs are going off day after day, there's not much of an audience (or, frankly, much energy on our own part) for a serious conversation on the issue. If you're feeling too happy and giddy about life, you can go to B'tzelem's web site and sign up for their depressing e-mail of the week. Any unwanted complacency will be gone in minutes, guaranteed.

But it goes on and on. Yesterday, after the attack in Netanya, a group of Israelis found the closest Palestinian and beat him with an iron rod until the police arrived and evacuated him to the hospital. He's in critical condition, though he's expected to live. Remember the bit about "light unto the nations"? Right.

And today, the evening news ran a story about a police crackdown on Palestinians being employed in Israel in violation of the law (since the territories are supposed to be sealed) and showed a video clip of three Palestinians hiding in an attic, with policemen and dogs searching everywhere and ultimately finding them. To be sure, some of these people are what Micha calls "bad guys," but most are just trying to earn a living. But anyone with half a minute of Jewish history education can't help but associate these pictures of people hiding in attics with the police and dogs searching them out with . . . well, you can't really say it. There's nothing comparable about the situations, but still, the visual similarity is enough to make you (me?) sick.

So, in the midst of this situation, is there a bright spot? Well, there are humorous moments. Purim is coming up (Hamas has promised some special holiday explosions for us, so stay tuned), so Micha got to pick a costume. Elisheva took him out, and he picked a policeman's costume, complete with shirt, hat, handcuffs, and, yes, revolver. We've long had a "no guns" rule for our kids' toys, and I came home from work to find this gun in the house. I was none too pleased and said, "Why are we allowing guns in the house now?" My wife gave me a look that only spouses can give each other, which, roughly translated, read "Now, what planet do *you* live on? Do you know what he sees every day when he goes to school in the Old City? What, exactly, Mr. Liberal Schmiberal, are you trying to hide from him?" Or maybe it was "*You* take him shopping, and *you* get to pick." But it wasn't supportive, of that I'm certain.

And on a more serious level, the collapse of all the rules, expectations, assumptions, and hopes has led to a renewed introspective mood among some, a mood that I think is positive. We went to a lecture three or four weeks ago on a rainy night. Ruth Gavison, one of Israel's premier political philosophers, was lecturing at the Jerusalem Hilton on "philosophical justifications of Israel's existence." Not a new subject, but interesting because she was once believed to be on the radical left and was now embarking on a new project of justifying Israel's existence in modern political terms, in the terms used by liberal democratic theory.

This is an important issue because in the ongoing conflict between Jews and Arabs over this land, it all boils down in the end to "Who says it's yours? It's mine." Many Jews have long argued, of course, that God promised us this land in the Bible. But that isn't a particularly convincing argument to secular Israelis, to say nothing of Arabs and others who have their own traditions and for whom the Bible's promises are not terribly compelling. Other Israelis have used the argument that "we used to live here, but were evicted by the Romans, and now we're just getting our rightful land back." But that argument, too, is less compelling to Israelis than it used to be. How long do you have to be gone before you no longer have a claim on a place, many Israelis now ask themselves. A colleague of mine told me that years ago, when she was young and idealistic, she happened to be in Norway representing Israel at a conference. She began a conversation with a young Norwegian woman who worked in Norway's foreign office. Eventually the conversation turned to the Arab-Israeli conflict, and to the question of what, if anything, gave Israel the right to this land. My colleague, raised in the intellectual elite of Israel's secular society, responded with the position she'd been taught from an early age: "This was our ancient homeland, and we were evicted by force. Now we're back to claim what's rightfully ours." The Norwegian woman looked at her with astonishment and said, "That's absurd. Do you have any idea how huge a kingdom the Vikings had? How do you think the world would respond if Norway suddenly announced that we want all that territory back?"

My friend told me that even today, decades later, she still shudders at that conversation, and at how little she had to say in response. That problem, and the question of how to justify our being here when there clearly was another people on this land when we began to arrive in large numbers during the early parts of the twentieth century, is a critical one for people here, so Gavison's lecture topic struck a nerve. The lecture was held in the Hilton's largest ballroom, and they had a thousand chairs set up. And despite the freezing rain and generally dreary mood about town, it was standing room only. Young and old, men and women, religious and secular, left and right, native Israelis and immigrants, had all turned out to hear her. And I thought, what a very cool thing. More than a thousand people in a city of only six hundred thousand inhabitants, all coming to hear a quasi-academic lecture on political philosophy.

As with any crisis, this whole nasty state of affairs has brought Israelis closer together. No longer is "How are you" a simple phrase. People pause and then answer, "OK, considering." Or something like that. And people actually stop to listen to the answer. I saw a friend this morning and, realizing that I won't see him again until next week, said to him, "Have a happy Purim." He paused and said, "I'll settle for a quiet one."

That's all we want. A few weeks of quiet. No one expects solutions, or certainly peace. But quiet would be nice. Nice, but not likely. Sharon will probably take office in two days now that his government is coming together, and Hamas has promised more suicide bombings in "honor" of his becoming PM. And then, two days after that, Purim—and fireworks promised from Hamas. Maybe the police will stop them all. Maybe. Purim is, after all, a holiday about securing Jewish safety when it seemed least likely.

So in the next few days or a week, a lot is likely to change. Hopefully, at least some of it will be for the better. In the meantime, if it's your holiday, have a happy Purim. Here, we'll settle for a quiet one. Actually, though, if it's quiet, that alone will be enough to make it happy.

Something Inside Has Died

Day in and day out, news reports of a shooting, an explosion, and victims. And then the same drill. A quick call home to make sure that everyone in our immediate family is accounted for, and later, throughout the day, checks to verify that our friends and neighbors are OK. A quick summary of the attack on the evening news, and all is forgotten.

It's not forgotten, of course, by the kids who're now orphans, by the teenagers who will live the rest of their lives without a limb or with horribly disfiguring wounds, or by the parents who will bury their children the next day. But there's a limit to how much anguish any one of us can internalize, and so I notice that we—and our friends as well—do the inventory of the people we care about, and then we move on. No one talks about it, no one remembers their names. Because, after all, we're OK.

But it begins to strike me, as I think about it, that there's something sickeningly narcissistic about the way we're all reacting. What, I ask myself, has happened to us here? Is this what it's boiling down to? "I'm OK, so everything's OK." How can a society function that way?

But how can it function any other way?

. . .

Remember Annata, the refugee camp close to Jerusalem that I visited a couple of years ago, where we heard the story of Nabil and the IDF's destruction of his house? I think about him a lot lately.

For two years, ever since I went to Annata with the group opposed to home demolitions, I've been on their e-mail list. An occasional report, sometimes a request to help with fundraising, and mostly announcements of future events and activities. Until recently, though, I hadn't been hearing much from them.

Now, with the Intifada in full throttle and the army clamping down on Arab villages in a whole variety of ways, including roadblocks created with deep trenches, people can't get by, food can get scarce, medical treatment in these villages is completely unavailable, and, not surprisingly, Israeli liberal groups are mobilizing in a whole new and intense way.

Now the e-mails from this group are coming in pretty regularly, asking us to sleep in one of these villages for a night so that the army can't shoot at them as easily.

I have this sense that I should go. After all, the people in these villages are probably not the snipers or the bombers, and they don't deserve to suffer. The same values that got me to go to Annata in the first place, I figure, should get me out there this time. But I know I'm not going to go.

It's not only that it's dangerous, or that any decision to go to one of these villages would involve a major argument with Elisheva (though that prospect is not particularly appealing). But what is it, I wonder? In part it's because I only *assume* that the people there are not the snipers or the bombers. But the army is making a different assumption. How do I know? Who am I really helping here?

But more than that, I don't have the strength. I don't know for sure who's shooting at us, but someone is. Until our kids get home each day from school, Elisheva is a nervous wreck. Each time during the day that I hear the thud of what sounds like a sonic boom (probably from fighter planes breaking the sound barrier), or the rush of sirens, I instinctively look out the window of my office in the direction of our house, just a few blocks away. No smoke coming from that direction, and I get back to work.

We're on edge all the time, and it's wearing. Each hour's news broadcast, each morning's paper, each logging on to the web, is a fear-filled moment—what has happened that I haven't heard about yet?

Here, too, there's a limit to the angst that I can take. The Palestinians in these villages deserve to be protected and advocated for, but with everything that we're facing, it's not my first priority to run to *their* aid. My wife, my kids, are also the victims of this conflict, and right now they're the ones I've got to be here for.

There are simply too many victims: the Israelis who've been murdered, the Palestinian kids who've been sent out to "fronts" when responsible parents and leaders would have kept them in school, and, perhaps no less tragically, even the now shattered will of much of the Israeli peace movement. It's as if gravity has been suspended. Everything we thought we knew, every assumption we'd made about the world, has been undone. Still reeling from that discovery, still trying to figure out how to live in the aftermath of that, none of us has energy for the causes we used to think were literally part of who we are.

. . .

Something dark and terrifying is happening here. The months of endless assault on our sense of security, the daily fear for our kids and our spouses, is eroding the caring and selfless parts of ourselves of which we were once most proud.

I wonder how much of the "old us" we'll eventually get back. I don't know yet, and it's clear that it will be a long time before we understand what the long-term implications of this will be for the people we're becoming.

But even now, long before the end, it's clear: Parts of all of us have already died.

March 2001:
What a Difference an
Election Makes

Palestinians Delicately Begin Debate on
Circle of Violence

Palestinians delicately begin internal debate about violent nature of their intifada, for first time since late last September; some Palestinians are speaking out only against militants' use of residential neighborhoods as a base, especially after wave of bystander deaths in Al Bireh, outside Ramallah, during last few weeks; but broader question of intifada's direction is being broached, too; some Palestinians are gingerly asking if their leaders have a strategy that justifies devastating loss of life, property, mobility and income—gingerly out of concern that their questioning be mistaken for disloyalty to nationalist cause and for some out of fear of gunmen themselves.

New York Times: Sunday, March 11, 2001, page A1

Greetings from Jerusalem, where the biggest change is the weather. With few exceptions, it's been gorgeous and warm for the last couple of weeks—a fitting metaphor for the change in mood that's also taken root. Since things were so incredibly lousy when I wrote a couple of weeks ago, I figured it was only fair to let you know how much better things have gotten.

Even Ariel Sharon's most ardent supporters don't credit him with the change in weather, but the coincidence has been remarkable. He came into office a day or two before Purim, amid prevailing despair. And since then only one murder on the road to Gilo, but virtually no other terror incidents and certainly nothing serious (though two huge car bombs *were* defused). The territories have been fairly quiet and the Labor Party is busy licking its wounds and trying to figure out how to make a comeback, so even the politics are quiet.

As you'll remember, many of us laughed at Sharon's campaign jingle in the days before the election: *"yesh li bitachon ba-shalom shel Sharon"*—"I've got confidence in Sharon's peace," which also translates as "I've got security in Sharon's peace." No one's laughing now; the mad dash to make peace with people who're attacking us is over. The Palestinian Authority is talking openly about moving to a massive nonviolent Intifada, some Palestinians are now admitting that they're worse off than they were in September, and in general Israel is coming out of hiding. For these few days alone, it almost seems, it was worth electing this guy.

But of course this is the Middle East, and things are never as simple as they seem. So, a brief "rewind" back to Purim. On the day of Purim, as we were preparing to go out and deliver *Mishloach Manot* (little baskets of food that it's customary to deliver to friends on the day of Purim), we told the kids that they could each pick a few friends to deliver to as well. Among others, Micha said he wanted to deliver some to Nomi, a girl in his class he's never mentioned before. So, somewhat puzzled, we added her to our list. After doing all the deliveries in our neighborhood, we headed out to Nomi's house, which just happens to be in Gilo. Gilo, you'll recall, is the neighborhood about a mile or two from our house that has been shot at for months now from the neighboring Arab village (Beit Jala), and is the neighborhood that CNN insists on calling a "settlement" (because it is technically over the green line) even though Jerusalemites see it as a neighborhood, not even an outlying suburb.

When we got to her house and delivered the Purim goodies, Nomi's father asked Micha if he wanted to see the tank in their backyard. Micha, normally very excited about such things, didn't respond but followed us to the back porch where, literally, about twenty yards from their sliding glass door, was a tank, an armored personnel carrier, a whole pile of sandbags, an Israeli flag fluttering in the wind, and a group of soldiers lounging around waiting for the "nighttime festivities." Micha took a look and then wanted to leave, which was very different from his usual infatuation with tanks and the like, but I attributed it to his being shy in front of Nomi. Back to the car we went.

In the car, returning to our neck of the woods, Micha was unusually quiet, and I asked him if he was OK. He kept looking out the window and didn't say much. But seconds later, as we were driving along, he said firmly but softly, "At school, Nomi says her mommy cries at night when they shoot at her house."

Elisheva and I looked at each other and said nothing. But we both realized right away what a toll this whole mess has taken on these little kids. We send them off to school, with backpacks, lunches, and Pokémon cards, assuming that these little second-graders are basically oblivious to everything that's going on. And suddenly we realized that they know all about this, and that they talk about it among themselves at school. Now we understood why Micha wanted to bring candy to Nomi, and why he wasn't excited about the tank. Because this was real, and she was hurting. And he knew it. It was quiet in the car on the way back to the center of town.

There was, as I have mentioned, one shooting incident on the Tunnel Road just on the other side of Gilo, where a fifty-nine-year-old man from Efrat was killed by Palestinian snipers on his way to work. The next day, I had to go to a conference in Be'er Sheva, and after the driver picked me up at home, he said something like "Too bad you don't want to go by the Tunnel Road; it would save you a lot of time." Since the only other person in the car was my colleague who actually lives in Efrat (and who therefore goes that route every day), I was in a bit of a pinch. Truth is, I hadn't been on that road since the whole mess began, but somehow it just seemed ridiculous at that moment that we have to waste time because we're afraid of getting shot at in our own city. To hell with it, I figured. So, I said, "I don't mind the Tunnel Road; let's save the time." "Good decision," he said. "Besides, the safest time to take the road is the day after someone's killed. They never do it two days in a row."

We made it, obviously, and without incident. For me, the return to this part of the country, which I used to drive all the time, was a return to normalcy. And this return to normalcy has given us all a chance to breathe a little easier, and for me, to even be reminded of why I always used to hate leaving Israel when I'd come for visits years ago. I had to speak at the King David Hotel a week ago Shabbat, and walked from our house in the middle of the afternoon. As I walked to town, there were literally hundreds of people out for their Shabbat afternoon walk, lots of kids in their youth groups walking to or from some activity, people sitting in parks, and the Old City off to the right shimmering in a golden Jerusalem sun. I used to love coming here for Shabbat, and used to hate the thought of getting back on the plane to go "home." It was good to have that walk to town, because after all these lousy months, it reminded me of what it was that drew us here.

I was home one morning this week, taking advantage of the warm weather, sitting on the porch with a laptop doing some writing. On the street below, an old Arab peddler with a cart went by, calling out in Yiddish, *"Alte zachen, alte zachen"* (roughly translated as "old things, old things," a variation on "rags, clothes, bottles"). An Arab conducting business in Yiddish, in a modern Israeli neighborhood. I couldn't help but laugh at the absurdity of this Arab calling out in Yiddish to a population that speaks only Hebrew and some French or English, but there you have it. Sharon's in office for two weeks, the weather gets better, and even the Arabs are speaking Yiddish.

On the way to work on Friday morning, just at the front entrance to our building, there was a group of people surrounding a man I know named Balfour Hakak. He's one of the reigning experts on Jerusalem, and every Friday morning he gives a tour of a different neighborhood, rich with history and always with reference to classic Israeli literature that refers to this site or that. And here he was, with his charges, pointing at our very new building. I didn't stop to listen, but he was obviously telling them what was here before this office building. And I was reminded of what I used to tell Avi as we'd ride our bikes around town and people would take pictures of us from buses: To the rest of the world, this isn't a home, but a stage, and we live on it. For these few days, it's been great to have it feel like a home again.

Having said that, it's still a crazy home. I received an e-mail the other day from a human rights organization I used to be involved with, asking for people to bring shovels on Friday morning and to travel together to a small Palestinian village on the other side of the green line that's been completely cut off by IDF trenches. The people in the village have no medical care, no one can get to school, etc., and in general they're cut off. The e-mail said that this is no way to treat a civilian population, and Jewish values demand that we do something. So bring your shovels, they said, and we'll fill in the trenches.

What was interesting about the e-mail, though, was a note at the end that this "should be" pretty safe. But, they noted, there is some danger. Fine, but think about it. What's the danger from? The very people we'd be going to help! The whole thing struck me as noble but absurd. We'd spend an entire day filling in a trench or two that the IDF bulldozer would open up again in an hour. And we'd have to do it in fear of being shot at by the people we were trying to help. No thanks.

I didn't go, but I was sad about not wanting to go. When we first got here, I did lots of stuff like that. Now, two years later, I knew instinctively I wasn't going. Not that the need is less; there are a lot of people suffering in those villages, and the closures are not just strict, they're brutal. And not because of the alleged danger, because I genuinely don't think we had much to worry about. But more because like a lot of Israelis, I'm torn. I still care about all the things that I cared about when I went to those villages in the spring of 1999, but I'm also sick of putting my kids to bed to the sound of gunfire. The closures cause untold pain and suffering, but it's been quiet at night. The army's clamping down—quietly, but very, very firmly—and the result is that we're all breathing much easier.

That's the craziness. All the values that I was raised on—values, by the way, that I was taught were Jewish values—tell me to go fill up the trenches. But I also know that with those trenches filled up, someone will get out and try to hurt us, just because we're Jews trying to live in a Jewish country. Jewish values or Jewish safety. The saddest thing about this place is that now we often have to choose. It's a horrible choice to have to make, and now I make a choice radically different from the one I used to.

But, I said to myself as I clicked "delete" on that e-mail, the situation out there is horrifying, but at least now, Nomi's mommy isn't crying at night. For me, for now, that's good enough.

Well, on to Pesach. Happy scrubbing!

Jephthah's Daughter?

- - - - - - - - - - - - - - - - - -

Sometimes, these days, I wonder what's happening to us. Can a land emit a poison, a toxin that confuses, that obfuscates, that virtually guarantees that we become something other than what we want to be? Is there something about this land, or our passion for it, that blurs the vision? What is it about this land that blinds us to the very real and often devastating cost of our love for it, that leads us to ignore the horrific and repeated story of death for the sake of keeping it, a death that often inexplicably robs us of our children, and our children of their lives?

Is it possible that a place can blind us to the fact that our children are just that—children who need our love and protection, not pawns in the battles we choose to fight? And is it possible that no matter how one might try, that poison seeps in and vanquishes us? Does the land itself turn us into Jephthah, whom we scarcely remember?

> **11** *Jephthah the Gileadite was an able warrior, who was the son of a prostitute. Jephthah's father was Gilead;* ²*but Gilead also had sons by his wife, and when the wife's sons grew up, they drove Jephthah out. They said to him, "You shall have no share in our father's property, for you are the son of an outsider."* ³*So Jephthah fled from his brothers. Men of low character gathered about Jephthah and went out raiding with him.*
>
> ⁴*Some time later, the Ammonites went to war against Israel.* ⁵*And when the Ammonites attacked Israel, the elders of Gilead went to bring Jephthah back.* ⁶*They said to Jephthah, "Come be our chief, so that we can fight the Ammonites."* ⁷*Jephthah replied to the elders of Gilead, "You are the very people who rejected me. How can you come to me now when you are in trouble?"* ⁸*The elders of Gilead said to Jephthah, ". . . If you come with us and fight the Ammonites, you shall be our commander over all the inhabitants of Gilead."* ¹¹*Jephthah went*

with the elders of Gilead, and the people made him their commander and chief.

¹²Jephthah then sent messengers to the king of the Ammonites, saying, "What have you against me that you have come to make war on my country?" ¹³The king of the Ammonites replied to Jephthah's messengers, "When Israel came from Egypt, they seized the land which is mine, from the Arnon to the Jabbok as far as the Jordan. Now, then, restore it peaceably."

¹⁴Jephthah again sent messengers to the king of the Ammonites. ¹⁵He said to him, "Thus said Jephthah: Israel did not seize the land of Moab or the land of the Ammonites. ¹⁶When they left Egypt, Israel traveled through the wilderness to the Sea of Reeds and went on to Kadesh. ¹⁷Israel then sent messengers to the king of Edom, saying, 'Allow us to cross your country.' But the king of Edom would not consent. They also sent a mission to the king of Moab, and he refused. So Israel, after staying at Kadesh, ¹⁸traveled on through the wilderness, skirting the land of Edom and the land of Moab. . . ."

²⁸But the king of the Ammonites paid no heed to the message that Jephthah sent him. . . .

³⁰And Jephthah made the following vow to the LORD: "If you deliver the Ammonites into my hands, ³¹then whatever comes out of the door of my house to meet me on my safe return from the Ammonites shall be the LORD's and shall be offered by me as a burnt offering."

³²Jephthah . . . attacked them, and the LORD delivered them into his hands . . .

³⁴When Jephthah arrived at his home in Mizpah, there was his daughter coming out to meet him, with timbrel and dance! She was an only child; he had no other son or daughter. ³⁵On seeing her, he rent his clothes and said, "Alas, daughter! You have brought me low; you have become my troubler! For I have uttered a vow to the LORD and I cannot retract." ³⁶"Father," she said, "you have uttered a vow to the LORD; do to me as you have vowed. . . ."

—THE BOOK OF JUDGES (perhaps aptly named)

Thousands of years have passed, and the story continues. Not only because we continue to tell it, but because we are the same actors. The denial of rightful place. The sense of betrayal, of entitlement. War. Historical narratives on both sides that prove the land is really ours. And the passion—the destructive, murderous passion—that comes from our love of the land, and which then consumes our children.

In the last week of March, Shalhevet Pass was killed in the Jewish quarter of Hebron. She was ten months old. A Palestinian sharpshooter leveled his rifle in the direction of the Jewish quarter, located her in his sight, and sent a bullet into her skull.

What does one make of all this the morning after?

"Animals, and maniacs."

"What is that supposed to mean?" Elisheva asks me when I mutter while reading the paper.

"Anyone who would shoot a baby on purpose, just like that, is an animal," I reply. "And those people who live in Hebron, they're maniacs. Ridiculous—living in a dangerous place like that to make a point. Knowing their kids could get shot. Who gives them the right? Bunch of lunatics."

"And just what the hell do you think we're doing?" comes the icy response. "If the shooting comes here, are you picking up and leaving? Even if it gets dangerous for the kids—as if it isn't already. You know you're not going anywhere. And not only because everything you have is here, just like them, there. But because you think it's yours, and no one's going to force you out. Because you've said it dozens of times: You're not going to be the first Jew in history to give up on Jerusalem. Well, it's the same with them. They just chose a different spot not to give up on.

"That's why you're upset. Because you're just like them. Because we're really no different than them."

Deuteronomy's Greatest Hits?

We did end up taking the kids to Ben Gurion's house on Election Day, just as we'd planned. They liked it, though I think that in the short run, the Sega Rocket Ride at the local amusement park made more of an impression. For me, though, the library at Ben Gurion's house is still amazing, no matter how many times I've seen it.

Beyond the literally thousands of books in the place, what I like about Ben Gurion's house is that his desk still has his copy of the Hebrew Bible on it. It's my favorite part of the house, this desk with the worn little book on it, falling apart at the binding with the pages yellowed and frayed. There's something about the image of the founder of the country dealing with all of the international intrigue, internal politics, military strategy, and nation-building that neonatal Israel required, and still referring to the Bible day in and day out for counsel, for solace, for an anchor in the turbulent times in which he lived.

I used to be jealous of him when I went to that house, jealous that he knew the book so well, envious of a worldview that let him find such comfort and grounding in those frayed and battered pages. This time, though, I'm more cynical than jealous. Would he still do that today, I wonder, opening those pages with a sense that they tell the story of the people for whom he's writing the next chapter?

Now, suddenly, I suspect not. Not in the middle of this. Those pages, that story, are becoming a bit tough to swallow these days. Whether it's sitting with the kids when helping them with their Bible homework, listening to the Torah reading at shul, or working on something in my study, too often the pages to which Ben Gurion apparently turned for solace and guidance just make me sad. Or angry? Or is it just abandoned? Deuteronomy isn't working for me these days.

1 *39Moreover, your little ones who you said would be carried off, your children who do not yet know good from bad, they shall enter it; to them will I give it and they shall possess it.*

My children didn't know good from bad when they got here, perhaps, because they hadn't ever witnessed real evil in the States. But here they've seen the pictures of bodies outside malls, the corpses lying under sheets at the bus stops. "Your children who do not yet know good from bad"? I don't think so.

"To them will I give it and they shall possess it." This is how you possess the land? Tell that to Shalhevet Pass, who was consciously and intentionally shot in her head. What about her possessing the land?

. . .

Or this.

12 *29When the LORD your God has cut down before you the nations that you are about to enter and dispossess, and you have dispossessed them and settled in their land, 30beware of being lured into their ways after they have been wiped out before you! Do not inquire about their gods, saying, "How did those nations worship their gods? I too will follow those practices." 31You shall not act thus toward the LORD your God, for they perform for their gods every abhorrent act that the LORD detests; they even offer up their sons and daughters in fire to their gods.*

What about the abhorrent acts that we do, that God must detest? The gods to which we offer up our sons and daughters?

Shalhevet Pass was killed on Monday, March 26, 2001. In Israel's tradition, she should have been buried later that day. Or the next day at the very latest. But her parents left her unburied for a week, saying they would not lay her to rest until Ariel Sharon promised to recapture the hill that had been given to the Palestinians and from which the sharpshooter had fired. That's what you do with your child's corpse? That's how you pressure the prime minister? "You shall not act thus toward the Lord your God." Indeed.

. . .

24 [16] *Parents shall not be put to death for children, nor children be put to death for parents: a person shall be put to death only for his own crime.*

Children die only for their own crimes? What about Muhammad Jamal Al Dura, caught in a crossfire no one has yet figured out? Imam Hiju, killed in her home by errant Israeli artillery? Shalhevet Pass, murdered by a sniper who didn't care that she was only a baby? Or Kobi Mandel, savagely murdered and beaten beyond recognition by Palestinians who hated him just because he was a Jew, or an Israeli?

How many hundreds of Palestinian kids have been sent to the front by their parents, or Palestinian Authority operatives, told to miss school and throw rocks at frightened soldiers? Don't their parents or the PA know that those kids are going to get hurt, that some are inevitably going to be killed? And what about the Israeli kids waiting for the bus to go to school when some guy walks up to them, speaks with them for a minute or two, then pulls a string or pushes a button, blowing them all to smithereens?

. . .

I don't know, Ben Gurion. I know that it's the book that tells our story. But parts of it really aren't working for me these days. Were things that different back when you sat at that desk? Or is it me? What did you see that I'm missing here?

Two-Wheelers and Tombstones

Even in the midst of this "situation," childhood continues. Kids, after all, are lucky not to have the perspective that allows them to appreciate how much everything has gone to pot. So they do their thing and keep growing up.

Micha has finally learned to ride a two-wheeler, and his training wheels are off. No small accomplishment, it strikes me, in a country where it seems there isn't an empty parking lot or a flat place to practice for hundreds of miles. A few yards here, a semi-open path there, and he's figured it out. He's ready to rock.

For months he's been asking if we can go mountain biking when his training wheels come off, and even though his little bike with the tiny tires and no gears is about as suitable for mountain biking as my beat-up Nikes are for climbing Mount Everest, I promise him a mountain bike ride. So the first day we have available, we decide to go to Har Ha-Ruach ("Wind Mountain"), about twenty minutes outside Jerusalem, where there's a trail that's bumpy enough and steep enough to count as mountain biking but sufficiently passable that it won't frustrate him too much.

We head up the Jerusalem–Tel Aviv highway, then turn off into Abu Ghosh, the large Arab town we pass through to visit my brother, Yonatan, and to Har Ha-Ruach. From the back, Avi asks, "Abba, are you sure it's OK to drive here?"

"Avi, haven't we driven here a million times before?"

"Yeah, but not since the whole thing started."

It's true, I realize. We've sort of been hibernating since October, and we haven't been out to my brother's house since then. He's been to see us many times, but we haven't been out here in ages. The kids haven't been in an Arab village for months—since October 2000—and Avi's nervous about being here.

"Don't worry," I tell him. "Relations with this village have been great since '48. There's never been trouble here."

"Why?"

"I have no idea. We're fine. Relax."

So much for a casual family outing. But we do get to Har Ha-Ruach without incident, park the car, unload the bikes, top off a few of the tires with some air, and head out. Micha's doing great, having the time of his life, incredibly proud to have joined the august clan of riders. And he's good, really good. Those tiny tires don't seem to stop him from going anywhere. He's made of pure muscle and grit, and soon we find ourselves pretty far out on the mountain, somewhere between Nataf, where my brother lives, and Kibbutz Ma'aleh Ha-Hamishah ("The Ascent of the Five"). The road levels out and we're pedaling along. Avi's itching to go faster, I'm watching out for Micha, and Micha's just in heaven.

A couple of hundred yards farther along the road, pretty much in the middle of nowhere, on a stretch I don't recall ever having ridden, I suddenly notice a large rectangular stone with some inscription on the side of the road. Always curious about this sort of thing, I stop the bike and lean over to read. It says something like "On this spot, on the 5th of Kislev, 5698 (9 November 1937), five members of Kibbutz Kiryat Anavim were attacked and murdered while working on this road."

I've always wondered whom Kibbutz Ma'aleh Ha-Hamishah was named for. I once asked someone when we had a faculty conference at the Guest House in Ma'aleh Ha-Hamishah, and they laughed and said, "I have no idea. But with a name like that, in this country, it has to be five people killed doing something." Now, it turns out, that's true. The 1930s were not a great decade in this region. There was a tremendous amount of tension: Arabs attacked Jews, Jews retaliated against Arabs, and neighborhood battles and general lawlessness characterized the time.

I'm reading the inscription on this little monument, stuck here in the middle of nowhere, when I hear the boys say, "Come on, Abba, let's ride." But I don't want to just let it go, and try to explain to them what happened here. "Abba! Really. Let's ride. Enough of that stuff."

Enough, indeed. And we set off again, pedaling our way back to the car, but it's hard to let it go. Even on virgin two-wheeler expeditions, history smacks you in the face. You can't even take your kid out for a bike ride without explaining that this Arab town is OK, only to find a monument to five dead Jews along the trail. This just isn't a normal place. To live here is not to tell a story, but to live one. Living here, you become the story, and it takes over. There's no avoiding it, there's no escaping. There's no way not to repeat it. The story is here to stay, and we're part of it, like it or not.

On the way home, back to Jerusalem, I wonder how much of this Micha will remember. He's euphoric about having been mountain biking and doesn't seem in the least bit affected by our little unexpected history lesson. Is it just normal for these kids to see monuments to dead Jews wherever they go? Have they become so accustomed to it that they don't even see it anymore? Are they immune at this point? To the implicit message that the danger lurks around every corner? To the repetition of the story? To the fact that even if it's not the case that all the world's a stage, this place certainly is?

I look at the three kids in the rearview mirror, and two are playing Game Boys, one is reading. Nothing of note happened, their postures seem to be saying. Or do they just get it already, knowing that that's what's happened here, and that's why we're here?

Or more likely, it strikes me, are Game Boys and novels the best way to avoid thinking about another history lesson they didn't want to hear in the first place?

April 2001:
"That's the Way It Is"

A quick letter as Yom Ha-Shoah (Holocaust Memorial Day) ends and the country begins to gear up for Yom Ha-Atzma'ut (Independence Day) next week.

Truth is, what's new is that there's nothing new. For the first few months of the Intifada, or low-scale war—call it whatever you like—people were genuinely addicted to the news. Here at home, we had the radio on all the time, watched the nightly news, ran outside to get the paper first thing in the morning, all to see if anything had developed in the last few hours. Sometimes it had, sometimes it hadn't, but deep down, I think we were looking to see whether anything had happened that might indicate that this whole nightmare might soon be over. But that didn't come to be, and now, I think, there are very few people who believe that the end will come anytime soon.

Remember how Walter Cronkite used to end his nightly broadcasts with "That's the way it is"? Well, this is the way it is. And like it or not, this is how it's going to be. Sensibly or not, this is what we brought our kids to. This is what our kids will have to live with, probably for the long haul.

A few nights before Pesach, we all sat down to the table, and out of the blue Avi asked, "So when do you think this whole thing is going to be over?" I think we were both a little taken aback because we hadn't heard him talk about it at all for a few weeks, and in some ways, I think we both assumed that he was oblivious. But we were obviously wrong. This is clearly eating at him, but there wasn't much to tell him. But I told him the truth. The first Intifada lasted for many years. And this one's just begun.

The real truth, though, would have been more harsh, but I didn't have the stomach to tell him. That truth would have been that the first Intifada, whether we want to admit it or not, pushed us to make far-reaching compromises, really got the peace process started. You couldn't do more than Barak did, and the response couldn't have been more clear. When it was time to finally reach some difficult compromise and end the conflict, Arafat decided to create a "diversion" of sorts, the diversion we're still living with now. The kids no longer ask about peace. I think they know the answer. Nor do the boys ask if this will all get worked out before they have to go into the army. I think that they know the answer to that, too.

Life does, though, have its lighter moments. We had a bit of work done on the house a few weeks ago, some painting, a few additional electric outlets—minor stuff. We used the same contractor we'd used for our remodeling, and about a year to the date from its completion, he showed up with a small crew for a few days of work. These men were the same ones we'd seen every day for months last year, Palestinians who live in Bethlehem, people with whom we'd had very nice relationships back then. But a lot has changed in a year.

As Shlomo, the contractor, was working on the electricity, I asked him how things were going. "Not easy," he said. There are days the army shuts down the border, so he can't work because he has no crew. He can't schedule anything at all, and his workers are hurting. Then he added, with a slight grin, "You know, of course, that it's now illegal to bring these Palestinians to work in Israel. So when I pick them up, I'm breaking the law. And now that you know, so are you."

Whatever. So the day went on, they got to redoing the plaster in the living room, and suddenly we noticed a ton of flies or some sort of mosquito all over the place. It was unpleasant, obviously, and Shlomo remarked that they were all over his house too. He turned to Mahmoud, the Palestinian plastering the wall, and asked, "Mahmoud, you have the bugs at your house, too?" Mahmoud, scarcely looking up, said no. "How's that possible?" asked Shlomo, knowing that Bethlehem is only a few minutes away from here. This time, Mahmoud stopped working, looked up, and said, "It's simple. The kids in the neighborhood throw stones at the soldiers. The soldiers fire tear gas at everyone. The tear gas kills all the mosquitoes. Life is good in Bethlehem."

A chuckle, and everyone went on with their business. They finished, left to go home, and we sat down to dinner. It got dark, and within the hour we heard the thunder of tank shells again. "Where's it coming from this time?" Avi asked. I told him, "It's too loud to be too far. Turn on the radio and we'll hear." And sure enough, at seven o'clock, the news reported that tanks were shelling Bethlehem in response to some people who shot at some soldiers (no one injured). "Bethlehem?" asked Avi. "Isn't that where that guy who was here today lives?" "Yup," I responded. And you could see Avi processing the rest himself. A real person, a worker who made our house look nice, a man who's kind to the kids whenever he's here and who has a sense of humor. He went home, and now we were shelling his neighborhood. The confusion on Avi's face was beyond painful.

The other day, after another terrorist incident, Israel invaded Gaza in a wildly popular but now much maligned military venture that cut Gaza into three districts. Reading the paper the next morning, Elisheva said, "I'm really glad we did it, but it's no solution. Where will it lead? What good will that do? They'll just hate us more, and more people will die."

That's it. There's really no solution. Well, there's one. We could pack up and leave.

That, of course, isn't going to happen. Not many hours ago, as Yom Ha-Shoah started, Israel television showed the annual memorial ceremony at Yad Va-Shem live. About 8:45 P.M., as the ceremony was winding down, we had the TV on. We had some friends over, and the adults were watching on and off, but the kids had gotten bored with it. Tali was at the computer working on a paper for school, the boys were playing Ping-Pong on the terrace with a friend, and we were standing around as the army orchestra began to play Hatikva [Israel's national anthem]. It grew quiet in the room. Tali stopped typing, and the adults stopped talking. As Hatikva was being sung, we could hear the sound of the Ping-Pong ball going back and forth, and suddenly the incredibly close sound of tank fire. It was surreal. At Yad Va-Shem, they were commemorating the memory of six million Jews and were singing the Israeli national anthem. At our house, Jewish boys were outside in the Jerusalem evening, playing Ping-Pong. And about two miles away, Israeli tanks were firing away, so powerfully that the house almost shook.

The contrast between the memorial service for Yom Ha-Shoah and the sounds of tank shelling at the very same time brought home to all of us that that's why we're here. We're here, in part, because having a country of our own means that that can never happen again. Little Israeli boys do not have to raise their hands in surrender, and now, if we need to, we fire back. Not all Israelis think we should be firing, and most of the world thinks we shouldn't. But at that moment, those questions struck me as minor. The fact is, we can if we need to. And that makes all this worth it.

I watched Avi and Micha playing Ping-Pong, oblivious to everything going on around them. Gone were the days when they'd run up to the roof to watch the shelling, or when they'd come downstairs, scared, telling us they couldn't fall asleep. They just wanted to play. They scarcely noticed the tanks firing away, and living with shelling outside and Hatikva on national television just seemed normal to them.

Il y a la guerre en Isräel

For two years now, the boys have been going to school in the Old
City, at a public school just a few hundred yards from the Western
Wall and the Temple Mount. Usually they get driven to school and
brought back home by a minivan that picks them up at home, so we
don't actually go there often. But if they miss the bus, or have to get
picked up early for some reason, we do drive into the Old City, and
each time we do, I'm filled with wonder at the different world that
exists just seven minutes or so from our home.

Our neighborhood, Bakk'a, is made up of narrow streets and
old Arab homes, to which some modern Israeli construction has been
added. But despite its quaint and mildly Mideastern look, it's a relatively modern place. As we drive out to the main road that runs just
by our street, we pass the chic cafes that have sprung up in the last
few years, restaurants surrounded by lush gardens, the dry cleaners,
the camera store, and antiques shops. There's the butcher and the
health food store, the used book shop and the veterinarian's office,
where the kids love to look longingly at the various pets we've never
let them get.

But five minutes later, as we make a right turn up to the Jaffa
Gate of the Old City, we enter a different world. The gate's been
widened for cars, of course, but the streets themselves are still
exceedingly narrow. As we climb the hill to the actual entrance to the
city, we pass the young Arab men peddling pita bread, rolls, and
other baked goods on open carts, sometimes drawn by a donkey.
Straight ahead as we enter the gate is the Muslim Quarter, which we
used to frequent when I was a kid, but which has seen too many stab-
bings of Jews in recent years for us ever to go in there now. But still,
it's quaint and alluring. There are elderly Arab men, wearing kaf-
fiyehs (originally the traditional headdress of Bedouin Arabs, now
worn by many others), sitting at backgammon tables, smoking and

idling away their days as if nothing has changed in the hundreds of years since these city walls were built. Arab women, wearing their traditional black and embroidered dresses, walk seemingly without concern, their backs erect, with bushels of vegetables or other wares balanced precariously on their heads.

The Muslim Quarter is closed to traffic, though, so we follow this sole cobblestone road to the right, past the Citadel of David, once a fortress, today a museum, and in the last century, the site of the grand ceremony marking the British general Allenby's capture of Jerusalem in 1917, wresting control of the city from the Turks. The road narrows even further and takes us into the Armenian Quarter. Pedestrians have to flatten themselves against the walls on either side of the road as our car barely crawls by, for the roads here were built for donkeys, not automobiles, and with large stone buildings constructed on either side, with no sidewalks at all, there's absolutely no way to widen them. Eventually we weave left again, past the Armenian pottery shop and the tourist shops with postcards and Jewish, Christian, and Muslim knickknacks on the left, with more elderly men sitting outside, and Zion Gate on the right, where Israeli soldiers battled the Jordanians in both 1948 and 1967, eventually capturing the Old City during the 1967 Six Day War. Another hundred yards and we're in the Jewish quarter, but still high enough up the hill that the main thing we see is the golden Dome of the Rock, one of the holiest sites in the world for Muslims. Below the Dome, out of our view as we park in the parking lot, is the Western Wall, just down the stairs from our kids' school.

To get from the parking lot to the school, we walk the dark alleyways, winding and turning in a seemingly endless maze that we could never navigate until our kids showed us exactly how to go. That's what I love about their going to school here—just minutes from western Jerusalem, they feel completely at home in a different world, a world that still preserves the smells, sights, and sounds of hundreds of years ago, a world of alleys and corners and virtually hidden passageways that they've come to know like the back of their hand. The thousands of tourists who used to throng the Old City before the violence brought tourism to a virtual end would take pictures, stand back and take in the exotic scenery, as we would run after our kids as they trotted off to school, to their friends, to a different world in which they felt completely comfortable.

At times, when we would gather for a school play or some other meeting, other parents and I would marvel at the fact that our kids go to school here and see nothing wrong with taking life in the Old City very much for granted. In our first years here, not that long ago, we parents would share with each other our awe at the realization that what for many people is a mysterious tourist site is home to our kids, and home to us in ways that we would never have expected even a few years ago.

. . .

It's another parent-teacher night at the boys' school. As always, the teachers are a bit late, so we cool our heels and wander around. Why is it that this is the first time I notice the barbed wire around the perimeter and on the roof? It's rusted, and clearly not new.

Conversations in Los Angeles with friends about the pros and cons of the various school options we had there suddenly come back. Teachers, proximity. Cost. School philosophy. And, of course, physical plant and safety. I force myself not to laugh. The worst of the bunch back there didn't compare to this dilapidated building. This is a dump by those standards. There aren't half a dozen parents from back there who would send their kids to a place that looked like this. And of those six, how many would be able to get beyond the barbed wire? Honestly, we too would have thought this nuts.

Some stirring in the hallway. Maybe it's our turn now. We head to the classroom, but the second-grade teacher's not ready for us yet. But it's only going to be a minute, so we hang out closer to the door. I notice the bulletin board just outside the door, which has little kids' pictures with flowers, trees, Jewish stars, and the like. It doesn't seem very noteworthy, until I look more closely and see that the writing is in French. At the bottom of the pictures, it becomes clear. These are little pictures some kids in a Jewish day school in Paris have made to cheer up our kids. I laugh. I never knew that anyone actually ever did anything with those pictures. I remember making them myself when I was a little kid. We drew our pictures for the "poor Israeli children" and never saw them again. To think that some of them actually made it to an Israeli school's bulletin board strikes me, thirty-something years later, as ridiculous and funny. I don't know why.

Then I read the wording on one of the pictures. It's a little girl's handwriting (she's signed it "Jessica" at the bottom), and she has clearly worked hard to make it as legible as possible. It's a labor of love: *Je sais qu'il y a la guerre en Isräel mais gardez confiance car dieu regard tout dans le ciel et sachez que les tefillot des enfants gagnent tout les prières. Jessica.* ("I know that there's a war in Israel, but be confident, because God is in heaven and sees everything, and know that the prayers of children win out over all other prayers. Jessica.")

Two things strike me right away, cynic that I am, or have become. The first, and it's obviously not her fault, is the theological absurdity of the line "Children's prayers are more powerful than all other prayers." A lot of kids have died here, Israeli and Palestinian. I'm sure that they all prayed. Were they answered?

I wonder about the fact that in her French, Jessica has used the Hebrew word *tefillot* for prayers. I wonder why. Probably because that's the language her teacher uses back in Paris. But what about all those Arab kids? Have we forgotten to teach our own kids that Arab kids also pray? That they, too, have become miserable in the past months? That what is so painful about this situation is that it's not a simple matter of right versus wrong, simply good against evil? There's something about using a Hebrew word for prayer that suggests we're the only ones suffering, and I find myself getting angry.

It's the same reaction I have when American friends come for a visit and begin to pontificate about what Israel should or should not do, with a simplicity and a conviction that shows no awareness of the

complexity of the situation, or no moral depth. "How could we possibly give Hebron back?" one asks after I gave a lecture a few months
ago. And I wanted to ask him, "Who's the 'we' here? I don't see *your*
kids in the army. I don't think *you* have to watch your children get
more and more callous as they're asked to do things that military service among a resentful and sometimes hostile population almost always
requires. If you did, maybe you'd realize that this isn't so simple."

Or the person who wrote me after one of the e-mails made its
way around the States: "Why so many question marks in your letter?
Don't you get it yet? They're out to destroy you, and unless you
destroy them first, you won't make it. Keep your powder dry." It
infuriates me. From a leather recliner in Forest Hills, New York, it's
easy to be an armchair hardliner. "It's true that we didn't start this
latest round of violence, and it's true that we offered a reasonable
peace deal—or at least the start of one. But the story's more complicated than those simple—but true—facts. Come over here and live in
this, see its never-ending complexity," I find myself muttering when
I listen to those people, "and then let's see how sure you are of who is
right and what we should do about it."

For some reason, Jessica's choice of the word *tefillot* for "prayer"
strikes me as a similar claim—real prayer is Jewish prayer—and I
find myself almost furious. And then, when I look at her picture, the
finely detailed flowers and the handwriting she's worked so hard to
keep neat and legible, I wonder why I've gotten so angry in the space
of just a few seconds. Maybe she didn't mean anything of the sort.
Maybe she's never even thought about this at all.

A little girl in Paris does her best to make us feel better, and we
end up seething at her. It's not her fault. It's not our fault. And the
world doesn't seem to think that it's the Palestinians' fault, either.
So whose fault is it? Whom should we get mad at? Jessica—you're
just in the wrong place at the wrong time.

. . .

But there's one other thing about Jessica's little picture. *Je sais qu'il
y a la guerre en Isräel.* "I know that there's a war in Israel." How

do you know that, Jessica? Who told you there's a war going on here? You know what, you're right. But you're making me wonder, how come we keep telling our kids we have a *"matzav,"* a "situation"? How come they live here, and you live so far away, and yet you know the truth?

But you're right, Jessica. We brought our kids to a war. Do you have any prayers for that?

A Challenge for Robert Frost

Jealousy. The sense that there's simply not enough for everyone. That's been the theme of this land, once called Canaan, then Palestine, now Israel. The blood that flows today is a continuation of the struggle between the children of Isaac and the children of Ishmael:

> 21 The LORD took note of Sarah as He had promised, and the LORD did for Sarah as He had spoken. ²Sarah conceived and bore a son to Abraham in his old age, at the set time of which God had spoken. . . . ⁹Sarah saw the son whom Hagar the Egyptian had borne to Abraham playing. ¹⁰She said to Abraham, "Cast out that slave-woman and her son, for the son of that slave shall not share in the inheritance with my son Isaac."
>
> ¹¹The matter distressed Abraham greatly, for it concerned a son of his. ¹²But God said to Abraham, "Do not be distressed over the boy or your slave; whatever Sarah tells you, do as she says, for it is through Isaac that offspring shall be continued for you. ¹³As for the son of the slave-woman, I will make a nation of him, too, for he is your seed."
>
> —BOOK OF GENESIS

Two nations emerge from Abraham, and both claim this land. And too often, each has tried to justify its claim to this land by denying the legitimacy of the other.

At the first Zionist Congress in Basle, in 1897, the now famous phrase "a people without a land for a land without a people" first achieved prominence. It was, many observers now say, an attempt to convince world Jewry to rally support for the fledgling Zionist movement without worrying that harm might be done to another people.

But there was, of course, another people here, and from the very beginning of the Zionist movement and the first waves of Jewish immigration to this land, relations were strained. The British thought that they could finesse the issue. In October 1917, when their government issued the now famous Balfour Declaration, the British made it clear that a Jewish state would have to take the legitimate rights of the Arab populations seriously. The declaration said it as simply as could be:

> His Majesty's Government view with favor the establishment in Palestine of a national home for the Jewish people and will use its best endeavors to facilitate the achievement of this object, it being clearly understood that nothing shall be done which may prejudice the civil and religious rights of existing non-Jewish communities in Palestine or the rights and political status enjoyed by Jews in any other country.

Of course His Majesty's Government learned that that was much easier said than done. Riots and violence in the 1920s were more vicious and bloody than any before, and with time, the British realized that they could not govern Palestine. So they decided to leave, and on the 29th of November, 1947, the United Nations voted to adopt the Partition Plan, which created one state for the Jews, one state for the Arabs.

The territory allocated to the Arab population (today called Palestinians) was much larger than anything that is now being contemplated. The Jews didn't get very much. They got a small area adjacent to the Sea of Galilee, a narrow strip along the coast, and the area of the Negev, an arid desert that to this day is scarcely populated. The three areas were connected by small strips of land that seem barely defensible.

But the Jewish leadership accepted the proposal; Arab leaders didn't. Arab countries attacked, and by the time the War of Independence was over, the State of Israel had been declared and had captured much of the territory that had originally been allocated to the Arab state in the plan the Arabs had rejected. Eight years later, in

1956, another war, and Israel captured the entire Sinai Peninsula, only to be forced to return it to Egypt almost immediately. Eleven years later, the June 1967 Six Day War. This time Israel captured the Sinai again, the entire West Bank of the Jordan, and the Golan Heights. And this, now claim the Palestinians, was the beginning of the "occupation." Is there an occupation? Of course there is. But who forced it on whom? That part of the story they rarely mention. Just like the early Zionists who preferred to pretend—or perhaps even believe—that there was no one here before they arrived.

Six years later, another war. Egypt and Syria attacked Israel on Yom Kippur in 1973, and for a brief period Israel lost portions of both the Golan and the Sinai Peninsula. But eventually the tide turned, and Israel recaptured what she had lost in the surprise attack.

Anwar Sadat was the first to recognize that he would not get his land back by force, so he chose a different—previously unthinkable—path. He proposed peace.

Sadat visited Jerusalem for the first time in November 1977, and eventually a peace agreement between Israel and Egypt was signed. Israel returned the Sinai to Egypt, and gradually Israelis began to assume that other parts of the captured territories would go back as peace agreements were signed with Jordan and Syria as well. But Jordan signed an agreement asking for very little land back, realizing that by this point, the land it had lost in 1967 was sought by the Palestinians as their own homeland. And Syria showed no interest in a deal at all.

The conflict with the Palestinians continued—bloody and vicious—for years, until the Oslo Peace Accords were signed in 1993. In paving the way for Palestinian statehood, Israel effectively repudiated—without ever saying so—the "people without a land for a land without a people" slogan that had first been used a century earlier. Egypt and Jordan had recognized Israel's right to be here, and Israel had effectively recognized the legitimate rights of a Palestinian people.

It seemed that everyone was giving up something, and that regional peace would soon be a reality.

But then, in November 1995, Yitzchak Rabin was assassinated. Benjamin Netanyahu was elected prime minster shortly thereafter, and the Netanyahu government, which had been suspicious of Arafat and his genuine intentions all along, slowed down the process of returning land. Relations between Israel and the Palestinians soured, and with time, Israelis lost patience with the policy that seemed to be letting the dream slip away.

In the next election, Netanyahu lost to Barak, who together with Clinton tried to push through a deal to end the conflict. But Camp David failed despite Barak's far-reaching offer, and Arafat—whom Rabin had called "our peace partner" and who received the Nobel Peace Prize—unleashed the El Aksa Intifada in response.

Arafat's Intifada has killed the peace process. No longer is it ailing; it is dead. Now, months into this conflict, very few Israelis believe that there's anyone to make a deal with. Arafat, even most former leftists believe, is an unrepentant terrorist, an inveterate liar who says one thing to the world in order to convince the U.S. and Europe that he is genuinely seeking peace, but something very different to his own people, whom he subtly and not so subtly encourages to continue the killing. He cannot make a deal because, unlike Sadat and Israeli prime minister Menachem Begin, and unlike Rabin and Jordan's King Hussein, Arafat will not—or cannot—compromise. We've shown how much we're willing to move; he hasn't conceded anything. But he's also a vicious dictator, and the more moderate elements of the Palestinian population have no chance whatsoever of gaining control of their side of the process. So the peace process is history, and Israelis, desperate for an end to this, are trying to think "out of the box."

There will be no negotiated settlement, they now say, for there's no one to negotiate with. And there will be no military solution, for short of annihilating millions of Palestinians, which no one here even considers, or forcibly moving them to a different location, which very few consider and which the world would obviously never tolerate, the army can do little. So, say some, it's time to take matters into our own hands. It's time for a "unilateral separation."

The theory behind this new idea is simple: They need a state, and we need peace. But we'll never be able to negotiate our way to a settlement, so let's do it on our own. We draw the borders we think make sense. We pull back from Gaza, from large parts of the West Bank, and we build a wall. "Here's your state," we say. "Good luck. We hope you're successful. But these are the borders. Stay on your side, and we'll live reasonably civilly side by side. But if you cross the border, or continue the use of violence, the response will be more punishing than anything we've done to you before."

It's the old biblical adage from Numbers 23, taken radically out of context: "There is a nation that dwells apart." Or to quote Robert Frost, several thousand years later, "Good fences make good neighbors."

. . .

But it's not nearly as simple as that. When people start to think about this only remaining solution, they realize that even this is fraught with problems. True, we don't need Palestinian consent for this, and that's a large part of what makes the option attractive. But we do need internal consensus about what to do, and that we don't have.

What shall we do about the very small settlements in Gaza, where there are a million Palestinians and a few thousand Israelis, who make up about one percent of Gaza's population? Most Israelis say that we should uproot those settlements, that the strips of land we would have to keep to make those settlements contiguous with Israel would effectively divide Gaza into three parts, infuriating the Palestinians. It's time to get out, most Israelis say. But the settlers there disagree. And they say they're not going to budge. Suddenly Israelis realize that "unilateral separation" might mean Israeli soldiers forcibly removing Jewish settlers from their homes. And the settlers are armed. The entire country shudders to think what this might lead to.

Or what about the West Bank? Barak was willing to give virtually the whole thing to a future Palestinian state, but Sharon and others say that that is dangerous and foolhardy. We need a strip of land just to the west of the Jordan River, they insist, to prevent Jordanian, Syrian, or Iraqi tanks from rolling across. There is no reason to assume that Palestine would stop them, argues Sharon, so we have to have the capability to do it ourselves. But Palestinians say that this leaves them with a country surrounded by Israel, cut off from the other Arab countries.

And how will we connect Gaza and the West Bank? A tunnel? A bridge without access to Israel?

And what about the large Israeli Arab populations, especially those in the Galilee, who have never been treated adequately by Israel? Today they are about twenty percent of Israel's population, but that could grow, and they could exercise a great deal of control. They're bitter, and certainly not committed to the idea of a Jewish state. So how do we protect both the democratic dimension of Israel and its Jewish character? Some Israelis say, when we build this fence, let's give back even parts of the Galilee, well inside the green line, and make those Arab villages part of the new Palestinian state. Let's cut into our flesh now to save our soul later on. But what if the Israeli Palestinians don't want that, others ask? Will we have an armed confrontation on that internal front as well?

And what about Jerusalem, the thorniest of the problems? Palestinians say that East Jerusalem has to be their capital, but numerous Israeli governments (including Barak, who offered exactly that) have campaigned with a promise that the city will never again be divided. What do we do with the Temple Mount, sacred to both Jews and Muslims? Clinton had proposed giving the Muslims the surface of the Mount, and Jews the subterranean sections. A Solomonesque proposal, and clever, but it made Israelis wince. With Palestinians in control of the Temple Mount, how could we be certain that they would not shoot at worshippers at the Western Wall, effectively making life in the Jewish quarter untenable? After all, isn't that exactly what happened with Beit Jala, which we gave back, and from which they've been shooting at Gilo for more than a year?

In the face of no prospects for a negotiated solution, "unilateral separation" seems like the only sensible solution. But the more we think about it, the more we realize that this, too, is hopelessly complicated and might tear Israel's fragile society completely asunder. The Palestinians aren't our only problem. We, ourselves, have no consensus about how we'd like to end this.

. . .

A question for Robert Frost: It may be true that good fences make good neighbors, but what do you do if the neighbor who wants to build the fence cannot even decide where he wants to put it?

Lag Ba-Omer, Then and Now

- - - - - - - - - - - - - - - - -

A quick trip to the States for work, and right back to Tel Aviv airport. I land in time to get to Jerusalem for Lag Ba-Omer, and to say hi to the kids before they disappear into the night with their friends to light bonfires. The news in the interim hasn't been good. More of the same shootings, which have become boring, but also the horrifying deaths of two Israeli kids from Teko'a, aged thirteen and fourteen. They were found dead the day before in a cave not far from their homes, bludgeoned to death, horribly mutilated. On a walk just outside their small village, which is only a short drive outside Jerusalem, they were apparently happened upon by some Palestinians and murdered. The funeral, which took place earlier on the day I arrived home, had to be delayed for two hours while forensics experts worked to see which body was which. One shudders to imagine their last moments. It's too much to contemplate.

· · ·

It turns out that they're just about Tali's age. Her youth group, Bnai Akiva, has mostly girls and boys from our neighborhood. The girls attend school at a variety of institutions not far from where we live, while the boys, for the most part, go to school in Efrat, the "primo" religious high school in the area, where they dorm during the week and come home a few weekends a month. A few of the boys had been in class with the boys found in the cave. Now, for the first time, Tali's going through something kids shouldn't have to know. She's watching her friends grieve—not talk very much, but struggle with the horror and loss. Tali, too, won't talk about it, but it's in her eyes. Something's changed. The circle of this violence now has her inside it, too. Had we stayed in L.A., I know, I'd have a much more innocent daughter.

And I remember our first Lag Ba-Omer here, two years earlier, in much better times. The innocence. The sheer joy of it all. Watching our kid grow up before our eyes, with a confidence that we'd never seen. And I think of all that the last few months have taken from her, never to be returned.

. . .

But still, out she heads to her bonfire with her friends. Comes back at 10:00 P.M. to pick up some more food and paper plates for the dinner they're making outside, and is in a much better mood. When will she be home? Probably in the morning, she says. "It's really fun." (Meaning, "Don't even think about giving me a curfew.") And we're fine with that. Because that's the strange thing about Jerusalem. Your kids have to go to sleep to the sound of shooting, and the house occasionally shudders with the thud of tank shells landing only a few miles away. But they can still be out by themselves at all hours of the night, and there's nothing to worry about. It's a safe city. We'd never have let her stay out by herself this late in L.A., with or without other friends. Here, we don't even bother to ask if anyone's walking her home. It doesn't matter. She'll be fine.

Who's Killing Children?

Shabbat afternoon and the Gordis family is hanging out, reading in the living room, when Avi notices a few draft pages of an article I'm writing about this whole situation lying on the coffee table. The front page has a working title of "They Kill Children, Don't They?" and he picks up the pages and scans them.

"Is this the title?"

"I don't know. Just an idea I'm playing with."

"Who's killing the children? Us or them?"

What do you say to that? So I say nothing, grunting something that I hope will pass for an answer. Tali, though, has overheard the conversation, and apparently decides that her brother deserves an answer.

"Both. We kill their children, and they kill our children."

"Was it always that way?"

"Who knows. But that's how it is now."

And out the door she walks, to spend Shabbat afternoon with her friends.

And I'm left there to ponder that brief exchange. We kill their children. They kill our children. Are we also killing our own children?

. . .

The next morning, I'm getting ready to go to work, and Elisheva is sipping coffee at the dining room table and reading the morning paper. The headline reads "IDF Gunship Missiles Kill Two in Jenin," but I've heard that already, saw it on the web in the morning, and have barely glanced at the paper.

"Disgusting," she mutters.

"What's that?"

"This attack yesterday."

"What attack? What'd they do now?"

"Not them, us."

"What's disgusting? We were after some chief Fatah guys."

"So what? We wounded schoolkids on the way home. No one should be allowed to fire anything when they know that there are kids around."

"That's a nice theory. Do you want to win this war, or watch it go on?"

"There's no winning this war. There's no solution to this shit. And given that fact, we shouldn't be killing kids."

. . .

That's true, as far as it goes, but not much of an operating policy, it seems to me. After all, too often the Palestinians are putting their own kids where they want them and need them. So what are we to do? Kill? Or die? Is that what's happening here? Lose this undeclared war, or become people who can't bear to look in the mirror?

Or both?

. . .

We've been married a long time, Elisheva and I, for half our lives. We were together for most of college, got married right after graduation, went to graduate school together. We moved to California, had three kids, have remodeled more houses together than we care to recall. By and large, we've come to see the world through very similar eyes. We like the same movies, the same art, the same architects, the same furniture. We're politically similar and religiously pretty much on the same page. We're not identical twins by any stretch of the imagination, but over the years, and especially since our mid-thirties, there hasn't been much that's very important that we've reacted to in radically different ways.

Until now. There's something about the stress of living with this war that has us disagreeing regularly. I can't tell if it's bickering just for the sake of having something to argue about—better, perhaps, than both of us admitting that this is now feeling completely hopeless—or if we're actually becoming somewhat different. But there doesn't seem to be any consistency to the sides we take. One day she's the one who's critical of Israel, or the IDF, or the people who make up this country. The next day I'm the one who's out of patience and she's become the great Zionist propagandist.

. . .

In school, Micha is learning about Samson, the biblical hero of the Book of Judges, who slew beasts barehanded and at the end of his life killed three thousand Philistines as he seized the pillars of a temple and brought the building down, killing himself and his captors. Micha's enthralled with the story. On a family hike near Ein Gedi by the Dead Sea, he and I are climbing over rocks and he is regaling me with stories and songs he's learned about "Shimshon Ha-Gibbor," Samson the Hero.

"Abba, did you know that when he destroyed that temple, he killed three thousand Philistines, and that was more than all the other people he'd killed in his whole life?"

"Wow. Really?"

"Yeah. And do you know what he said as he was planning to kill them all?"

"No, what?"

And what follows is a song about how Samson will get revenge for all the bad things that have been done to the Jewish people, how through him God will right the wrongs that have been done to us. I'm torn between being pleased that he's so taken with what he's learning in school and being distraught over the subtle message. But I say nothing.

A bend in the trail and I meet up with Elisheva, who's walked ahead with Avi. "Are you following this Samson crap he's learning at school?"

"Why's it crap? It's in the Bible, isn't it? Don't you want him to learn that?"

"Of course I do, but this glorification of Samson is a bit much, isn't it? There's more than a little nationalistic twist to this reading, it seems to me. Seems a bit odd to be glorifying this person as a hero, to have the kids singing songs about all the people he killed."

"So what? I think it's great that they're giving these kids something to believe in."

"And what exactly is that 'something'?"

"Oh, come on. You can't expect the whole world to buy into your hypercritical, self-analytic, 'we shouldn't be doing this and we shouldn't be doing that' worldview, can you? How many people want to live with the inner turmoil you seem to revel in? He's a little kid. Don't you want him to be able to believe that we're right, that he's on the side of something good? And that something grander than us will protect us? Don't you think he has a right to believe in something?"

"I'm not suggesting that he be consumed with inner turmoil, and I wasn't looking for a fight. I just think it's a bit weird that of all the stories in the Book of Judges, this is what he has to be singing songs about."

"Well, when Avi was his age, the only hero he had was Michael Jordan. Is that what you'd prefer? When I see Micha climbing over these rocks, singing songs like that, I'm thrilled that we brought him here, and that he has something to believe in."

. . .

But by the time we begin the drive back to Jerusalem the next evening, the tides have turned again. We're heading north on the road that hugs the western edge of the Dead Sea, and watch the flickering lights of Jordan off to the east in the night. Not long later, we come to the intersection where the road to Jerusalem turns to the left, so we turn and head west. We pass the turnoff to Jericho, which we used to take when we headed north, and now, were we to try it, would be absurdly dangerous. But we're not headed north, so we continue straight up the hill to Jerusalem. There's virtually no radio reception here, just bits of Jordanian radio, which I don't want to hear. So I try to find Israeli news, but aside from some static-filled chatter about the IDF's recent destruction of some Palestinian houses, nothing seems to be new. So I pop a cassette into the player.

A few minutes later, Elisheva leans over and turns off the music.

"Why'd you turn it off?"

"I'm not in the mood."

"What's with you?"

"I'm depressed, and I don't want to hear the music. That's all."

"What're you depressed about? It was a great couple of days, wasn't it?"

"I just can't take this news and all that discussion of the destruction of those houses."

I decide to say nothing, and she eventually continues.

"It was such a stupid, cruel, inhuman thing to do. I don't believe the army for a second when they say it was necessary. And I don't believe that those houses were uninhabited. We're getting disgusting. The only way that we're going to survive what they're doing to us is to be better than them, to avoid sinking to their level. If we're going to act like them, I don't think I can take it."

She's right about the houses, it strikes me, but wrong to equate us with them. I'm thinking about how to remind her that I don't see Israelis blowing themselves up in the middle of Palestinian marketplaces. But Avi interrupts.

"Will you two cut it out? I'm tired of hearing about all this. Ema, turn the music back on. The rest of us want to hear it."

. . .

Elisheva does nothing, so I turn the music back on. She's staring out the window, presumably at the Judean hills, gorgeous even in the dark of night. She says nothing, and I'm not sure what I can say that will comfort her. So I, too, am silent.

Something about her profile reminds me of her when we were much younger, in college, when it seemed we never exhausted what we had to talk about. Long phone calls at the end of the day from New York to Boston where we were each in school, letters in the mail that we've still got stashed away in shoeboxes somewhere all these years later, long walks in Riverside Park when she'd come to visit, when hours seemed to pass in the flash of a second.

It struck me as ironic, and sad, driving up the hill to Jerusalem, that here we were, living where she'd always wanted to live, more in love with each other than we've ever been, and there was nothing to say, no comfort to offer. This war is killing more than our children.

May 2001:
Wedding Halls as the
Perfect Metaphor

Latest Disaster Tests Resiliency of Jerusalem's Residents

This is a city accustomed to coping with crisis. But as sirens screamed through the night, with ambulances racing to a collapsed wedding hall in which at least two dozen people died, Jerusalemites struggled to deal with what some described as crisis overload.

New York Times: Saturday, May 26, 2001, page A6

It's a couple of days before Shavu'ot, a couple of hours before Shabbat. I'd planned to use the morning to prepare some of the materials for my teaching on Shavu'ot, but we've received a few e-mails in the last days asking what's happened to our communications, and this morning a call or two to make sure that we're OK in light of the events of the last few hours. Given that, and the fact that I'm not at all in the mood to prepare for Shavu'ot, I'll jot down a few items from the past few days and try to get them out before Shabbat.

Bottom line, we're all OK. None of us was at the wedding in Talpiyot last night. The kids are in school, Elisheva's out doing errands, and I'm home. Another crappy day in Jerusalem.

As you've undoubtedly heard by now, the big news this morning is the collapse of a wedding hall on Derekh Beit Lechem in Talpiyot last night. It's Israel's largest domestic disaster of this sort. For those of you who know Jerusalem and know where we live, it's about a five-minute drive from here, probably less. I was exhausted last night, and went to bed early. As I was getting ready to call it a night, we suddenly began to hear sirens, which isn't unusual these days. But as they continued to scream by for more than half an hour, Elisheva said that something must be going on and we should watch the news. I had no interest in more shooting, and told her so. She went downstairs to watch TV, and I went to bed and slept through the continuing sirens with no problem.

This morning when our alarm clock went off, she told me about the wedding hall. A complete disaster. At present, one channel is doing nothing but constant broadcasts from the site, from hospitals . . . and updates from the morgue. The scale of this thing is unprecedented. They had to bring ambulances in from Ashdod, Ashkelon, the center of the country, and from the other side of the green line. There are urgent calls for blood. When they don't kill us, we kill ourselves through sheer negligence and stupidity.

At breakfast this morning, after the kids had gone to school and Elisheva was reading the paper and sipping her coffee, she said that the wedding hall is a metaphor for the whole country—one layer collapses and destroys everything below, killing everyone in its wake. Pretty grim, but then again, these are grim days in Israel, in ways in which the American media (which we read voraciously) doesn't begin to capture. Even *Ha-Aretz* and the other web sources of Israeli news don't begin to give an impression of what's going on.

So, a few vignettes from the last couple of days.

I was in Tel Aviv on business this week. One evening, I had a beer with a friend at one of those trendy Tel Aviv pubs. He'd just gotten back from *milu'im* (his annual month of reserve duty) and was chatting about what they'd done. He's in his mid-thirties, and said it was the hardest *milu'im* they'd ever done. Usually, he said, they run around, shoot a bit, and basically have a decent go of it. This time, though, it was serious. They kept them for the full month, which is in itself unusual, and partook in intense war games. Tanks, APC's, helicopters, planes, the works. The task was to "retake the Golan" after three days of Syrian control. The IDF, quite obviously, is busy preparing for the worst.

My friend told me that in the middle of one exercise, as he and a buddy were dragging a crate of artillery shells up a steep incline and not having a very good time of it, he muttered to his friend something like "This sucks. When the real thing comes, you can drag this thing yourself." To which his friend responded, "Don't worry—in the real thing, we'll both be dead in the first seven minutes."

Really cold beer, in a great little pub, so we both chuckled, but it's the kind of gallows humor that has begun to pervade Israel. There's a sense that something is about to happen, and it isn't going to be good.

Interestingly, this friend of mine, who made aliyah almost twenty years ago, has always struck me as a classic *oleh* (immigrant to Israel). He came from England, served in the army, went to college and graduate school, got married and has four kids. He's extremely politically active—the works. And, he's leaving. Not for good, he says, but for three to five years, because he just can't take the intensity anymore. For me, that revelation was much more distressing than any other part of our conversation, because he'd always struck me as one of the diehards. He says he still is—he just wants a break. I think he's much more representative of the larger picture than we commonly suspect.

Yesterday we had the Jerusalem Fellows at Rabin Square, the spot where the prime minister was murdered. We were there to talk about how one handles what's happened to Israel in the last year in educational settings—not an easy issue. Virtually every one of us had been there numerous times, so we were just standing around taking it in, quietly without much talking, when a gentleman in his late fifties or early sixties walked up and said, "You want to know the real story? The truth? You want to know why I spit on this monument every time I pass it? Because the bastard deserved it."

Now, to understand what happened next, you need to know the

story of the *Altalena*. In June 1948, a ship named the *Altalena*, bearing arms for the Irgun (Menachem Begin's military wing), approached the shore in Tel Aviv. Ben Gurion, intent on molding all the various forces into one army, refused to allow the ship to dock. After several days of negotiation, shooting broke out. To this day, there are conflicting accounts of what, exactly, was being negotiated, and of who shot first, Ben Gurion's troops (under Rabin's command) on the shore, or the Irgun people (under Begin's command) on the boat. But the upshot was that the boat caught fire and, with all the arms on board, exploded and sank, as much of civilian Tel Aviv watched from the beach. It was a cataclysmic event back then, the first major episode of Jew killing Jew in the not too long history of this country.

The man who had just walked up to us went on. "My father was on the *Altalena*. And Rabin, that bastard, gave the order to shoot. He killed my father. My whole childhood, I suffered without a father because of this criminal. Let him rot in hell." And off he walked.

No one said much until a member of our faculty, a well-known left-wing columnist for *Ha-Aretz*, completely enraged, screamed back, "Sinking the *Altalena* was the best thing that Rabin ever did in his life!" Thankfully, the other person was out of earshot and nothing more happened, but the little exchange cast a pall over the rest of the day. Israel is a little place with simply too much history, and someone always hates someone else because of it.

It was clear, as we sat in the little shade we could find and ate sandwiches, that people didn't have much to say when talking about Rabin. It surprised me, but I soon realized why. The sense of tragedy that used to accompany any mention of him has dissipated. It's not because time has passed—we Jews are very good at perpetuating memory. It's dissipated because we used to think that with his death, the peace process also died. But now, most of us believe he was wrong. Noble, but wrong. Arafat wouldn't have behaved any differently at the end with Rabin than he did with Barak. He wouldn't have signed. And he would probably have resorted to violence, because that's what he's good at, that's how he achieved his position on the international stage, and because, quite frankly, he apparently has an image of how to be a revolutionary but not a sense of how to become a statesman. And in the meantime, because of Oslo and the rest, they're armed, organized, legitimate. And they're killing us.

The inability of a group of highly educated, extraordinarily articulate people to say virtually anything about Rabin was telling. There's just nothing to say, a real sense that we can't get out of this predicament. There are four million Palestinians in the refugee camps (there were seven hundred thousand in 1948); they're ready for massive armed confrontation, and we're not. People here murmur that if this were happening in Syria, they'd have put down the revolt months ago. That's true. But we don't want to be Syria. We want to be better, different, and we can't. This is an ugly, dirty war, and we're being ugly and dirty enough to bring the world's wrath down on us, but not nearly ugly and dirty enough to win. To win, we'd have to wipe them out, and though we could, we can't and won't. This is going to go on for a long time, and like my friend in the pub, people are tired of it.

The rabid right-wingers and left-wingers among the Fellows, and among our friends, don't even argue anymore. The left-wingers think that the settlements are stupid and won't last any more than other colonial attempts have, but they don't think that getting rid of them will end this war. And the right-wingers think that we should stay there, because if we leave there, the front lines will just move closer, and the left-wingers know that's true. As a settler friend of mine said to me last Friday after the blast in the Netanya mall, "Even if we did leave the settlements, where would we move to? Netanya?" The right- and left-wingers don't argue because ironically, we all know the truth. There's no peace to be had. They want us out of here. So we can either pack our bags and go back to the States and Europe, or we can prepare to fight it out for the foreseeable future. Some of us will leave, some will stay. (That's not a hint, by the way. We're staying.) Some of us will die and some will live. Some of them will live and some of them will die. And in the end, there will still be millions of them left who think that the building I live in belongs to them, and they'll never sign anything that doesn't give them the right to this street. And we'll never sign anything that does. That's the extent of it.

So, no one here expects things to get much better, or any better for that matter, very soon. We'll have to just keep slugging it out. The world will condemn, American Jewish organizations will issue statements about supporting us (while staying far enough away, of course, to make sure that no one gets hurt in these emotional demonstrations of support), and life will go on.

On the bus back from Tel Aviv yesterday, it suddenly struck me that it's possible that this country won't make it (and that was before the wedding hall event). No one here wants to fight forever, but no one here thinks that the Palestinians will compromise on anything. They've been told over and over again that it's all theirs, and they're willing to fight for it. We moved into a very bad neighborhood, hoping that we could do some sort of regional urban renewal, and it's not working. That bus ride, with a few quiet moments to think about everything I'd seen and all that's been happening recently, was the first time that I seriously envisioned the whole enterprise collapsing, people leaving, no one coming (certainly not from places where Jews are welcomed), the world turning against us, the war of attrition going on endlessly, the backbiting that comes from the frustration and rage getting even worse, and in the end, our either signing a deal that we shouldn't, or not fighting as hard as we'll have to, or whatever.

I wondered if I should share that thought with Elisheva, and decided against it. She's depressed enough as it is (unlike my euphoric tenor!). But last night, right after dinner, she looked up and said, "Did it ever occur to you that this whole country could be one big failed experiment?" So much for not burdening her with my worries. . . .

Shabbat shalom and *chag same'ach*. Here, we'll do our best.

August 2001:
Berkshires Liberation,
But a Tighter Noose

There's nothing like a bomb going off where you live to remind you that it's your home they're trying to blow up.

It was Thursday afternoon, my last afternoon in Israel before heading out to the States for a long overdue and much needed summer vacation. Elisheva and the kids had been there for five weeks already, and it was time to join them and head out to the Berkshires and Maine for a couple of weeks of hiking, relaxing, and plain old peace before heading back to Israel for the beginning of the new school year.

I decided to do early check-in at the Inbal Hotel, where El Al had set up a temporary check-in operation for a large American group that was leaving the same night I was. I wasn't staying at the hotel, and wasn't officially part of the group, but was told that I could check in there anyway. I figured it would be much easier than dragging my bags to the airport later that night. So I joined the line at the Inbal, and discovered that El Al and airport security are not much more efficient in Jerusalem's best hotels than they are at the airport. The line was long, the progress slow, and I glanced at my watch and noticed that even though it was almost an hour away, I was likely to be a few minutes late for a three o'clock meeting I'd set up at my office. I decided to call my secretary and ask her to delay things for a few minutes. I dialed her number, but instead of hearing the familiar ring, the phone beeped back at me. I looked at the screen on my cell phone and saw the cryptic message "System busy." I hit "redial," but again, no luck. System busy. And again, and again. After a few dozen tries, I knew. Something had to have happened. That's the only reason that the system gets tied up like this. An immobilized cell network always means the same thing in Israel—something's gone terribly wrong, and people are frantically trying to find each other to make sure that the people they care about most are OK.

I asked one of the people on line if she'd heard any news lately.

"Of course" was the response.

"What's happened?"

"They bombed Sbarro Pizza on the corner of King George and Jaffa. Four dead and several dozen injured."

It's strange what you think when you find out that a bomb has gone off in the middle of your city, less than a mile from where you're standing. And it's never what you're supposed to think or feel. Maybe because we all knew this would happen sooner or later, or because the violence has become so constant, the dread so persistent, that something like this didn't sound as bad as our worst nightmares. Four dead, I thought. It could have been worse.

It *was* worse, of course. As the afternoon continued, the death toll mounted. Four, six, ten, nineteen, later reduced to fifteen with several more people in very critical condition. Well over a hundred wounded. Six infants dead. Five members of one family—both parents and three kids—dead. Two other kids from the same family are in the hospital, but they'll survive.

And the city is in a subdued shock. The war's come home. This isn't about the territories, we all know. It's about our right to be here—in any part of this place. This isn't about settlers, or the expansion of settlements, but about the fundamental right of the Jews to be here. That's why the corner of King George and Jaffa was the perfect place for the attack. It's Times Square, or Michigan Avenue. The heart of the city. The ultimate statement that there is no square inch of the country that's not a battleground.

Interestingly, people weren't as hysterical as I would have expected them to be. Earlier in the week, I'd made dinner plans with friends for that night, and we kept them. The restaurants were full, people laughing and enjoying each other's company as if nothing much had happened. The cynical remark you often hear on nights like that is "Well, tonight's the safest time to be in a public place. Today's bomb has already gone off." The chief of Israel's police was equally stoic. "Well, we've foiled most of their attempts in the past few weeks, but when you're in a conflict like this, you have to expect that the enemy will also score some victories. Today, he was successful."

What are we being told here? That this is normal? That the sounds of these ambulances racing across the city, sirens blaring, is the way we're supposed to live? That you might be blown to bits when you're sitting around enjoying a slice of pizza? That fifty-six years after the chimneys of Europe stopped spewing the bodies of Jews into the sky, Jews get blown up the chimney of a pizza oven (I do not exaggerate here—the news said that that's what happened to a couple of victims)?

Is this what it's come to? Is there no place on the planet we can simply be and be comfortable? A week earlier, Talia called from the States and said she wanted to come home early, even though she would miss the family vacation. She's had enough of it there. "Abba," she said as she described her conversations with some of the kids who were her friends before we moved, "I really don't want to talk to these people anymore. They all pretend to care about what's going on, and they ask what life in Israel is like. But then when I start to tell them, it's clear that they don't want to be uncomfortable. They'd rather talk about something else. But what else is there to talk about? I think I should be back there. Israel's having a tough time—I think it's time to come home."

After some consultation, Elisheva and I decide to let her come back. We'll miss her on the vacation, but she's on the cusp of adulthood, and she's got a right to decide that she needs to be home. This, after all, is what we wanted, isn't it? That our kids would see this land as home? So we changed her ticket, helped her pack up, and she's on her way back. But what should we tell her? That nothing's safe? That she can't leave the apartment? That she should be nervous every waking moment? That this is the "home" to which we've brought her? We murmur something about staying away from busy public places, and don't push it. What's the point? It's all so unpredictable anyway. Why have her be scared when there's nothing much we can do to protect her—or anyone else—in any real way?

Eventually I reach the front of the line, check my bag in, and head off to the meeting at work. A few last hours of work, that dinner with friends, and then off to the airport. In the lounge, I desperately search for some up-to-date news. But all the internet terminals in the lounge are out of order—nothing there. CNN, playing on the TV in the lounge, says nothing more than we already knew. The big question isn't what happened, but what's going to happen. After the suicide bombing at the Tel Aviv "Dolphinarium" disco in June, we did nothing. Twenty-one dead kids, and no response. Today, the reigning wisdom says, Sharon can't get away with that. So something's bound to happen, and many of us are anxious to know what it will be before we board the plane and are insulated from the world for twelve hours. But there's no news to be had. Sharon and his cabinet are still meeting, and nothing's been decided.

With more than an hour left till boarding, I decide to cool my heels in the music shop at the airport. I buy some CD's for the people who have hosted our family during the summer and, checking out, notice a two-CD set called "Songs of Remembrance" that looks decent. Truth be told, I don't even examine it that carefully. On a day like today, with the sounds of the sirens still ringing in my ears, some music to erase that sound seems like just what the doctor ordered. So I add those two CD's to my pile, pay, and go back to the lounge.

The flight is uneventful. Fortunately, I sleep most of the way. I've only got a few waking hours with no news of the world to wonder what's going on down there. We land, I wait for my bag, then head out to Hertz and rent a car. Driving into Manhattan, I tune the radio to WINS. Though it's been almost twenty years since we've lived in New York, "You give us twenty-two minutes, we give you the world" is still engraved in my memory. But the world doesn't seem to include Israel today. It's all local stuff—nothing about the Middle East, which might as well be in a different galaxy. I swing into the Upper West Side, pick up Elisheva and the kids. We load up the car for our vacation, and out we sail to the Berkshires.

We take the Taconic Parkway. Talk about culture shock. This is a different planet. Two straight lanes in either direction, green on all sides. No military checkpoints. No Arab villages on the side of the road where your antennae have to be a bit more sensitive. Trees without end, farms that look as if they've known only peace and predictability for hundreds of years. I flip on the cruise control—the ultimate statement that life is predictable, even, calm. With time, the boys in the backseat grow bored with my telling them to look outside and see how beautiful the green is. "More trees in this one view than in the entire State of Israel," muses Avi, possibly correctly. But the trees eventually lose their allure, and the boys are in a different world, their headphones and

Game Boys making them completely immune to my persistent requests that they look out the window. With time, Elisheva also falls asleep, and it's just me, with another two hours of the Taconic to go.

I remember the CD's that I'd bought at the airport, and pop the first disc into the player. There's something about the lyrical melodies, Israel's "oldies but goodies," that gets me musing. What happened to that country, that place full of hope, that place that always felt happy and so replete with promise? How did we get where we are? With nowhere to turn, nothing to do?

Because that, of course, is where we are. None of the options are any good. Every Israeli has had this conversation hundreds of times, and the latest iterations of the discussion now replay in my mind as we cruise past the lush farms, the never-ending woods, this reality wholly unlike the one in which we live. We could unleash a full-scale war and probably win, but win what? Recapture the land we've given back since Oslo? And then what? Just to be back where we were before the peace process began? To what ultimate end?

My cell phone goes off. In America, it seems, the circuits are not busy. It's a very close friend, also on vacation with his family, now in the Midwest on his way to Canada. He just wanted to say hello. It's hard being here when everything is falling apart over there, he says. We chat for a while, until the inevitable part of the conversation arrives. What's the end of this going to be, he wonders. "How should I know?" I tease him. "You're the one who convinced us to move there in the first place. You're the one who should have the answers."

"I never thought I'd end up apologizing to someone for playing a role in their decision to make aliyah," he muses sadly. "You're forgiven," I quip. We both know we're mostly kidding, but only mostly. The conversation's too uncomfortable. We wish each other good vacations, and hang up.

We got to West Stockbridge, and had a fabulous time there and later in Maine, in Acadia National Park. The kids hiked and biked, went kayaking on the Atlantic, didn't watch the news, and seemed more relaxed than I'd seen them in months. I wondered if it was being out of Israel that made them so carefree, or if it was just being on vacation. I hoped it was the latter, but I wasn't sure.

Monday we headed back to JFK, and decided to treat our kids to a few hours in the business-class lounge (only one of our tickets had been upgraded, but there's no point in living in Israel if you don't acquire the skills to talk your whole family into the lounge!). We got the kids something to eat, and Elisheva and I instinctively grabbed copies of the Israeli newspapers that were lying there. Micha looked at the paper, which had the blaring headline "Seven Dead in Two Days," and asked, "Is there still fighting in Israel?" Yes, we said. "Is it worse than when we were there?" About the same, we lied. "When will it be over?" No answer to that one.

The flight was fine, if long, but the re-entry has not proven as smooth as we might have hoped.

After we had finished unpacking last night, I came across those CD's that I'd bought the night I left here. The music sounded like a better idea than the depressing chatter on the radio, so I popped the second CD into the player on the nightstand. Folded clothes, hung up shirts, listened to the music.

In a short while, the last cut on the CD. It was Ehud Manor's famous lyrics, sung a cappella by a single haunting female voice:

> *Ein li eretz acheret*
> *gam im admati bo'eret.* . . .
>
> I have no other place to go
> Even if my land is burning
> One Hebrew word burrows
> into my veins, into my soul
> with an aching body
> a hungry heart,
> This is my home.

That's pretty much it, I realized. This place, this intolerable, stressful, violent land, is home. It was beautiful out there in upstate New York and Massachusetts and Maine, with those verdant hills and placid farms. But it's not home. It's been just about a year since this latest round of violence started, and we're sadder and wiser for the time that's passed. We know that peace isn't around the corner. We've learned how deep run the hatreds. We've discovered anew that there are no easy solutions. The left is gone, the right is paralyzed. The neighbors are nasty. And we're all stuck in this together, with no place to go.

That, of course, is the real point. There's no other place to go. Israel's the only spot on the planet that we have a shot at calling our own, so we can't walk away from it. No matter what. Because the words of that song call it like it is.

Ein li eretz acheret, gam im admati bo'eret.

I've got no other place to go, even if my land is burning.

That, it strikes me, is why it will somehow work out in the end. Because it simply has to.

December 2001:
Almost Hanukkah, and
Here We Go Again

Terrorists Strike in Jerusalem Center. At Least 6 Dead, 160 Wounded in Kikar Zion Suicide Attacks

At least 6 persons were reported killed and some 160 wounded when two Palestinian suicide bombers detonated themselves in the heart of Jerusalem last night close to midnight. The two explosions at the foot of the Rehov Ben-Yehuda pedestrian mall were followed shortly afterward by a car bomb on nearby Rehov Kook, which apparently did not cause many casualties. The mall had been packed with the usual Saturday night crowd of mainly teenagers out for the evening. The bomb scene was gruesome with overturned tables, bloody chairs, and bodies and body parts strewn on the ground, in one of the worst attacks in Jerusalem in months. Police speculated that the number of casualties would probably turn out to be similar to those in the devastating Sbarro pizzeria attack in Jerusalem and the Dolphin discotheque bombing in Tel Aviv several months ago, when a total of 36 were killed.

JERUSALEM POST: Sunday, December 2, 2001, page 1

There was a rainbow in the sky yesterday morning (Monday), the "morning after." No rain on the quick walk to the office, barely any mist, but a huge rainbow over the whole western part of the city.

237

When I got to work, people were gathered around the windows, staring in awe, in virtual disbelief. No one said much—no one had been saying much for more than a day. Then someone said, "Maybe it means something." A moment of silence. And then another responded, "I wish I could believe in things like that." And the group dispersed.

It had been quiet for a while. Shootings every day, of course, and a couple of people killed every week, but nothing "major." We'd gone to sleep pretty early on Saturday night. And since I'd bought us a little RadioShack "sound machine" on a recent trip to the States to drown out the nightly sirens, we didn't hear the wailing of the ambulances that many of our friends later told us had woken them up.

So when I got up at 5:00 A.M. on Sunday to go bike riding with a friend and decided just to check the web before heading out into the frozen Jerusalem morning, I had no idea what had happened the night before. For a moment, after I logged on and saw the pictures of the dead teenagers, the bloodied bodies, the destroyed stores, and the remains of the suicide bombers on Ben Yehudah Street, I literally felt nauseated. I *thought* that Tali had been home when we went to sleep, but I couldn't remember for sure. I ran up the stairs to her room, opened her door, and thankfully found her fast asleep in her bed. She's been known to go to the Ben Yehudah scene, or some other public spot, at night with her friends. Mercifully, that night she had too much work.

It seemed virtually sacrilegious to be going bike riding after news like that, but my friend was already on his way over, and at 5:10 in the morning, you can't exactly call to cancel. But filling water bottles, checking tire pressure, adjusting helmet and all the rest, I couldn't help but feel that there was something perverse about going out to have some fun just hours after all this, when the hospitals were still filled with mutilated teenagers whose only mistake had been forgetting that we live in a war zone, and that they're the targets. That's the strange thing about Israel. It seems so normal most of the time that you can actually forget you're at war. Then you feel guilty for forgetting.

After a couple of months of relative quiet (more than three months since the Sbarro Pizza bombing, for example), we'd all forgotten. And that made the reaction that much stronger. In a meeting with a staff member later in the morning, I noticed that he seemed distracted. "You OK?" I asked him. "Basically," he said. "My wife's part of a phone tree for the students in her school, so we were up all night contacting people. So I only slept for a couple of hours. And I'm not used to waking up with a blood lust."

One of my secretaries looked completely washed out. Turns out her sister lives at the corner of Ben Yehudah and Jaffa, the precise spot of the first of Saturday night's bombings. And she couldn't reach her until 4:00 A.M., so she, too, was awake all night. I told her to go home and get some rest. "What should I go home for? To watch the news and cry?" she asked. And she started to cry.

The office was depressing, but luckily I'd already made plans to work at home for part of the day. So after we called all the Fellows to make sure that they were OK, I went back to the house to try to finish an article I've been working on that's way past deadline and taking longer than I'd expected. After a couple of hours of work, I decided to take a break and flipped on the TV. Israel doesn't have a twenty-four-hour news station, so I was preparing to change the channel to CNN when I suddenly realized that there was live news being broadcast. The Haifa bus had just blown up, and there were more pictures of more bodies, more disconnected limbs, tattered clothing, a shredded bus that had been blown clear across the boulevard onto the sidewalk of the opposite side of the street, and sobbing soldiers doing their best to get people onto stretchers before they, themselves, began to throw up. And then, of course, the rising death toll. Seven, with fifteen *"pezu'im anush"*—mortally wounded. Then ten dead, ten very critical. Then twelve, then fifteen, where the number rests at present.

Now, hours after Sharon's speech and the beginning of the responses, it seems obvious that something had to be done. But it wasn't obvious. We did nothing after the Dolphinarium, nothing after Sbarro. People here were afraid that the same thing would happen—or more precisely, wouldn't happen—again. How much has changed it's still too early to tell. But at this early stage, with Sharon having called the Palestinian Authority a terrorist state, it seems (but who knows) that the peace process is now officially dead. There's no "partner," and, he's suggesting, something new is about to happen.

No one really knows anything about where we're headed. But it's the only thing on people's minds. My regular Monday morning *chavruta* (study session) is with a man who's a dyed-in-the-wool left-winger. He was part of the student takeover at Columbia in the '60's, pretty counter-establishment in many ways decades later. As we were finishing up our studying for the morning, I said to him, "Well, let's hope we hear some good news." "Good news," he said, "would be war. And yeah, let's hope."

That's the irony these days. With peace having collapsed, lots of intelligent people are genuinely hoping for war. But war's a hard thing to hope for, it still seems to me. The costs are horrifying, on both sides.

Days before the latest bombings, Israelis were wrestling with the deaths of the five Palestinian kids who were killed last week when, while on their way to school, they stepped on or played with some explosive device that the IDF had left not far from their homes. At first, of course, the IDF denied having anything to do with it. Then they admitted that they had put it there, but said that it had been intended for terrorists trying to cross over the border. But lots of Israelis wondered, what kind of a country puts explosives where kids might get to them, "hoping" that only terrorists get killed? Is this what we've come to? many Israelis asked. What about all those lectures these soldiers get in basic training about illegal orders, and how they're expected to refuse to comply with them? Does anyone listen to that these days? A serious debate was just beginning to emerge.

Now, of course, no one seems to care anymore. After all, the IDF didn't actually intend to kill those kids, but Ben Yehudah was targeted precisely because it was filled with kids. Ten dead, the youngest fourteen and the oldest twenty. Tragically, most people have now forgotten about the dead Palestinian kids. There's a limit to how much you can worry about.

But there's also a limit to how much you can deny. Since we're now in Kislev, the month of Hanukkah, Avi's school's monthly theme is "heroism." Last week, before the world changed again, they had a speaker at school on the subject of heroism. This speaker was injured in an army training incident almost thirty years ago, and lost both legs. Since then, he's gotten married, has had children, likes to ski down the Hermon, cycles on a bike that he pedals with his arms, etc. Avi was obviously deeply touched by this person, and talked about him all through dinner.

That night, though, as I tucked him into bed, Avi made reference to my recent attempts to get drafted, and asked, "Abba, why do you want to be in the army?" I explained that I wished that there didn't have to be an army, but that if there is one, then I think I ought to do my share, just like all the other men in this country. "Aren't you afraid?" he asked, at which point I realized what he was really asking. "Are *you* afraid?" I asked him back. "Well," he said, "I just wouldn't like to be crippled for my whole life."

It's not the stuff a twelve-year-old boy should have to think about as he goes to sleep. So I lied and told him I was certain that he'd be OK, that accidents like that in the army are very rare. And I rubbed his back as he fell asleep, wondering just what in the world was happening to him beneath the veneer of this loving, smiling, basically happy kid.

Sunday night, after the two explosions in Jerusalem and the bus bombing in Haifa, we were at the dinner table again. With the news clearly on his mind, Avi asked what *"patzu'a anush"* (mortally wounded) means. He knew what the words meant—he wanted to know what it meant medically. I was tempted to tell him it's a euphemism for "not dead yet," but even I knew better. So I told him it meant that the people were still alive, but that they were so badly hurt that doctors weren't sure they would be able to save them. Avi was quiet for a minute, and then said, "If I was hurt that badly, and I'd be crippled or in pain for the rest of my life, I'd just rather die."

OK, sweetie, no problem. Would you pass the salad dressing, please? What, exactly, do you say to a twelve-year-old kid just getting old enough to understand what this is, what it is that his parents have brought him to?

Last week was November 29th, the anniversary of the United Nations vote on the Partition Plan that ultimately created the State of Israel. There were years here when November 29th was a pretty big day, marked with celebrations, school assemblies, public speeches, the works. This year it was hardly noticed. A very few people (my wife among them, not surprisingly) put Israeli flags on their cars. A few schools mentioned it. But beyond that, nothing.

Why is that? Because fifty-four years later, nothing about the United Nations (which knew the fate of the three kidnapped soldiers captured in October 2000, but let their parents wait for a full year before learning that their kids were dead) seems worth celebrating. Because fifty-four years later, after five or six wars (depending on how you count), we're still bleeding, we're not actually any closer to a workable solution, and we may be headed back into war. Because fifty-four years later, there's ten percent unemployment, the hotels are completely empty, there are literally no tourists, there's no peace and no peace plan. No one's quite sure what to celebrate.

Even Hanukkah might be tough this year. Because we're about to do it all again. The Jews are going to try to get the bad guys out of here, whatever that means. But the truth is, we don't know what that means. Thousands of years have made the Hanukkah story seem simple—we were right and they were wrong. We were smaller in numbers, but we won. That kind of confidence, about all sorts of issues, is hard to find here these days. No one here thinks we're a hundred percent right, and no one has any idea how you win this. There are some people who are despondent.

Which reminded me of a brief conversation that I had with a man at shul on Yom Kippur. There's a tradition that at the recitation of Yizkor, the memorial service that's recited on Yom Kippur (in addition to a few other times during the year), people who don't *have* to say Yizkor (i.e., people who haven't lost a parent, sibling, spouse, or child) leave the service while Yizkor is being recited. It's kind of a silly custom, based apparently on an old superstition, and I remember that when I was growing up, my father always told me that *his* father, a pulpit rabbi, used to tell people not to leave, that they should say Yizkor for the six million. I remember my father telling me to say Yizkor for the Israeli soldiers who had died in the previous year. And as a kid, I never walked out during Yizkor.

But where we daven now, everyone who can, leaves. It's just the custom, and if I were to stay in, people would assume that something awful had happened and would worry. So I walk out. But each time I do, I hear my father and my grandfather telling me that it's silly, just a superstition, and I'm slightly worried that I'm going to get "caught" on my way out the door.

This year, just as I was about to exit, one of the older men in the shul grabbed my arm. "Do you see all these people leaving for Yizkor?" he asked. Assuming that I knew exactly what lecture was coming, I told him that yes, it was a lot of people. Then, his eyes brimming with tears, he said, "It's such a wonderful thing. When we founded this shul in the late '40s, we were all survivors of the death camps. No one walked out during Yizkor. Everyone had lost most of their family. And then came the wars here, and more people died. And still no one could leave during Yizkor. And now, look. There are more people outside than inside. That's why this is such a wonderful country."

I think of that little exchange almost every Shabbat when I see him. It reminds me why we're here. I know that not everyone at my office believes that rainbows mean anything, but I still believe in this place. I'm a dinosaur, one of the last classic Zionists. I believe that the Jews are better off because we have this little spot of territory, because in the end, everyone needs a home. I believe that this nutty, scary place is the only response to Jewish history that makes any sense. I do believe that though we've got a long way to go, we've built something pretty miraculous here.

And most of the time, I also believe we'll be OK.

January 2002:
The Good News About Pretzels

There was some good news about President Bush's close encounter with a pretzel a few days ago—it was the leading headline on Ynet, the web site that many Israelis use to monitor the news, for a good few hours. It's been a long time since we've had an innocuous headline, and for a few blessed moments, it actually seemed like an aura of normalcy might be returning to our lives. Life is good when someone falling off a sofa is the lead headline. Until a couple of days ago, this was the most quiet we'd had in almost a year and a half. No suicide bombers, no mortars fired at settlements, and relatively few shootings. It's ended now, as it was virtually guaranteed to, but even so, the good news is that the biggest story of late is the huge story that was made of the *Karine-A*, the arms boat that Israel intercepted and seized.

Though the boat and its shipment were the subject of much discussion at the most senior levels of government, many of us found the whole thing somewhat funny. Of course what could have been done with all those weapons and explosives isn't that funny, nor is the fact that there's now incontrovertible proof that Arafat is still gearing up for a massive confrontation and that Iran is helping him. That, to be sure, is more than a bit troubling. But still, the sense of exhilaration that the Israeli press had about this—and the implication that this was a brilliant military operation—was rather ridiculous.

Of course Israelis have been longing for some good military news for months, so it's easy to understand why people were so thrilled about this air and sea operation and its success. But as one British colleague of mine said at work last week when he overheard a discussion of this daring raid, "My God, we sank the *Bismarck*. It's hard to get excited about capturing a rusted floating bathtub."

And he's basically right. One look at the photos of this vessel they called a boat made it very clear that if the Israeli army, the most powerful and technologically advanced army in the Middle East, couldn't capture this thing, we weren't going to be here long. But no matter. The press is abuzz. People are sending out e-mails with "first-hand accounts" of the brave sailors who boarded the ship, the wizard pilots who hovered their helicopters over the boat, something akin to the accounts of the 1948 battles and those of the wars since then that are now part of the Israeli sacred core curriculum. The weapons are arrayed at a press conference for all to see. And no one bothers to note that Hemingway's "Old Man" on the sea could probably—with just a bit of help—have done exactly the same thing.

What's not nearly as funny is how quickly we squandered the

public relations gains of this brilliant military coup. As a reprisal, the IDF sent tanks and bulldozers into Gaza and demolished—according to some accounts—dozens of homes that were still in use. It was an incredibly stupid thing to do, and morally perverse in my estimation. Of course there are some die-hards here who continue to insist either that it was sad but necessary, or that the homes were not occupied and weren't that numerous anyway, but very few people believe any of that. Most Israelis are pretty ashamed of this latest stunt. Lots of people now say—perhaps only in frustration, but they say it nonetheless—that Sharon and Mofaz just hate Arabs and enjoy the conflict. It's been freezing here—literally—and that has only added to the sense that destroying homes is incredibly unwise and so ethically troubling as to be shameful. More and more, you hear people (even those who voted for Sharon) saying, "He has absolutely no plan except to keep Arafat trapped in Ramallah and to make sure that any prospect for serious dialogue is going to be squandered." I, for one, have no idea what's up, but one thing's very clear—we're stuck.

Israelis are now even beginning to deliberate the wisdom of the targeted assassinations that generally receive high approvals. They're wondering, mostly because the latest one was clearly the reason for the renewal of shootings at Israelis (not that some other excuse wouldn't have been found eventually, of course, or that this terrorist didn't deserve to die—the list of people he had killed made the front page of all the papers, with dates, names, and all the details). Israelis are wondering about these assassinations because there's some question as to whether we're not killing off all the Palestinian future leadership this way, thus making it impossible to achieve some agreement in fifteen or twenty years. On my way to the airport last night (more on that below), one rather thoughtful commentator said basically the following: "Killing Israelis is how one rises in the ranks of Palestinian political leadership, too. If we keep killing off the Palestinians who kill Israelis, they'll have no legitimate leaders in the eyes of their own people, and then, in a decade or two, when we're ready to talk, there'll be no one to talk to."

I had quite a few questions for this fellow. Are we really talking about fifteen or twenty more years of this? And should we let these murderers remain free so that they can be groomed for leadership? What do we do in the meantime? But somehow he made some sense, and it was sobering.

It wasn't, unfortunately, the only sobering moment of the last few days. A couple of days ago, we took some Jewish educators who are studying here at the Mandel school for a couple of weeks to the Galilee for some meetings. The theme for the two weeks was basically "the creation of collective memory," and one of the elements that we scheduled was a visit to an Arab Israeli town, to give them a sense of how Israeli Arabs tell a very different story of what happened here in 1948. And for part of the afternoon, we arranged for them to meet in small groups with Palestinian Israeli high school kids.

We met in the high school of this town, a very nice and well-maintained building (which we noticed had no heat at all). We broke into small groups, and my group had about three American visitors, three Palestinian Israeli kids (we used to call them Israeli Arabs, but they now want to be called Palestinian Israelis), and two Mandel staff. As our discussion began, one of the kids said, "Wouldn't you rather see the village than sit here?" So off we went, this ragtag group of American and Israeli Jews, walking through the Arab village.

As we meandered through the village on our tour, we gradually broke into smaller groups, and within a few minutes, I found myself walking through the streets and alleys with a young woman named Karawyn, a smart, articulate, attractive sixteen-year-old eleventh-grader, just a couple of months older than our daughter, Talia. Karawyn walked me through the town, and as she did, an occasional car drove by. The looks on people's faces as they saw her walking through town by the side of a Jew wearing a *kippah* were extraordinary. They seemed not to be able to tell if she'd lost her mind or was in danger. Kiddingly, I said to her, "I guess there aren't lots of people wearing *kippot* who wander through the village, huh?"

"Jews never come here," she replied.

"Never?"

"Never."

This, of course, in the heart of the Galilee.

We walked and talked. She's a very interesting person, the youngest of thirteen kids, the child of religious Muslim parents, none of whose kids are religious (sound familiar?). She wants to be a pediatrician, and hopes to go to either Haifa University or Be'er Sheva for medical school. "Is that realistic?" I asked her. "Why not?" she replied. "Lots of people from this village have become doctors." Good news, I thought, so I pushed the conversation further.

"When you see people like me," I asked, "do you see an enemy?"

"Not at all," she replied. "You're not an enemy—you're just a regular person. The enemies are Sharon and Peres." Somewhat amazed that she'd group the two of them together (which said a lot about how little she knows about Israeli politics, even though she's a full Israeli citizen), I asked why they were enemies. "Because the Jews occupied us in 1948, and they want to keep the occupation."

I wasn't sure what she meant, so I pushed her further. "So you want to end the occupation?"

"Not really. I like being Israeli. I know my rights, and I make sure that I get them. But I'm a minority in my high school class. Most of the kids do want to end the occupation."

"You mean that they want to live in a Palestinian state?" I asked.

"Right."

"So if there were a Palestinian state in the West Bank and in Gaza, they'd want to move there?"

"No. This is their village. They want to stay here."

"But don't they understand that this village is part of Israel, inside the green line, and no one anywhere is talking about giving this village to a Palestinian state?"

"They understand that, but they want to end the occupation."

Now we were clearly getting close to the critical point, so I pushed. "And how do they want to do that?" And suddenly her demeanor changed. We'd been walking shoulder to shoulder through the village, looking straight ahead, just chatting, and she'd been totally relaxed. She stopped walking, backed away from me, looked down at the ground, and said, "You should probably ask them."

I didn't meet "them," of course, but the point was clear. The kids who are her classmates, full Israeli citizens, want to end the occupation. And when you ask a kid who has grand plans for her life how they want to do this, she won't tell you. Because she knows that when she does, you're going to realize that though you're citizens of the same state, you are enemies—potentially mortal ones. I wondered what kind of life she lives, sharing a class with them and hoping to be in the medical school class that one day my own kids could be in. And I realized, of course, that her community is fully twenty percent of the population of this country, without the West Bank and Gaza. There's a lurking sense of desperation now that has the entire country—not just Sharon—paralyzed. Of late, I've even noticed that it's considered bad manners to talk politics at the dinner table or with guests. No one wants to discuss it, no one wants to think. There's nowhere to go, nothing to do, so let's talk about the best place to buy all-weather outdoor Ping-Pong tables.

At times, though, you can't put the "situation" out of your mind, because it grabs you, stares you right in the face. Like last night, as I was driving Tali and two of her friends to the airport. She's made Israel's national high school debating team, and left last night for the world championships in Singapore. Recently the five team members decided that it would be a pity not to stop for a week in Bangkok, and for a day in Hong Kong on the way back. So she's off for three weeks to the Far East and a much needed reprieve from the pressure cooker she lives in.

We have a large van, so we offered to drive two of the other kids and their luggage, and one of the fathers came along for the ride. We were supposed to be at the airport at eight in the evening, so we left at six-thirty, leaving exactly twice as much time as should be necessary in case there was traffic. Thirty minutes later, when we should have been halfway to the airport, we hadn't even made it out of Jerusalem. Traffic was going nowhere. We listened to the seven o'clock news, which said that a major traffic accident on the Jerusalem–Tel Aviv highway had the road completely blocked, and the police were asking people to use alternate routes.

"What alternate route is there?" I asked the other dad.

"The Modi'in road, I guess," he said, referring to the new road by Modi'in, well outside the green line, a road I used to drive all the time but haven't been on in a year and a half. It's a road on which many Israelis have been shot and killed by Palestinian gunmen in recent months.

"You want to do it?" I asked him.

"I guess we have to—they'll miss the plane," he responded. So without saying anything to the three girls who were chatting in the backseat, we headed north to the Begin highway, out to Ramot, and on towards the green line. It's just a matter of five or six minutes to the line, but we were both nervous. He said, "You know, with all the traffic stopped on the highway, this road is likely to be well traveled now. It should be OK."

And for a while there were, indeed, lots of cars, and we both relaxed a bit. But as soon as we hit the green line (not marked in any way, but you somehow basically know where it is), we suddenly noticed that we were the only car on the road. Not another car to be seen. It was about twenty kilometers, I estimated, until the road led us back into Israel, so I just basically floored it. As our speed climbed above 120 kilometers per hour, and reached towards 130 or so, the girls noticed that we were going fast. "Why are you driving so fast?" Talia asked. And looking out the window, she saw that she didn't recognize the road and asked, "Where are we, anyway?"

"We're taking the Modi'in road," I responded, "because the highway's shut down." "Is this safe?" she wanted to know. The other dad responded, "Absolutely. No one's been killed here since yesterday." I looked at my watch, remembering that the funeral of the thirty-year-old woman (mother of two) who'd been killed there was at noon. Great. She's been buried for seven hours only. Maybe it's too soon for another shooting in the same spot.

"They told us in school that driving fast actually makes it easier for them to shoot at you," one of the other kids chimed in. I wondered why exactly they were even discussing this in school, and why driving fast would make it easier. It didn't make sense. I knew that there were two ways these shootings are done. Either the gunmen hide in the hills by the road, which I noticed were completely black even with my brights on, or they overtake you from the side in a different car and shoot as they pass you. So I kept speeding along, watching in the rearview mirror for a car trying to catch me. If it did, I figured, I'd wait just until it was close, then hit the brakes and make them pass me. Would this have worked? I have no idea. This wasn't part of the driver's ed course I took in the suburbs of Baltimore twenty-five years ago.

Anyway, we obviously made it without incident, except for the blood pressures of the two adults in the car. We got the kids checked in and sent off, and walked back to the car. "How do you want to go back?" I asked my friend. "The highway's apparently blocked in both directions."

"They made the flight. We'll go back on the highway and sit if we have to. No point tempting the fates twice in one night." So that's what we did.

I got home an hour later and, eating a late dinner, recounted to Elisheva the little drama of our drive to the airport. "How in the world did Michael let you take that route?" she wanted to know.

"There was no choice—the kids would have missed the plane."

"That's insane. Do you know how many people have been killed on that exact road?"

"Well, you do get to have your picture on the front page of the next day's paper, you know," I said, trying to add a bit of levity to her growing fury.

"You're not funny, you know."

"Well, what would you have done then, with the kids in the back, worrying if they're going to miss their flight and mess up their trip?" No response.

No response—that's the point precisely, because this is simply no way to live. As I was eating my dinner quietly at the table and we were both reading the paper, she suddenly said to me, "You know, I'm getting totally sick of this place. I'll never leave, because I couldn't live with myself, but I just can't stand it." This time, I was the one who had no response.

And that's where we are. Not unlike that tub that we captured—basically shipwrecked. I don't think there's a sane person in this country who believes that there's anyone to talk to, that they're going to stop killing us, that we're going to stop making them hate us more, that there's any consensus even among Israeli Arabs (as we used to call them) that the Jewish state has a right to exist. And yet we don't want to be anywhere else, and besides, most of the people here have nowhere else to go.

So people basically live from day to day, hoping that it will stay mostly quiet, that the latest shootings won't be the beginning of the next round of incessant violence, and that, if we're lucky, maybe the headlines will continue to be about George W's eating mishaps. That's a good kind of danger to have to live with.

March 26, 2002:
Great Town, Ghost Town:
The Night Before Passover

Last Thursday was cold and windy, exactly the weather you don't want here these days. Not because of the cold, but because the cold means that everyone is wearing heavy coats, and that, in turn, makes everyone nervous. You can never tell what's under someone's coat, so when everyone is wearing parkas, everyone could be a bomb. It's enough to make an already jittery city simply intolerable.

I got in the elevator early in the morning at work, and as soon as I'd stepped in, an Arab guy (sometimes you can just tell; it's hard to explain how you know, but you do) got in right after me. He, too, was wearing a bulky overcoat and was carrying a backpack. He didn't look at me, and as the door closed, I wondered for a second if "this was it." But, I figured, as I was the only other person in the elevator, it probably wouldn't be worth his time and effort. And as it's only a five-story building, I figured that one way or the other, I wouldn't be in suspense for long. He got off before I did. But despite the early hour, by the time I got to the fifth floor, let's just say that I was completely awake.

Later in the day, we had afternoon meetings at our other building on Graetz Street. We took about a half-hour break, and I decided to use the time to run to the hardware store to pick up some things that had long been on my to-do list. A five-minute brisk walk and I was on

Emek Refa'im. It was the middle of the afternoon, and except for the occasional soldier or security guard, I was virtually the only one on the street. All the restaurants, which a year ago would have had lots of customers even in the middle of the afternoon, were empty. Not almost empty—literally empty. Yoja, the Thai-food place—empty except for a guard with an M-16 sitting in front. Normans, the upscale burger place—so quiet that I couldn't tell if it was actually open. Same with Caffit, with Masryk, with the sushi bar, the new wine store—there was simply no one out. Jerusalem has become a ghost town. Businesses are closing, people are going broke day in and day out. Even when things aren't exploding, the city is caving in. Time isn't on our side.

I walked along the street and no one seemed to notice me. But not so on my way back. Now, with a bag from the hardware store, I was apparently much more interesting to each security guard I walked by. As I approached, with my own heavy coat and an unidentified bag in my hand, each one seemed to grow a bit more alert as I got closer, eyed me carefully as I walked by, and, I imagine, settled down a bit when it became clear that I wasn't about to blow myself up in front of their restaurant. But the whole thing struck me as a bit histrionic. True, it's been a bad few weeks in town, but still, to be that nervous, all the time?

Worried that I might be late for the start of our meeting, I kept walking, getting my thoughts together for the next few hours of work. I took a left off Emek Refa'im up the hill on Graetz towards our office, making sure to keep a good pace. And then, the deafening roar. It sounded like it was only a few yards away, but as I couldn't see any smoke, I knew it had to be farther. And as I was still able to wonder where it was, I knew I was okay. But I also knew what it was. They use a lot of explosives here for building purposes, as the ground is solid rock. But when they do that, the ground shakes. This time, nothing. No shaking, just a deafening explosion. And then quiet. I listened for what seemed like an eternity, and it was silent. Maybe, I thought, it really was nothing. And then the sirens. Siren after siren, unrelenting, just like the attacks themselves.

It wasn't a "major" attack. "Just" three people killed, sixty wounded, right on King George Street, across the street from our insurance agent where I'd been the day before. This is a town where a lot depends on luck and timing. Of the three people who weren't lucky this time, two were a married couple, on their way out of a prenatal doctor's visit. Rescue workers found the sonogram picture in the woman's purse. The couple's two other kids, now orphans, were at home in a town just outside Jerusalem. This was the stuff of the morning paper the next day, but the day following, it had all been forgotten. After all, if you focused on every victim these days, you'd never be able to get out of bed in the morning. You survive only because you can forget.

The problem is that being scared all the time and feeling sorry for yourself can also lead you to forget how much we've done wrong. *Kol Ha-Ir,* a weekly newsmagazine in Jerusalem, ran an all-black cover the week before last, with white lettering in a biblical typeface. It was a quote from the book of Micah, Chapter Three, that in part said:

> *Hear, this, you rulers of the House of Jacob*
> *You chiefs of the House of Israel*
> *Who detest justice*
> *And make crooked all that is straight . . .*
> *Assuredly, because of you*
> *Zion shall be plowed as a field*
> *And Jerusalem shall become heaps of ruins*
> *And the Temple Mount*
> *A shrine in the woods.*

Admittedly, *Kol Ha-Ir* is always slightly left of center, is usually critical of the army, and always hates the mayor. So some of this was expected. But no matter what one's political position is, the starkness of the warning—and the fact that it had obviously been said here before, to no avail—hit home for many. What the IDF did in the West Bank last week was incredibly problematic, even if necessary (whether it was actually necessary, and whether it worked, are matters of heated debate). The stories in that issue (and in much of the Israeli press, in fact) about soldiers moving from house to house in refugee camps by smashing through walls instead of going out into the streets (in order to reduce casualties), leading them to suddenly appear, in a pile of debris and dust, in the bedrooms of young, screaming children, are blood chilling. Whether or not we had to do that may not be the question. Those kids will never forget waking up as the wall came crashing in, as soldiers (they call them "The Jews") appeared in helmets and with M-16's, and it won't take a seething father much more provocation before he decides that he, too, will kill Jews to make a better future for his kids. It won't make him "right," but when it happens, it also shouldn't surprise us.

The suffering here seems to know no bounds these days. For anyone. There's plenty of it in the refugee camps, and there's plenty right here in town. The table of contents of that same issue of *Kol Ha-Ir* included a story about how local high schools are dealing with the deaths of so many of their recent graduates, another story about how waiters and waitresses in Jerusalem feel knowing that they're sitting ducks with cafes and restaurants now the target of choice. It contained an article about non-Jewish tourists to the city (the Jews, it seems, don't like the idea of blowing up), and one about a recent memorial at the Moment Cafe and an interview with its owner, who organized it. And on and on.

The other problem with forgetting as a coping mechanism is that you can also forget how wonderful life here used to be. And, because of that, the occasional respite from the tension and worry is more welcome than can be described. Like when our alarm company showed up on Purim day for our annual security system check. The same two technicians, in their Evron Security t-shirts, but also with Viking helmets replete with horns. It was the first time in weeks that I'd seen the kids giggle in pure joy. Or later that day, when I took Tali to the mall to get her a cell phone (after months of her patiently explaining the matter, I finally did understand that meaningful existence for people between the ages of fifteen and seventeen simply cannot be had without a more stylish phone), and all the salespeople were dressed in drag, or as monks or whatever. There was incredibly tight security everywhere, but people seemed to know how to have a bit of fun, anyway. On the way back from the mall, Tali even said, "Wow—it's nice to see people having fun for once."

People seem to be struggling to remind each other, and themselves, why we're here. Pesach helps. Yesterday was a gorgeous day. Warm, almost hot in the morning. And a day in which it seemed that the whole city was getting ready for Pesach. I took the car to the car wash early, figuring I'd get there before the line started, but no such luck. The line stretched out into the middle of the street by the time I got there. But it didn't matter. Everyone seemed to revel in the fact that even in the midst of all this, the whole city was still getting ready for the holiday. Later in the morning, when I drove to Talpiyot (about five minutes away) to one of the central locations where the rabbinate had set up huge pots of boiling water so you can get your silverware, wine cups, pots, etc., kashered for Pesach, the sidewalk was filled with people waiting on line, talking amiably. It was, I thought, Jerusalem at its best. The rabbinate actually doing something to be helpful (a major break from their normal policy), and people of all sorts—"black hats," knitted *kippot,* women in pants, men without their heads covered, and even some Philippine women who were doing this for the houses in which they worked—all getting along just fine. Enjoying the unexpected spring, people were content to hang out on the sidewalk, their pots and pans in tow, living a bit of what used to be taken for granted in Jerusalem.

This is, even after all these months, a great town. It's filled with people who've moved here from everywhere, and all for more or less the same reason—to live in a Jewish city, in a Jewish country. Walking with Avi today to yet another hardware store (pre-Pesach, what can you do?), we passed two Ethiopian women carrying boxes of matzah. I think that Avi barely noticed, but I couldn't help but muse on how different were the two countries from which we came, and, despite our abiding differences, the fundamental similarities in the reasons for which we're here. We passed another couple speaking French. And an elderly couple speaking Yiddish. A brief reminder of the miracle that Jerusalem is, wounded and suffering though she may be.

It reminded me of the party our shul had on Purim. Everyone crowded into the home of one of the members who lives nearby. Music, food, some skits. It had been a bad week, though to be honest, I forget exactly which catastrophe had taken place in the days preceding Purim. But then I saw, among the crowd, a dozen or so of the older men and women—all of them survivors of the Nazi death camps, sitting together as a group. I watched them watching the little kids who were way too wild, way too noisy, and saw them smiling the whole time. These elderly couples seemed to relish each screaming, wild child. For, they knew, the alternative to wild kids need not be tame ones. It can be no kids. And I felt terribly humbled. After all they'd been through, who was I to let this war get me to feel sorry for myself? A bit of perspective helps.

And that perspective seems to crop up all the time in this town, this place made of memory. We were at a wedding a couple of weeks ago: an elegant, joyous, perfect evening. True, I did have to get frisked to get into the hotel, and true, as we were dancing in circles, you couldn't help but notice the extra security men on the perimeter of the room watching attentively for anything that seemed out of the ordinary. And true, when a balloon or two popped, people stopped for a millisecond, realized that all was okay, and went on.

The ceremony took place in the courtyard of the Inbal Hotel. In keeping with a common Jerusalem custom, before the breaking of the glass, everyone present sang, in a quasi-mournful tone, the verse from Psalms, "If I forget you, O Jerusalem." The singing took a couple of minutes, so for a moment or two, we didn't have to focus on what was happening under the chuppah. As I looked around, I saw the security guards watching over us, and higher up, the rows of Israeli flags on the roof of the hotel, fluttering in the wind. And all around us, even in these moments, hundreds of people huddled together in the crisp

Jerusalem night, gazing at the bride and groom, singing "If I forget you, O Jerusalem."

As slow and quiet as the song was, it felt like an act of defiance. Like a statement to "them, out there," that we're here to stay. That everyone here is frightened, and for good reason, but few are leaving. This is the era, we seemed to be singing, that separates those who're willing to risk for a Jewish future, and those who, quite frankly, are not. It's the era in which we're seeing who is willing to tough it out, and hopefully will live to see the end of this. Perhaps I felt that way because of all the people who refuse to come here now, who have been convinced by American Jewish life to believe that meaningful Jewish existence and personal safety go together. They don't—at least they haven't for most of Jewish history, and they certainly don't go together here, now. None of us here want to die in this war, but some of us will. We know that. And most of us, I think, understand that you don't get meaning without risk.

Jerusalem conversations this week (at least in the circles I travel in) made much mention of the decision of March of the Living, the annual pilgrimage of American Jewish teenagers to Eastern Europe and Israel, not to come to Israel this year. And of the suggestion (later abandoned, apparently) of one region to go to Berlin (instead of Israel) to witness Jewish rebirth. The irony that American Jewish parents would send their kids to Auschwitz and Berlin, but not to Israel, was lost on no one. Another region is apparently going to Ground Zero after Eastern Europe, instead of coming to Israel. Think about what *that* really suggests. And then there was apparently a full-page ad in the *New York Times* last week, supporting the IDF Reserve officers who are refusing to serve in the territories. (A complicated issue, with what seems to me their honorable moral stance at odds with the need for a functioning military in time of war.) But here, few people seemed to have patience for what they described as armchair liberals in the comfort of the Bay Area or the Upper West Side taking a public stand on an issue that most Israelis believe is too complex and subtle to be easily summed up, and certainly not on one page of the *Times*. One person in shul, who had seen the ad, said, "They just left out what should have been the final sentence on the page: '*Now*, I'm *really* not going to make aliyah.'" A widespread giggle. Not because people disagree with the point of the ad, but because most people here can't figure out what people who're not assuming any of the risk are doing weighing in.

That risk changes everything. Occasionally, it even creates moments of humor. The morning after the foiled Caffit bombing, *Ha-Aretz* carried a front-page story noting that anyone who captured a terrorist in the act of trying to kill people would receive a prize of $5,000. Reading the paper, Elisheva laughed and said, "Hey, look at this. If we each capture a terrorist today, we can redo the living room." I didn't know whether to be more worried about the terrorists or her budget for what I'd thought was going to be one sofa and a bookcase. Or Avi's morning parting words to me as he heads off to school on his bike: "Bye, Abba, keep low and keep moving. Love ya." It's all sick humor, but I suppose that it's part of the way we get through the day.

But not all of it's funny, of course. Elisheva told me the other day that she wanted the car by 10:00 A.M. (as my office is a five-minute walk from home, there's absolutely no reason for us to have two cars), because she was going to get her hair cut. Simple? Not really. Because she knows that I know where she gets her hair cut—downtown, right by Ben Yehudah, now virtually deserted because of all the attacks there. And, for a moment, I debated whether I should say anything. But I didn't. If she'd wanted my advice, I realized, she would have asked for it. But she didn't. She simply said she needed the car. Meaning, "I'm going down there—it's my town, and they can't take it away from me." She did go, and as she got there a bit early, made a point of wandering around the completely deserted stores. She talked to the guy who cuts her hair, and asked him if he's frightened being in that store-front all day on that street. "Terrified," he said, "but I'm not leaving." Neither are we.

Yesterday, driving up the same Graetz Street I'd been walking up when I heard the bomb go off, I saw a parked car, and watched a young mother in her thirties and her two kids get out of the car. The kids were carrying a small cage with what looked like a little puppy, and the mom had her arms full of pet supplies. I'd been listening to the news, a depressing activity here at any hour of the day, and for a moment, the idea of buying kids a new pet in this setting seemed utterly absurd. But then, of course, I realized that it was the perfect thing to do. She was giving them exactly what they needed. Some restored innocence. Pure love. Fun. A diversion. And a reason to look forward to tomorrow.

Tomorrow is why we're here today. For tomorrow night, when we sing "Next Year in Jerusalem," those of us who live in Jerusalem will really mean it. If we're alive next year, we'll be here. Jews have been singing that line for too long with no hope of realizing it for us to simply walk away because it's unpleasant, or frightening, or even a bit dangerous. Life, this city has taught us, isn't about pleasant, or comfort, or safety. For those of us who've chosen to stick it out here, it's about purpose, even defiance. It's about saying that, yes, we want this to end. Yes, we're willing to give up a lot to make that happen. Yes, we've made terrible mistakes in how we've handled Israeli Arabs and Palestinians under our control.

But no, we won't leave. We won't confuse our having made mistakes with our having no right to be here. And we won't allow our wish for normalcy to delude us into thinking that normalcy's the goal. It's not. The goal is long lines at the car wash before Pesach, alarm guys dressed up for Purim, hundreds of men and women packed into synagogues in every neighborhood on the Shabbat before Pesach to hear the annual Pre-Passover Sermon, long lines with pots and pans, and even magazine covers that quote the prophets to critique the army and the mayor. The goal, quite simply, is Jewish life like it can't exist anywhere else. And from that dream, very few of us will walk away. No matter what.

As all of us say and, as some of us mean, "Next Year in Jerusalem."

April 2002:
Declaration of War

Sharon's Words: "Israel Stands at a Crossroads"

Following is a transcript of Prime Minister Ariel Sharon's televised address in Israel yesterday. The speech was recorded and translated from Hebrew by The Associated Press.

Citizens of Israel:
The state of Israel is in a war, a war against terrorism. This is a war that was imposed on us. It is not a war that we decided to embark upon. This is a war over our home.

New York Times: Monday, April 1, 2002, page A7

Needing Israel

[Op-Ed from *The New York Times*, April 13, 2002]

- - - - - - - - - - - - - - - - - -

JERUSALEM

Tuesday was Yom Ha-Shoah, Holocaust Remembrance Day, an agonizing day. In the afternoon, at work, we gathered in a circle while some colleagues quietly read the names of relatives who had been exterminated by the Nazis. Some had long lists; one even brought pictures. During the ceremony, word spread that a group of Israeli Defense Force soldiers—thirteen, it would turn out—had been killed in an ambush in Jenin. Another, in Nablus, fell to friendly fire.

It is hard to describe what fourteen soldiers means in this small country. People make frantic calls to find out where their husbands and fathers are. Then the hourly news announces to the entire country the location and time of each funeral. At such moments it feels that living here makes one part of an extended family.

No one in that family wants this war. But very few people here think we can do without it. Israelis understand why we're fighting. We also know why our soldiers are dying. There are significant pockets of armed resistance in the Jenin camp, but there are also lots of civilians. So we can't just bomb from the skies. We send soldiers house to house, only to watch as Hamas fighters use those same civilians as shields. On Tuesday we paid a heavy price.

We had fourteen funerals because we won't fight this war the way the Russians fought in Grozny or the way the United States fought in Afghanistan—from the safety of the skies. Hardly a building in Grozny was spared in the bombing; the Russians knew the price they'd pay if they tried to fight on the street. If Israel hit a hospital from the skies the way that the Americans did not too long ago in Afghanistan, just imagine the world's reaction.

Palestinians say we won't let their ambulances in Jenin. Yet two weeks ago Israeli soldiers stopped a Palestinian ambulance with a child in the back on a stretcher, and under him soldiers found an explosive belt. Palestinians say that we're not letting them clear their dead from the streets. The Israeli Army claims that's a lie, that the Palestinians are leaving the bodies there intentionally for good footage on CNN. Who's telling the truth? I don't know.

Last week, when the siege around the Church of the Nativity began, many Israelis understood why we couldn't just shoot our way in, but the frustration was palpable. If it had been Israelis in a church, or a synagogue, and Palestinians on the outside, how long would the siege have lasted? Everyone here knows the answer. When the Palestinians burned down the synagogue at Joseph's Tomb in October 2000, the Vatican didn't speak up.

When they later destroyed an ancient synagogue near Jericho, European liberals didn't lose sleep.

The siege outside the church began in foul weather. According to reports on Israeli radio, some soldiers stood for hours in the driving rain, making sure that none of the armed Palestinians inside would escape. All that afternoon, the residents of Bethlehem pointed at the rain and shouted: "Get out of here. We hate you. The world hates you. And look, even the heavens hate you." Maybe the world does hate us for having the audacity to protect ourselves, for meaning it when we say "Never again." Maybe the world is secretly delighted that no war can be made to look civilized, so the Europeans and the Palestinians can point their fingers at us and say, "See, they do it, too." Then maybe what they did won't seem so horrific, so unforgivable.

One thing important to Jews is remembering. We won't forget the twentieth century and the world's complicity, and when we recall this week, in which we buried fourteen of our sons, brothers, husbands, and fathers who didn't have to die except for our decision to do this fighting the hard way, we'll remember the world's double standard.

On Tuesday night, my twelve-year-old son, Avi, told me about a Yom Ha-Shoah class discussion about whether the Holocaust could happen again—a session he said he found "stupid." Why? I asked. "Because we have a strong army," he answered, "America is our friend, and look out there—now we take care of ourselves."

The next morning I watched him head off on his bike to school, with pride, security, and confidence. That's a lot more than Jewish kids in Europe had a few decades ago. It's a lot more than some Jewish kids have in Europe this week. It's why we need this country. And it's why we'll fight to keep it.

The Circle of Death

- - - - - - - - - - - - - - - - - -

It's been a rough few weeks. The Passover massacre in Netanya. The bombing of the Haifa restaurant right after that. Israel's response in the form of Operation Defensive Shield with its invasion of Jenin, and then, the loss of thirteen soldiers in one ambush that has shaken the country to its very core. The boys seem to be coping OK. Micha doesn't talk about any of it and since we don't let him watch the news, we assume he's pretty oblivious. Avi reads the paper without saying very much, undoubtedly silently calculating the number of years until he's in the army, when he could well be asked to do something similar. Nonetheless, he's holding it together. Or seems to be.

But something's wrong with Talia. She's distracted, moody. We ask her what's wrong, but in her typical teenager fashion, we get one "Nothing" after another. Elisheva and I talk to her individually, and together, but we can't seem to get through. After a few days of trying, we begin to worry that something is really wrong.

We know that she feels close to the principal of her school, and often uses her as a sounding board. So we call the school. The principal takes the call, and I tell her we're worried about Talia. "I don't want you to violate any confidence of Tali's that you feel you shouldn't, but if there were anything you could tell us to shed light on this, it would be helpful." She invites us to come in to school the next morning, and we clear our schedules.

Morning comes and we walk to Tali's school together. The principal takes us right away and we give her a quick summary of what's been going on. We've got a great kid, but since the Massacre, and particularly since Jenin, it seems we're losing her. And we don't know what to do.

To my surprise, the principal smiles, and actually seems to relax. What we're telling her is obviously a relief. She was apparently worried that it might be something worse.

"Look," she says, "Tali's fine. That's the bottom line. She's fine.

"This is a tough time for all the girls in this school. You know how you feel, how you've been feeling for a year and a half since all this started. Now add adolescence to that, and multiply it by the hundreds of girls in the school, and you get a sense of what this place is sometimes like. But you need to understand—as hard as this is for everyone, it is sometimes harder for Talia.

"She's worked incredibly hard to be Israeli. Her Hebrew's perfect, she's got no accent. She's worked her way into this school, which is no small accomplishment, and she's doing wonderfully. She's debating internationally, she's a counselor in Bnai Akiva. She's popular. She's surrounded herself with Israeli friends, and from what I gather, she's distanced herself a bit from her previous American connections. She got here a few years ago as a complete newcomer and decided that she would make it. And she has, in spades.

"But then comes a day like the Jenin ambush. Throughout the school, there are rumors that there's been a terrible tragedy with the army, but no one knows anything official yet. The cell phones start ringing throughout the school, the rumors spread, and many of the girls are on the verge of hysteria. Many are trying to find out where their father, their brother, their uncle, their neighbor, their friend is. Almost everyone is on the phone trying to find out something. The lack of information is agonizing and many of them simply can't bear it.

"But in the midst of all this, Tali's cell phone doesn't ring. You know why? It's because you haven't been here long enough. She knows that the likelihood that she's going to know any of the soldiers killed in Jenin is small. And in many ways, she's relieved. What sixteen-year-old girl wouldn't be? But as relieved as she's feeling, she's also feeling inauthentic. As Israeli as she's wanted to be, at moments like that, she feels like an outsider. She feels different. And nothing she can do will change that.

"Because, you see, now she really has begun to understand. In some important ways, she knows she won't be fully Israeli until she's inside the circle of death."

. . .

The conversation continues, I imagine, but the rest of it's lost on me. I just want to get out of that office before she sees that while Tali may be OK, I'm not. We continue with the necessary pleasantries, but I'm not hearing anything anymore. I'm focused on the "circle of death."

In the States, I suddenly remember, our kids would watch the *Lion King* video and sing their favorite song from the movie, "The Circle of Life." And here, the principal is now telling us that no matter how hard she tries, Tali won't be fully Israeli until she's inside the "circle of death."

. . .

The meeting draws to an end, and I see Elisheva and the principal standing and saying goodbye. So I get up, too. I thank the principal for her time, and we escape into the school's front yard.

She's really excellent, don't you think?" Elisheva asks me.

"Yeah. She's good."

"No. Seriously. I think she really has a good feel for Tali, don't you?"

"Yes. I said yes."

"Well, do you feel better now?"

"Yup."

"Is that all you have to say? Why are you so quiet all of a sudden?"

I don't say anything. After all, what's there really to say? That, no, I'm not really comforted by the thought that we've brought our kids to a place where they won't really belong until they're crushed by grief? That I feel like finding my daughter and hugging her, and apologizing, telling her I had no idea that this was what it would all become? That, no, I don't feel better? That I'm worried that something pure and innocent in my kids is already dying, and that while the principal probably thinks she just put us at ease, my heart is breaking?

Elisheva takes my hand and we start the walk back home. A block away, she's going to turn left to the house, while I continue straight to the office. She leans forward and gives me a kiss, and says, "Have a good day."

"You, too," I say.

And I ask myself as I walk away, "What would make this a good day for Tali?" To keep feeling left out? Or to become authentic and to be inside the "circle of death"? Or, I wonder, maybe there's no such thing as a good day anymore. Have we come to a place where all the options simply break your heart?

June 2002:
Frogs in Hot Water

New Arab Bombing in Israel Deepens
a Sense of Dismay

Palestinian suicide bomber blows himself up in shopping center in Petah Tikva, Israel, killing baby girl and grandmother and wounding more than 40 people; Israeli public security minister, Uzi Landau, accuses Palestinian Authority of encouraging suicide attacks; the attack in this city near Tel Aviv came at the end of a day in which Israeli forces conducted operations in four Palestinian cities in an effort to choke off precisely such bombings, and it deepened public frustration at the government's inability to halt the attacks.

New York Times: Tuesday, May 28, 2002, page A1

I've been told, though I've never actually confirmed this with anyone who could be trusted on the matter, that if you take a live frog and throw it into boiling water, the frog will quickly leap out of the pot to save its own life. However, if you take the same frog and put it in a pot of comfortable water in which you gradually raise the temperature to boiling, the frog will become used to the increasingly dangerous temperature and, rather than leap out to save his life, will simply stay in the heated water and die.

Whether or not this little bit of pop science is true is really not that significant. What *is* significant is that the metaphor was used by someone with whom I was speaking recently about the situation in Israel. This woman, who recently left Israel and moved to Canada, said that when she lived in Israel, she felt like the frog. The water was getting hotter and hotter, we were all basically boiling to death, and the real problem was that we didn't even notice anymore.

There's something to that, unfortunately. When we take a moment to think about what life here has become, what's really scary is not what's happening on a day-to-day, or week-to-week, basis, but rather, how accustomed we've become to all this, how normal it seems to be living in a place where things simply seem to explode without a second's notice. The unthinkable continues to happen, and more and more, we scarcely notice.

A couple of weeks ago, there was a *pigu'a* (terrorist attack) in the evening. I forget already which one it was, but I do recall that it happened before the evening news. Elisheva was in the States for a couple of weeks, so I was soloing during the kids' bedtime. I figured that there was no way I'd be able to get the kids to sleep on time if we had to process all this, so I purposely made sure that the television stayed off that evening and that none of the computers was logged on to the internet, and sure enough, got the kids to sleep without their finding out that the morning paper would have more photos of dead people on the front page.

But the morning was bound to come, and when it did, I woke the kids and Avi was the first downstairs to breakfast. Without thinking, I asked him to go outside and bring in the paper, which he did. Then, he unwrapped the paper, saw the pictures of the victims on the front page, and looked at me and said, "Hey, there was a *pigu'a* yesterday?"

"Yup."

"Strange. I didn't hear about it." And turning the page, he asked, "Where's the weather page? Can I wear shorts today?"

I didn't let him wear shorts, because it was way too cold, but I was struck—and rather horrified—that we've now gotten to the point that half a minute after your almost-thirteen-year-old kid finds out that yet another bus, or restaurant, or park, or whatever, was blown up, he says, "Gee, I missed that one" and wants to know what to wear to school. It's no way for a kid to grow up, but hey, that's the problem with being a frog in hot water—you don't even know that you're already dying.

So you learn to look at the bright side. Take synagogue membership, for example. No more shelling out a couple of grand a year and hoping that there's no building campaign that you can't say no to. Here, the dues are only about $50 to $100 a year. A pretty good deal. Until recently, that is.

Not long ago, our shul asked all able-bodied men (which amazingly, they apparently believed includes me) to take turns with guard duty during services. Avi hates when I do it. I try to tell myself that he misses me and just likes having me in the seat next to him. But he's too verbal to let it go at that. No, he says, that's not it. "Abba, I know what you're supposed to do. If someone is going to try to get in the shul with a bomb, you're supposed to stop them before they get to the door. But that means that you're going to be the one killed."

I'm never quite sure what to tell him when he says this. "But think of the bright side: then I won't be able to keep reminding you to follow the Torah reading" doesn't quite seem like the right approach, so I usually say nothing. Because he's right—being a twelve-and-a-half-year-old boy in Israel these days means having to deal with the fact that even going to shul can be dangerous. But no one thinks there's anything particularly extraordinary about that. That's just how you live here. More hot water.

The whole guard duty scene got even more absurd not long ago when someone decided that we all needed to get our rifle licenses renewed so we could legally carry guns while we're doing this guard duty. I was part of the second group to get this "training," which all of us had had before and which none of us needed. First, we had to go to a police station on a Thursday night to get a lecture from some police-person about the gun, safety, etc. Smart idea, except we've all heard this lecture before. But off we trudge, annoyed and whining about the waste of time. A few folk and me, plus one guy from our shul who had just returned from a few weeks in Jenin. He, too, was required to hear this lecture on how to use an M-1. A fabulous use of his time.

We get to the police station on Thursday night, and meet our "instructor." She's about twenty, if that, nibbling on a croissant the whole time, and quite frankly, gorgeous in that typical Israeli-earthy way. Suddenly, my shul buddies think this training is a superb idea. I'm virtually hysterical watching these forty-something-year-old guys who half an hour before had been grumbling about having to do this, now listening with the attentiveness that should have been accorded a lecture that finally explained the theory of relativity.

"When you aim correctly, there are exactly five points of contact between you and the weapon. The butt of the gun should be in the soft spot just inside your shoulder. Everyone get it?" Of course we got it, but I could tell that most of the group was profoundly disappointed that she didn't go one by one to point that spot out more specifically for each person.

We go through the "five points of contact," and then she looks at her printout and says, "Tomorrow, it seems, you're going to be tested on firing from a crouched position. Everyone familiar with that one?" Nods. "Anyone need a review or a demonstration?" Needless to say, Mr. Just-Back-from-Jenin was suddenly very interested in learning about this, too, and he said, "That would be helpful." She gave him a quizzical look, licked the crumbs of the croissant off her fingers . . . and proceeded with her demonstration. When it was over, she complimented us on our attentiveness; I thought I was in the twilight zone.

I was actually on the verge of getting annoyed with the stupidity of the whole thing (though I wasn't entirely certain whom to blame, as it wasn't clear who was playing with whom), when I realized that I'm probably just too serious. If you're going to live in this absurdity, shouldn't you learn to laugh at it? Maybe—unless you're just laughing as the water keeps getting hotter.

Then our "instructor" told us to be at the firing range at 9:15 the next morning.

"Where is it?" one of the people asked. So she told us, explaining that the firing range is just north of Ramallah and that we take the Modi'in road to get there. "But people have been shot all along that road," one person notes. "True," she says, "but tomorrow it should be OK."

"Why?"

"No reason. I hope it will be OK. Any questions? Good luck tomorrow."

Later that night, Mr. I'm-Not-Getting-Killed-on-the-Way-to-the-Firing-Range calls me to tell me not to pick him up in the morning. He's not going. "And I don't understand why you're willing to go," he tells me. "Because," I tell him, "we're invited out for Shabbat dinner tonight. It's a perfect Friday for me to spend doing this, since I don't have to cook." What I don't tell him, because he knows it as well as I do, is that if I wasn't willing to be a target, in one place or another, I'd have to stay in my house all day. And I'm not going to live that way.

"What're the chances that they're going to shoot at us tomorrow morning?" I ask with a chuckle. He says I'm nuts, and he's not going. I tell him to call me if he changes his mind. With Elisheva in the States, though, I do decide to print out a little note with my address and home phone and her contact numbers in the States, and I leave it on the dashboard in case anything should happen. The cops should know where to find my kids and how to reunite them with my wife.

The next day, at the range, things went smoothly. At one point, though, while five of us were waiting for our turn at the targets, we were hanging out with one of the instructors, and someone asked, "What, exactly, are the rules regarding opening fire?" It's not a bad question. All of us have guarded and have seen that we don't know everyone walking towards the shul, that there are people who do look a little odd but whom, everything else being equal, we probably shouldn't shoot on sight. But how long do you wait? Until they're right next to you? Until they make a move for the door to the shul? It's not clear.

"Well, the rules regarding opening fire are very unclear in these circumstances, it's true," we're told. But one thing has been made clear. If you decide to shoot, don't take any chances. Shoot to kill. No wounding.

Terrific—this should make Shabbat morning very relaxing, indeed. More simmering frogs, I guess.

I flew back to Israel from the States yesterday. In the lounge at JFK, before we boarded, people were talking a bit about the latest attack on the bus at the Megiddo junction and the killing of fourteen soldiers and three other civilians (at least at last count), but not with the same urgency as a year ago, not with the same sense of outrage. It was more idle curiosity, a quick glance at the Web to see if any response was in the offing, but at the same time, a sense that it didn't make much difference what we did, or whether we even did anything. We're used to it. After all, we're just frogs.

No one really wondered whether Sharon will hit back this time. If he's in the mood, he will. If George W. tells him not to, he won't. But you know what? Who cares? What difference does it make? Nothing we do will stop this. It's just the neighborhood we live in, the water we swim in. No matter how hot the water gets.

The frog in the water that's getting hotter and hotter has to hope for one of two things. It has to hope, if frogs hope at all, that either the water cools down, or he can jump out. But we don't know how to cool the water down. We've tried diplomacy, and it didn't work. We've tried massive military invasion, and it didn't work. We've tried to get the world to pressure the guy manning the stove, but to no avail. No one here has any idea what to do. Now we are going to build a fence. A big fence, pen them in, keep them out. But we're building it slowly, with no sense of the urgency that would seemingly accompany such a project if anyone really believed that it would save our lives, save this society. It will help, almost certainly, but for reasons that I cannot really fathom, no one seems in a rush to finish it. Could it be because we're no longer incensed at having to live this way?

. . .

I got to the airport, collected my bags, and met my regular driver out-side the terminal.

"How was your flight?"

"Fine, thanks. What's new here?"

"We've been burying people all day. What else do we do in this place? Here, let me take the suitcase."

Welcome back to the hot water, I guess.

A smart frog would therefore do anything he could to get out of the pot. But we're not frogs. We're Jews, and we ended up in this pot pre-cisely because there was nowhere else to go. The one clear lesson of the twentieth century was that we needed this place, because when push came to shove, we weren't safe anywhere else.

As our plane descended to Tel Aviv yesterday afternoon, the skies were crystal clear and both sides of the plane had a perfect view of Tel Aviv. The pilot got on the loudspeaker and, in both Hebrew and English, told people to look out the window. In English, he said, "We are now crossing the Israeli coastline, and you have a great view of Tel Aviv. . . ." But in Hebrew, he said it somewhat differently, beginning, "*Anu khotzim et khof artzeinu* [We're now crossing the shoreline of our land]." Not our country, not our state, though it can mean that, too. But "our land," the one little strip on this planet that's ours, at least for now. I doubt that the pilot meant to make a terribly Zionist com-ment at that moment. Had he, he probably would have phrased the English differently. No, it's just that the very nature of the Hebrew language communicates our attachment to this place, an attachment that is utterly intact, even if life has become absurd, even if the water is on the verge of boiling.

A twenty-year-old kid was shot and killed yesterday, driving along a road right near the firing range I went to a few weeks ago. His picture is on the front page of the morning paper today. But below the fold. A year ago, his picture would have been bigger, and it would have been above the fold. But that was then. That was when we thought there was something terribly outrageous about a kid getting shot in his car on his way to register for some school courses. Now, we know better. It's not outrageous. It's life.

Frogs might try to leap out of the pot. But most Israelis don't carry two passports; most have nowhere else to go. And most don't want to be anywhere else. Because if we can't be here, the implications for the future of everything we care about are too horrifying to be contemplated. So rather mindlessly, and certainly ineffectively, we'll probably just keep swimming around, knowing that it's getting hotter, and hoping against hope that someone will figure out how we can get out of this before we're boiled to death.

For now, though, a solution to this is far beyond anything that anyone here can even begin to imagine. So, we'll spend the day hanging out and cooking for Shabbat, hoping against hope that maybe next week will be a bit better.

June 2002:
Four Days, No Exit

Speech Stuns Palestinians and Thrills Israelis, Who See End to Arafat

Israeli officials express delight with President Bush's speech demanding ouster of Yasir Arafat as Palestinian leader before US backs establishment of independent Palestinian state; express hope Arafat will finally be ousted and new, peace-seeking Palestinian leadership installed; Palestinian officials are stunned; Israeli officials expressed the hope tonight that perhaps, at last, Yasir Arafat would be ousted and a new, peace-seeking Palestinian leadership installed.

But Ismail Abu Shanab, a leader of the militant group Hamas, which has been behind several recent suicide bombings, expressed a different hope: that perhaps, at last, Yasir Arafat and his Palestinian Authority would let real Palestinian violence explode.

New York Times: Tuesday, June 25, 2002, page A11

There's a reason they call it "terrorism," we've discovered again this week. For while they are, in fact, murderers, and while they do, obviously, kill far too many people, it's possible that the real impact of what they do on Israeli society is the terror and desperation they leave behind in everyone else who isn't killed.

This was quite the week. Tuesday, the bombing of the bus at

Tzomet Pat, about a mile or two from our house. Then Wednesday, the bombing of the bus stop in French Hill, on the other side of town. The city had already been reeling from Tuesday. When they hit on Wednesday, people seemed almost too numb to react. But not too numb to know that we're numb. The attacks, their relentlessness and their impact on literally everything are all anyone seemed able to talk about for the past few days. There was no escaping the talk of the town.

I had a lunch meeting on Thursday with a colleague and friend, someone who's been here for decades, who over the past two years has more than once used these regular lunches of ours to cheer me up, to assure me that things will get better. We met at Yoja, a Thai restaurant on Emek Refa'im, and immediately noticed that there was no guard. We both have clearly stated rules about where we'll eat—I need a kosher restaurant and he doesn't, but neither of us will eat in places where there's no armed guard. But it was hot, and we were tired. We got seated (not difficult, since we were the only ones there) and asked the waitress where the guard was.

"He doesn't come until 7:00 P.M., since that's when we're a bit more full."

"Have you informed the bombers that they're not supposed to blow this place up until 7:00?" my friend asked, trying to engage her in a bit of terrorism-inspired humor. No such luck.

"We don't have a guard. Do you want menus or not?" Israeli service brought to new heights by a national wave of bad moods.

We stayed, figuring that no terrorist was likely to blow himself up just for two guys in an empty restaurant. We decided to order beer with lunch. We asked her what kind of beer they had, and since they'd been out of several of our choices for main dishes, I kind of assumed they'd only have some lousy Israeli beer. But lo and behold, they had ice-cold Corona. Delighted, I said to her, "What a great country!"

Not amused, she looked at me and said, "No, it's not—it sucks."

"Well, you're here, aren't you?" I asked her.

"Not for long, believe me."

If the beer was going to be as icy as her response, it would be delicious, I thought. Great start for a relaxing lunch. As we were taking out our paperwork, my friend said to me, "Listen, we've got a long agenda, but I've got to tell you. I don't feel like being here. I'd much rather just go home, get into bed, put my head under the pillow, and pretend that I don't live in this mess." Which led us to a conversation about an interesting question: Why is it that when they blow up something in Tel Aviv, Hadera, Netanya, or wherever, we get angry and watch the news. But when they blow up something in our town, we become completely depressed, and virtually unable to function?

Elisheva answered that question for me this week when I asked her. It's simple, she said—the closer it gets to home, the more impossible it becomes to pretend that there's anything you can do to protect yourself. When they bomb a city an hour away, it leaves your defenses intact. You assure yourself, "Well, I never go there." But you can't say that when it's five minutes from your house. Then, you have to admit, they could just as well get you, too. And that's when everything begins to come unglued.

After this cheery lunch meeting, I had a meeting with a senior member of our faculty, a meeting I always look forward to but was a bit nervous about this time because I'm late with a chapter for a book that he's editing. It's already come back from the reviewers, and it doesn't need very many changes, but still, I'm late. As he churns out work with the regularity of a Swiss train, I was prepared for a mild chiding about not having the revised version in yet. But I shouldn't have been worried—he lives in Jerusalem, too.

At the beginning of this charming little war we're having, he, who's lived here his whole life (he's probably in his sixties), used to try to get me to see the long-term picture. He once said to me, "You just have to learn to wait these things out. We had frightening days right before the Six Day War, we were panicked during the first days of the Yom Kippur War. But it works out. We just have to be patient." I was actually looking forward to another one of those pep talks, and figured that would compensate for whatever mini-lecture I got about the chapter being late. I went to his office and asked him how he was. "Who knows? This is really out of control. It's hard to see any way out of this. You know, for the first time I can remember, nothing we do is working. I don't know . . . and I'm certainly not getting any work done."

I wasn't sure whether to be delighted that, given that start, I wasn't going to take any crap about the chapter being late, or horrified that he, of all people, was also now in the doldrums. The latter won out.

That meeting and the lunch were Thursday. It wasn't a great day, but luckily, we'd been invited to a wine-tasting party at our cousins' house in Ra'ananah, not far from Tel Aviv, that night. That, we figured, would offer some respite from the news, from Jerusalem, from a city-wide case of depression. We left the kids with instructions not to go out of the house, and drove up to Ra'ananah, armed with our bottle of wine, printouts from the Web about this particular wine, how it's made, etc. We were about six couples at the table, having a great time, studiously avoiding politics. An hour later, we were reading, explaining, looking, sniffing, and tasting the various wines, having a grand ole time. A friend actually called my cell phone from the States to check on how we were, and upon hearing where we were, told me she was glad to hear us all having some fun for once and said goodbye.

We were on the third or fourth printout of six when the woman sitting next to me answered her cell phone. People quieted down for a minute so she could hear, and we heard, of course, only her side of the conversation. "A *pigu'a* [attack]? Where? How many killed? . . . No, of course I'm glad you called. OK, we'll be home in a few hours. You OK? Thanks for calling."

So much for wine tasting. She filled us in on the little she knew about the attack in Itamar. Without saying much, people passed their printed sheets to the head of the table, while another person got up to go turn on the news. The carefree part of the party, it was obvious, was over. We stayed another couple of hours, had a great dinner, and chatted, but nothing was the same. And gradually, of course, the conversation turned to the other question constantly asked here, "What are we going to do?"

Silence, for the most part. No one knows. We just know one

thing—this cannot go on. One person suggested the fence. Another said that every time a bomber kills people like this, we have to exile a whole village. For good. Let these kids know they're causing a lot of suffering for people left behind. Kill their mothers and sisters, or their religious leaders. But do *something*. None of these suggestions would work, I suppose, and we're certainly not about to try any of them, but no matter. You listen to one or two of these discussions, and you realize that this is a country on the very edge of desperation. People here cannot take it anymore, and no one knows how to stop it. Neither does Sharon, of course, but few people here blame him for that. No Monday-morning quarterbacking of the prime minister these days. Everyone admits that they, too, have no idea what to do.

Friday, at least, was quiet. I decided to use the temporary reprieve to tell our neighbors that we're having about sixty people for dinner at our house on Tuesday night, for an end-of-the-year party for the Mandel Jerusalem Fellows. Shouldn't bother them too much, but especially since we've also hired armed guards for the building, I decided to tell them anyway. I happened to hear a group of them downstairs, sweeping the courtyard for Shabbat. Figuring that this would be easier once they were all in one spot, I went downstairs to chat. They were in the midst of conversation, which they continued even as I stood there. One was saying, "My friends say they're not afraid for themselves, they're just afraid for their kids. Some say that they're afraid of their kids growing up without a mother. It makes me feel guilty when people say that. Because, to tell you the truth, I'm not only worried about my kids. I'm worried about me. I don't want to die yet. I really don't."

Oh, hi. We're having a barbecue. That OK with everyone? This didn't seem like quite the moment for *that* conversation, so I said "Hi" and pretended I'd just gone out to get the mail.

Shabbat morning, I had guard duty at shul during the early shift. Initially, I was glad that I'd gotten the earliest shift, figuring that it wouldn't be so hot standing out there for forty-five minutes in the sun. So, I didn't even bring sunglasses. But I'd forgotten that this is the Middle East. It's always hotter than you think it's going to be, and the sun more glaring than you imagine possible at 7:45 in the morning. It was too late to go home and get sunglasses, so I figured I'd just make it through my shift squinting a bit.

The guy who coordinates this whole thing at our shul hands me a rifle and says, "OK, there are some changes in the procedures that I'm legally obligated to tell you about [meaning, This is going to be ridiculous, and you're free to ignore it, but I have to say this]. First of all, no loading a clip into the weapon unless there's a problem. Keep the clip on your belt. Second, here's the sequence of warning shots . . . and third, and this is the new part, if you're really convinced that there's a suicide bomber, they don't want us aiming at their torso, since that could explode the device. Rather, aim for their head or their hands."

It's nice to start Shabbat morning with a good laugh. In the five or so seconds that you probably have once you identify someone as being suspicious, you're supposed to get the clip out of its case, get it loaded into the gun, get a bullet into the chamber, flick off the safety, and aim for the guy's hands. And not miss. That's really great.

For some reason, I was reminded at that moment of how flight attendants always tell you that your seat cushion can be used as a flotation device. Have you ever, ever heard of a plane crash in which someone actually lived and then paddled away from the plane resting comfortably on a seat cushion? Neither have I. I seem to recall that because they float, they're just the first things to be recovered from the crash scene. The bodies get found a bit later.

The situations, it struck me in the blinding sun as I contemplated this new idiocy, were more analogous than it might seem. When the plane's going down, and you're a passenger, there's not much you can do. Ditto here. There's just not much that any of us can do.

Anyway, as I was standing there in the sun, musing on this terrific situation, one of the older men at shul, a survivor of one of the concentration camps (now, *there*'s a euphemism when you think about it—they weren't brought there to be concentrated) walked by on his way to shul. He stopped to say hello, and then looked at the gun and said, "You know, I was the first from my village to go back there after the war. When I got there, I decided that after all that we'd been through, a Jew should never be without a gun. So I bought a carbine and kept it in my house. I loved that gun. But then they started to make laws, and people had to turn in their weapons. So I hid mine in the ceiling rafters of my house. When I decided the next year to come to Palestine, I knew I couldn't bring it with me. So I left it there. A friend wrote me and told me that they tore down the house to build something new. I wonder what they thought when they found the gun. They probably wondered what secret crimes I'd been guilty of." He was silent for a moment, obviously thinking of a place and a time far away. Then he chuckled, and walked away. "Shabbat Shalom," he said.

I wondered briefly how long it takes to be able to laugh at something like that. After shul, I found myself outside with a few people chatting, and soon enough, there were four of us—this same guy, another survivor of Auschwitz, a friend my age, and me. And again, the same conversation—what are we going to do? One of the elderly gentlemen made a suggestion, and the following conversation between the two survivors of Auschwitz ensued.

"When they attack us like this, we have to show them we won't take it. We have to tell them we're going to burn down their village, and then, after they've had a chance to get out, we need to do it." (I decided not to point out that everything here is made of stone, and villages don't burn. They'd have to be bulldozed. This isn't Eastern Europe. But I decided to keep my profound construction-related insights to myself.)

"You think you survived all that, just to become exactly like the Hungarian soldier who burned down our village?"

"It would be different. He did it for sport. He laughed, and enjoyed it. We wouldn't enjoy it, but we have no choice."

"You know what? You think you could do it. But if the time really came, you'd find out that you don't have it in you. That's what makes us different. We can't do those sorts of things."

"OK, we were chosen to be different, but if we're not careful, we will have been chosen to be dead. What we learned is that Jews need to protect themselves, because no one else in the world will really care."

"Well, that's true, but don't overestimate what we can do here."

"So, then, what? Live with this?"

"Perhaps. We've been through worse, you know." And off he walked, saying "Shabbat Shalom" as he disappeared into the crowd.

Another uplifting conversation. And then, Shabbat lunch a couple of hours later. We had friends over, people who've been here seemingly forever, since the early '80s. He talked about how despite everything, he's still one of those old-fashioned Zionists who believes in the absolute necessity of this place, and his faith that it will all work out in the end.

They, like we, have a son who's having a Bar Mitzvah this summer. So gradually, the conversation turned to that, and then, to the question of which of their American family would actually show up here for it. Turns out, most are coming. But then, the woman said that, after the French Hill bombing on Wednesday, she called her mother and told her not to come. Why? we asked. "Because I don't want her to feel pressured to come to this place now. But she said she's coming no matter what. She said, 'If it's good enough for you, then it's good enough for me.'" She paused, and her voice cracked. Suddenly slightly teary, she continued, "You know what the irony is? It's really not good enough for me anymore." Suddenly aware that her children might be listening at the other end of the table, she kind of whispered, "I can't do this much longer."

OK, kids, who wants more dessert?

Ha'Aretz had a cartoon on the editorial page a few days ago showing a mother getting her school-age kids out the door to school, with their backpacks and water bottles, calling after them, "Be careful, kiddos. There are *hatra'ot* [warnings about imminent attacks] for today." The point being, of course, what are they supposed to do? Not go to school? Be prisoners in their houses? There's nothing they can do. Nothing any of us can do.

. . .

I figured that the beginning of the work week would afford a respite from all these conversations, but no such luck. On the way out of work this afternoon, two Fellows and a faculty person were sitting in the lobby, and called me over. "We're talking about the future of the Jewish state. Interested in a brief conversation?" Chuckle. But now that I've gotten used to being depressed, I figured I might as well sit for a moment. Three intelligent people, no ideas.

"We've got to get out of Gaza first. Clear out those settlements, and show them that there's a political solution for them if they just stop these bombings."

"Have you lost your mind? They *know* there's a political solution. They don't want it. Arafat just announced two days ago that he'll take the deal that Barak offered at Camp David. And this, after claiming for two years straight that Barak never offered anything at all."

"Getting out of Gaza won't do anything. We have to get out of the West Bank, too. It's no good for us to be occupiers, it's anti-Zionist [because Zionism, in this read, is about a Jewish majority in a Jewish country, and keeping the territories destroys the idea of a Jewish majority], and it isn't working."

"So what happens when we pull out?"

"They get a country, so what? I'm happy for them to have a state."

"But why, after all this, do you believe that they'll be satisfied with that? Don't you understand that they want one state here, stretching from the Jordan to the Mediterranean? They'll just use the cover of a state to mass arms, and wait for their next opportunity to unleash one of these terrorist wars. Or get some Stingers and shoot down an El Al passenger jet from just a few miles away once we get back to the '67 borders."

"If I accept what you're saying, then there's no hope."

"The fact that it means that there's no hope doesn't mean that I'm wrong, does it?"

"No, it doesn't. But if they don't want coexistence, and they're really willing to keep sending suicide bombers into the country, then we have to admit that even a wall won't work, that we'll live this way forever, and eventually, they'll win."

"What's so surprising to you about that? They had their chance for an agreement at Camp David, generous or not. But they chose to walk away and not continue the talks. Don't you get it? When the moment of truth came, they proved that they'd rather be revolutionaries than statesmen. And we're still trying to figure out how to get them back to the table. They're laughing at us. Time's on their side, and we're busy squabbling amongst ourselves as to where, exactly, the fence should be. We're absurd!"

One Fellow, writing a Ph.D. dissertation on civic education in Israel, quietly mused, "I think I've just figured out why I'm not making enough progress on this thing. It's a f—ing joke. We're not going to be around long enough to educate anyone about anything." I'd had about as much of this as I could take, and wished them all a nice afternoon.

In the absence of any long-term strategy, it seems the government is going to try to at least put the kibosh on the suicide bombers. Won't save the country in the long run, but just might make the next few weeks a bit more sane. We woke up this morning to headlines in *Ha'Aretz* that today they are beginning a massive call-up of reserve soldiers, who will be "training" for a few days and then sent to the territories. The *New York Times* is reporting today that Israel is preparing a "decisive and crushing" response to the recent wave of attacks, something far more powerful than Defensive Shield a few months ago.

If it's true, and if it happens, it'll be ugly. There probably won't be massacres, any more than there were in Jenin last time. But innocent people will be killed, and the pictures will not be pretty. But I don't expect that many people here will lose sleep over that. We would have, at the beginning. When it was suggested that Muhammad Jamal Al Dura, the Palestinian kid killed in cross fire while crouching with his father at the very beginning of this whole mess, might have been killed by Israeli fire, people here were beside themselves (German TV has since analyzed the entire tape, which most foreign media refused to release, and has claimed that he had to have been killed by Palestinian shooters.) "How could that happen?" our friends wondered back then. It couldn't possibly have been intentional, could it? How did we not stop firing if we knew there was a kid there?

But that was almost two years ago. A lot has died since then. A lot of Palestinians, many Israelis. Most of the liberalism that used to characterize Israeli society. And the sense that we ought to care what the world thinks. They've killed a lot more than almost 500 Israelis. They've actually killed who we used to be. They have, quite literally, terrorized all of that right out of us. And, it's become pretty obvious, they've killed hope, too.

So, it's not likely to be a pretty week. If the army actually does something, the world will pounce. CNN will have a field day, Saeb Erekat will talk about how they just want peace but we've destroyed their infrastructure. Colin Powell will urge us to exercise restraint (just as the U.S. has been doing in Afghanistan?). The Europeans will wring their hands, secretly delighted that they can turn the focus from their past to our conflict, and the pope will pray for peace. Kofi Annan will not try very hard to hide the fact that he hates us. The Arab states won't pressure Arafat, the United States won't freeze the Palestinian Authority's assets, the Palestinians will not decide they want a better future and get rid of Arafat—for their good, not for ours.

But ironically, we'll feel better. Because this paralysis is strangling the country, economically and in terms of morale. So we have to do something, anything. It won't really matter whether it works in the long run. Something has to change in the short run. Buses have to stop blowing up. Hitchhiking gathering spots can't turn into cemeteries. Fathers can't bury their wives and three of their children, with two others in the hospital, all in one day, as was the case in Itamar this week.

The other day, on the way home from an errand, Avi asked me in the car, "Abba, would you allow me to ride a bus?"

"You know that I do," I told him.

"Well, Ema won't, you know. Why will you?"

I was about to explain that I wasn't about to let "them" win, that I wasn't about to have us be safe because we can afford a car when lots of people here can't, that I wasn't about to hide in our house all day, but I didn't know how to say it without making it seem that I don't care about him. So I was quiet.

"You know what I think?" he suddenly added. "I think that when grown-ups really love Israel, they're even ready for their children to get killed for it. That's what I think."

And that's when I knew for sure. Something has to give. We've got to end this. No matter what it takes. Because, quite frankly, I'm not prepared to have my kid think that.

Enough is enough.

July 2002:
Have a Magical Day

7 Killed, 17 Hurt in Ambush of Bus by Palestinians

Palestinians in Israeli army uniforms carry out brazen daytime ambush of bus near Israeli settlement of Immanuel, killing seven people; 17 people are wounded as gunmen set off bomb and then hurl grenades, raking bus with gunfire to kill passengers trapped inside; an 11-month-old baby, her father and grandmother were among the dead, hospital officials said.

New York Times: Wednesday, July 17, 2002, page A1

I had to call one of the Disney hotels in Florida the other day, and after getting the information I needed, I thanked the woman I was speaking with. "You're welcome," she replied. "Have a magical day."

I was completely stunned. Of all the things that I've ever been wished, "Have a magical day" was undoubtedly the most absurd. I had no idea what to say. "You too"? I've never wished anyone a magical day, and didn't feel like starting then. It was one of those moments that reminded me how different life is in these two parts of the world, America with Disney, and Israel with, well, the news.

Here, we don't wish each other a "magical day." The new common greeting is "Have a quiet day." It's not a reference to noise, of course, but a euphemism. Even the evening news anchor, who until a year and a half ago used to end his broadcast with *"Erev tov"* ("Have a good evening") now says *"Erev shaket le-kulanu"* ("Let's hope we all have a quiet night").

It was, in fact, quiet for a few weeks. An uneasy quiet, to be sure, with a nervous second or two each time we turned on the news because we knew it wouldn't last forever. But it was quiet. People were coming out of their shells. The guard at the rebuilt Moment Cafe, which I drive by often, first got rid of the machine gun, and then, a few days later, was replaced by a kid who looked like he was sixteen years old. He was probably older, but he sure didn't look it. For a second, I was bothered that so quickly after a massacre at that very spot, people were letting their guard down. But then, I realized, that's exactly what's so unbelievable about the people here. They (we) have developed an ability to filter out huge chunks of reality so that life can go on. It's denial in a big way, but it works.

Friday afternoon, as I was doing some last-minute buying before Shabbat, I couldn't help but notice how full and bustling the sidewalks were. Everyone seemed to be scurrying with challah, flowers, and last-minute groceries. The coffee shops were packed, people were idling about on the streets, all as if nothing has been happening here for almost two years, all as if there wasn't a chance—even though there was—that one of the passersby might suddenly blow himself up. People just chose not to think about that. We're choosing to live. "Choose Life," Deuteronomy says. I guess we are.

But this choice to live requires massive amounts of denial. Denial of the constant danger, yes, but more than that. Part of what we've become adept at denying is the cost that having this quiet (until the last couple of days in Immanual and Tel Aviv, at least) is exacting from "the other" population. We know that just a few miles from here, 700,000 Palestinians are being kept under strict curfew, that the IDF has recaptured virtually all of the West Bank's major population centers, that the massive military presence just increases the hatred that they feel for us (if that's even possible), and that this is no solution. All of this is pretty clear, at least to the saner parts of this population.

But that's where the filter comes in—people don't think about it. It's not that we don't care, or that anyone takes lightly the brutal conditions created by curfews in this sort of oppressive heat. Rather, it's simply that now that our kids can walk the streets without fear, now that the newspapers don't (or didn't, until two days ago) have pictures of the latest victims on the front page each day, now that we don't have to worry what our kids will see if they turn on the TV when we're not around. We're breathing easier. And given a choice between being terrified and kinder, or a bit more relaxed and more brutal, most Israelis have acquiesced, I think, to a choice for the latter. Not a choice we're necessarily proud of, but to be perfectly honest, not one that keeps us up at night either.

In the midst of this calm, as people return to what resembles a quasi-normal way of life (until the next incident), this country has a way of reminding you that there's nothing normal about it. Especially on a day like today, Tisha B'Av, when we're fasting and mourning the destruction of Jerusalem and its Temple twice in the past, I'm struck by how much this country wants to stay alive.

At certain moments, it becomes clear that we're not entirely certain how to do that. Avi asked me not long ago, one morning as he was reading the paper, "What do they put in the paper in countries that aren't in a war?" It was a devastating question, but in these past few weeks, he's gotten his answer. Sort of. True, one can get easily discouraged about the ultra-Orthodox parties forcing the Knesset to change the day when daylight saving time will end so Yom Kippur will be over an hour earlier, despite the damage to the country's economy. Or one can be disheartened by the law recently passed in a Knesset reading that permits certain villages to be open only to Jews, allowing people to refuse to sell to Arabs there. Some people I know are distraught—I'm not. It's not that I like any of that. But rather than be distraught, I see a country in the midst of an existential crisis still trying to figure out how to be Jewish and democratic, how to be normal enough to survive and not so normal that there's no point in surviving. Sure we'll make bad decisions along the way. No one said that this project would be easy. With all due respect to Disney, it's not magic that is going to make this work.

A week ago today, we went to my cousin Eitan's "graduation" ceremony upon finishing basic training. It was a pretty brief ceremony, and a bit short on Jewish content for my taste, but it was still profoundly moving. They're just kids, these hundred or so "soldiers" who were lined up on the stage being congratulated for being professional, skilled, dedicated, disciplined, etc. Were they Americans, they'd have been spending this summer as their last break before college, or their summer between freshman and sophomore years.

But not these kids. The night before, they'd marched 50 kilometers in a heat that even the night couldn't dissipate, and had arrived at the Latrun army base in the morning just before the ceremony to get a bit cleaned up. They weren't dirty by the time we saw them, but they were haggard and exhausted. Happy to be at the ceremony, I'm sure, but obviously wanting a bed more than anything else. There were some speeches, a few songs, like "Machar"—"Tomorrow"—vestiges of an earlier Israel where tomorrow always looked brighter, where anything was possible, and Hatikva. They got their colored caps, tossed them in the air in a vague imitation of the Annapolis naval academy, and then picnicked with their families before going back to their units.

Midway through the ceremony, I glanced at Elisheva, who I could tell was upset. I asked her what was wrong, and she said she was fine. But I pressed, and she said, with just a hint of tear-filled eyes, "I didn't have kids for them to have to do this." I understood what she meant. We've got one daughter who'll be doing something like this in two years, and a son who'll be doing exactly this in five. And then another one.

I didn't want to disagree with her during the ceremony, so I didn't say anything. But I didn't agree. It's true, of course, that when we were having our kids in the San Fernando Valley, we didn't imagine that this was how they'd have to spend a few years of their lives, just when all their American friends are having the most carefree years of their existence. But it's not true, it seemed to me, that we didn't have kids for this. We did. We had kids who we dreamed would be part of something profoundly important, who would live lives dedicated to a tapestry much more grand than the years that they'll actually be physically alive.

And I looked at the background, just behind the stage where these kids were lined up. It's the old British police barracks, the Latrun fortress, that the Arab legions possessed during the War of Independence, enabling them to control the road to Jerusalem and thus preventing the Hagganah from breaking the siege on Jerusalem. Ben Gurion was adamant that the fortress be captured, and ordered the Hagganah's Seventh Brigade to take it. Yigal Yadin, the unit's commanding officer (who would later become an archaeologist whose best-known work would be the uncovering of Masada), insisted that they weren't ready, that many of the men didn't even have water bottles. But Ben Gurion insisted, and the fortress was attacked. After hours in the blistering heat, the attack failed. The men collapsed in the heat, and as they rose to get up off the ground, they were picked off by Arab snipers. Evacuating them—and the dead—took the better part of a day.

Another attack was launched shortly thereafter, with not much more success. Eventually, of course, the fortress fell, but it's an area with a great deal of blood soaked into the surrounding hills. On Thursday, as we sat in the amphitheater watching these kids graduate basic training, you could still see the shell- and bullet-pocked walls of the fortress right behind them. I wondered if the relatively new recruits knew where they were standing. I hoped that they did. And yes, I thought, this is exactly why we had kids—to be part of the larger story of this place and this people and of the struggle to unite the two. I can't think of any better reason.

That Shabbat, we were told on Friday night that on Shabbat morning there would be a break in services, for a Torah scroll from Berlin was being brought "home" to Israel. There's a long story to this scroll, which an uncle of one of the synagogue's members had taken with him to Antwerp when he fled Berlin. It eventually disappeared after his death and was subsequently found by our friend when he went to look for it in Antwerp. So that morning, before the Torah reading, we took a break. A small group went down the street and around the corner to the apartment where the Torah was being kept, and then, using a *tallit* as a *chuppah* (the traditional way of bringing a Torah to a synagogue), danced and sang as the Torah was brought to the shul. It was hot then, too, but everyone braved the heat. Most people danced, but as we got closer to the front courtyard of the synagogue, I saw the group of survivors of Auschwitz, who have been part of this shul since they got here in 1948, standing on the side, watching. There was something haunting about the looks in their eyes. I wondered what this sight made them remember. What lives cut short were suddenly coming back to them? Parents they never got to say goodbye to? Brothers and sisters who went up smokestacks, without even a burial spot? Children they couldn't protect when it mattered most? I wondered what it felt like for them to have one more piece of that shattered past brought home.

This morning, Tisha B'Av, that was the Torah we read from. After the regular service, and even after the hour and a half of Tisha B'Av *kinnot* (dirges), our shul added a few pieces about the Shoah. The last of them was read by one of those same survivors, who insisted on standing in the center of the room and reading it aloud, word after carefully enunciated word, as his voice began to crack and he could barely continue. Haltingly and with enormous effort, he made it through the whole thing, as the rest of the group was completely and utterly silent. He finished, but didn't move. He just stood there in the middle of the room, frozen. No one budged, and we just waited for him to go back to his seat. He did, but not before, mustering whatever voice he had left, he cried out, *"Am Yisrael Chai!"*, took out a handkerchief, started to sob, and, his body still wracked by uncontrollable grief half a century later, made his way back to the mourning stool he'd been sitting on.

Those are the moments that remind us all why we're here. Musing a bit about this day devoted to mourning all that's happened to

Jerusalem throughout the years, and reflecting back on that basic-training graduation ceremony at Latrun of just a week ago, on the long road this man had traveled, and on the road traveled by the Torah that has now joined him, it struck me: he's home. So is that Torah. And so are we. And that, for me, is magical enough.

August 2002:
Before They Kill Us All

At Least 7 Killed as Militants Bomb Jerusalem Campus

Powerful bomb tears apart bustling cafeteria at Hebrew University in Jerusalem killing seven people, including at least three Americans, and wounding more than 80; bomb was hidden in bag and left on table by Palestinian militants; school is one of few places where Israeli Jews and Israeli Arabs still mix, which has given students there sense of safety even as new violence threatens elsewhere in city.

New York Times: Thursday, August 1, 2002, page A1

We were at a *bris* today, a wonderful and much needed reprieve from the spate of death and attacks that has enveloped everyone here. It was a particularly moving morning, as many of the people gathered to welcome the new baby were friends of two of the Hebrew University students killed last week. The move from mourning to celebration wasn't easy, but it was welcome nonetheless.

There's a point in the *bris* when the baby always starts to cry. It has nothing to do with pain, for it happens long before the *mohel* actually does anything. Usually, it's because the baby's diaper is taken off, and he doesn't like being cold. In the States, people panic when the baby cries, and the *mohel* almost always makes some sort of joke to put people at ease.

The *mohel* today didn't make a joke. The baby just cried. Not loud, not long, but he cried. It didn't matter, though, because most of the adults were crying, too. Because of last week, because of last month, because of this whole year, and the one before that. And, frankly, because of what's probably going to be next year, too. We stood there with tears in our eyes, and without a joke to ease the pain, because the phrase uttered at the *bris*, *"le-hachniso bivrito shel avraham avinu"*— "to enter him into the covenant of Abraham, our forefather," is no laughing matter. It's no joke to be part of this covenant here. It makes you a target. It gives you enemies. It means that you have to constantly remind yourself that you're here for a reason, that you're here because you believe in something.

People who believe in as much as most of the people assembled at the *bris* this morning believe in didn't need a joke to make themselves feel more comfortable. We've long since learned that life isn't about comfort. It's about choosing meaning. And today, overlooking the Judean hills and the Old City, looking out on an extraordinarily beautiful view that masks the seething hatred and flaming passions of the people who inhabit that view, a brand-new, innocent baby joining this beleaguered but still-passionate community was exactly what everyone needed.

At one point in the *bris,* it's customary for those gathered to say, "Just as he has entered the covenant, so may he enter a life of Torah, of marriage, and of good deeds." What a simple prayer. That he live his life as part of a tradition, that he try to raise a family, and that he be decent. There's not much that's more important than that. At least to us.

When news of the Hebrew University bombing spread a few days ago, the TV newscasts showed partying in Gaza, with Palestinian adults and children celebrating the deaths and the mutilations. As if anything in the world was made better by this carnage. Those reports and the photos of those celebrations shook many people up here as much as the horrific deaths of the victims themselves. Tragically, we've become used to the death, to the funerals, to the fear that follows. But there are still sights that shock us. Like watching people taking joy in the blood, the death, the mutilated bodies of those who will live maimed for the rest of their lives. What in the world is there to celebrate?

I wonder. Do they also say "May he be committed to a life of good deeds" when their sons are born? Would they mean it, if they did?

When Salah Shehadeh was killed by the IDF in Gaza not long ago, and innocent kids were killed in the attack, Israel was divided. There were those who thought that the attack was stupid, or immoral, or unwise. And there were those who disagreed, saying "War's war—he wants to hide in a civilian center, that's what's going to happen."

But even those who said that this was the inevitable result of war didn't exult. No one did. Not one person here whom I saw or heard took any satisfaction from the deaths of those children. There was only pervasive horror at what had happened, even for those who tried to justify it. It was horrible. Plain, simple, horrible. We didn't celebrate; the mere idea never crossed anyone's mind. And that, quite frankly (all political correctness aside), is what makes us better than them. Much better. It's not what we're taught to say, those of us reared in the grand traditions of American liberalism and multiculturalism. But the problem, we're learning, is that those traditions work best in the placid environs of American Ivy League universities, and somewhat less well in cities in which people have a habit of being blown to bits because they decided to eat lunch.

Last week, I got a chance in the middle of the day to read through that morning's edition of *Yedi'ot Achronot*, one of Israel's three main dailies. It contained the summary of an interview with Sheik Yassin, the "spiritual" leader of Hamas. Yassin starts out by saying that Hamas will agree to a cease-fire (even if true, it's not quite clear what that's worth, since even Shimon Peres—still the arch-leftist who thinks that Oslo was a good idea and can still be resurrected—admitted that day that there are twelve Palestinian terror groups operating now, most of whom probably wouldn't abide by the cease-fire) under three conditions: Israel must return to the pre-Intifada borders, must release the

Hamas militants whom it's captured in recent days, and must stop the assassinations of Hamas leaders and the destruction of their homes. Doesn't sound bad—maybe he's softening up, at long last.

But then you read the rest of the article. Asked whether he's ultimately willing to have a Palestinian entity coexist with Israel if Israel would return to the pre-June 1967 borders, Yassin refuses to commit. Instead, he offers the following "clarification" of his offer for a cease-fire. "Israel was born in violence, and Israel will die in violence. Jews have no right to be on Palestinian land. What right do they have? Because 4,000 years ago in the time of Abraham a small band of refugees came here from Iraq? This land belongs to the Palestinians." That's the very same guy who's offering us a cease-fire. That's the guy who, no matter what we figure out with the Palestinian Authority, will still run Hamas, and who, no matter what we do, will always be able to blow up buses like they did the morning that article appeared. That's the neighbor we're going to be stuck with for as long as we can imagine. Not just him. But thousands and thousands of people just like him.

The relentlessness of this is starting to get to all of our kids. The TV was on the morning after last week's bus bombing, and as I was working at the computer, I didn't even notice that Talia, now just shy of sixteen, had come into the study and was watching the coverage, something we usually don't let the kids do. When I realized she was in the room, sitting on the sofa and taking it all in silently, I glanced at the TV screen that I'd been ignoring. There it was, as always: pictures of the destroyed bus, with video feeds showing helicopters evacuating the most grievously wounded and being greeted by teams of emergency crews at helipads on hospital roofs. And bodies, too, still lying by the skeleton of the bus, partly covered by sheets on the ground, legs and feet sticking out, gruesomely arranged waiting for some coroner to come and pick them up.

She sat there stone-faced, saying absolutely nothing, but it was clear that something had to be happening inside. Was it fear? Fury? Disgust? So I said to her, "You know, this will be over some day. I really believe that." And she turned to me and said, "I know it will. The question is whether it will be over before or after they kill us all."

She was silent for a few moments, and then she said, "Have you noticed how some posters now refer to the victims of the attacks? They print their names, and then instead of following their name with '*z'l*' [*zikhronam livrachah*—may their memory be a blessing], they print '*hy'd*' [*hashem yikom damam*—may God avenge their blood]. We're quite a peace-loving bunch, aren't we?"

Just when everything seems so dark that it's hard to move on, I'm reminded of how different we are from them. Even in the face of all this, even when she's worried that "they're going to kill us all," my daughter is worried that we're too filled with the desire for revenge, that there are elements in our society more militant than she has the stomach for. She may not yet know that *"hashem yikom damam"* is a classic Hebrew phrase, not the invention of modern Israelis. (She probably also doesn't know that some people interpret the phrase to mean that *God*—and not we—must be the one to avenge the blood, making it a kind of pacifist statement for some.) But no matter. She's decided that despite everything that they're doing to us, and to her world, our language is too violent. She knows what she believes, and it's not what they believe.

Last Saturday night, after Havdalah, I turned on the computer to check the Web and to see the news. The *Ha'Aretz* web site showed a photo of Israeli soldiers searching the bedroom of a frightened Palestinian family in Shechem, the soldiers in full battle gear and the mother and her child cowering in the corner. Avi was appalled. "Do we really have to do that?" he wanted to know. "I don't know," I told him, "I really don't know. People like us just don't have all the facts."

He thought about that for a moment, and didn't say anything. But then he said, "I would hate it if anyone came in our house and searched us like that. Whoever did that to us, I'd hate them forever."

And I was thrilled. Not thrilled, of course, that my kid has to wrestle with the question of whether the country he's moved to sometimes uses too much force—for that is a real question, probably not discussed enough in a country simply exhausted by death and fear. But I was glad that he still cares about being decent, about doing the right thing. I'm relieved that even though my kids have been scared—really scared—more days than I can count in the past two years, they still care about what's right, about what's honorable, about what being a Jew demands of them. Despite all the carnage, they're simply constitutionally unable to celebrate death, anyone's death—and that makes all the difference.

This will be over one day, that I know. And it will be before they kill us all, long before. When that happens, we'll have a society populated by people like our kids, kids who, despite everything, still hate death, still revere life. Our enemies, on the other hand, at least many of them, will have a new generation that was raised to celebrate when innocent American kids get butchered for the crime of visiting Israel, a generation taught that the way to resolve territorial dispute is to blow up buses, to shoot up the center of town, to bomb cars on the roadside.

So, I remind myself even on the worst days, and we've had more than enough of those recently, that we still have much to celebrate. Because we, too, have babies. But we don't want them to be martyrs. We just want them to live. To inherit and to preserve a tradition. To make families. And to be decent.

Standing in the crowd at the *bris* this morning, even as I watched a room full of adults crying not just for joy, but for all the pain and sorrow that this community has experienced in recent days, I just knew that things here will work out OK in the end. Not soon, but one day. And if our kids come out of this still hating death, still loving life, still desperate to be decent, no matter what price we'll have paid in the interim, we'll have won.

We'll have some of this land, and we'll still have our souls. And that will be enough.

October 2002:
Yehiel Tchlenov Was (Mostly) Right

Remember Yehiel Tchlenov? He was the guy who about a century ago, at the Sixth Zionist Congress, led the opposition to Theodor Herzl's idea that the Jewish state be created in Uganda. Having tired of the opposition to his idea of building the State in Palestine, Herzl began to endorse a "Uganda Plan," figuring it might be easier to get support for a Jewish state in a largely unpopulated portion of Uganda than in the politically complex Palestine. Tchlenov opposed the idea vociferously, and led a large delegation that stormed out of the hall. In the end, the "Uganda Plan" died, and Tchlenov, a too little known figure in Zionist history, got his way.

A century later. . . . It's been relatively quiet here for the past month or two. There've been some shootings and a few miraculously foiled suicide bombers. But mostly, it's "pre-Iraq time-out." We're off the front page of the *New York Times,* having been supplanted by the suburban Washington sniper, the Bali resort explosion, the apparently attacked French tanker, and American soldiers fired upon in Kuwait. If you didn't live here, you'd assume that "all was quiet on the mid-Eastern front."

But even when it's quiet, this is a war zone. Jerusalem traffic is routinely made even worse than usual by surprise security roadblocks all over town, the kids watch every adult get searched everywhere they go, and periodically, sitting outside on our terrace, they can still hear and see the army helicopters chugging their way over to the Old City and to the West Bank beyond, to do what, one can only imagine.

On Sukkot, we decided to give the kids a reprieve from all this. We figured they deserved a few days of life as it had been "before." So off we went to the Galilee for part of Sukkot to get away from it all. And it was in the Galilee, watching the kids run around and hike and relax as they never get to do in security-conscious city life, that it struck me that Yehiel Tchlenov had been right.

Even though we were staying in Tzippori, in the middle of the Galilee, we decided to take the kids to Rosh Hanikra, on the western edge of the country, at the Lebanese border. Micha had never been there, and it had been years since the big kids had gone. We figured that Micha would like the cable car, the cliffs, and the caves—and even the big kids were actually anxious to go back. So off we trekked to the northwest corner of the country (still—time-wise—a shorter drive than from our first house in North Hollywood to LAX), bought tickets and settled in for the introductory movie.

For the most part, the film explained the process of erosion, how the caves had been formed over thousands of years, yadda yadda yadda. But before it actually got to that part, the movie opened with a brief history of the various people who had lived in this place. And it quoted a midrash about how Abraham had come by that spot on his way from

Ur Kasdim (in what would today be Iraq) to Canaan, and then, on the screen, flashed the biblical verse that reads "And to your descendants will I give this land." I stole a glance at the kids at that moment; all three were glued to the screen. And I wondered, "Do they get it?" There's no such thing as a plain old nature reserve in Israel. There's no place here where history—their history—isn't at the core. Every national park and nature reserve tells *their* story, not someone else's. That's why this country couldn't have been built anywhere else. That's why it had to be here. That's why Yehiel Tchlenov was right.

Elisheva was also struck by that verse. On the way out of the movie, she said to me in a hushed tone after the kids had gone ahead, "That must be pretty off-putting for the Israeli Arabs who come here, no?" But I really wasn't in the mood for one of those angst-ridden conversations; the whole idea of the vacation, I thought, was to get away from that. So we didn't pursue it, though I knew she was right.

The kids explored the caves and the cliffs, and eventually made their way to the very southern end of the site. There, they found the tunnel the British had dug through the mountains, and the train tracks that were to be part of the rail line from Egypt to Europe, another one of those grand colonizing British projects. But this is Israel, and if there's a tunnel and British train tracks, there's got to be more. And sure enough, a few minutes later, the kids were reading the large explanation about how the Hagganah blew up one of the bridges on this spot before the War of Independence, to ensure that the Lebanese didn't use the tracks to ferry troops in for what was shaping up to be the battle over the Galilee.

So much for getting away from it all. Micha, of course, was fascinated by the rusted girders of what used to be the bridge, and wanted to know where they put the bomb, etc. But we could see the older kids processing, suddenly reminded that there's not a square inch of this country that hasn't been contested, that hasn't been fought over. Reminded that when you live in Israel, even on vacation, you can't get away from it all. Because you don't tell the story here, you live it. That's why Uganda made no sense. That's why Tchlenov was right.

The next day, they wanted to go horseback riding. We were OK with that, but thought that they should also see Tzippori National Park and its archaeological site, which they hadn't "done" in a few years. But there was no way we'd have time for both, and the kids made it clear that this was a no-brainer. They wanted the horses. "OK," I figured. "It's vacation. Whatever." So we went to the place where you rent the horses, hopped up, and set out for a trek out to wherever. Our guide led us up some hills and down, a turn here, a turn there, and at one point, got off her horse to open a gate that blocked the road.

We continued along and suddenly, we realized that we were actually in Tzippori National Park. Amazingly, the kids remembered all the sites. Sitting on our horses, Elisheva and I could hear them explaining to each other about the amphitheater and the various mosaics that had been uncovered. They remembered the stories that they'd heard about Rabbi Yehudah HaNasi, the redactor of the Mishnah, who lived here and is said to be buried here. And I thought of Tchlenov again. Here, you can't even go on a horseback ride without running into history. As complicated as it's always been here, and as sad as it's gotten over the past couple of years, there's still nowhere else we could have done this, nowhere else on earth where it would have made sense for the Jews to try to build a home.

The problem with this place, though, is that it's much too complicated for such unabashed self-assuredness to last very long. The day after we got back, we had a wedding to go to. The bride, a friend of mine, is an Israeli Palestinian, a Muslim, who was marrying a guy one quarter Syrian, one quarter German, and two quarters I-don't-remember-what. The reception was to take place at the Ambassador Hotel, in East Jerusalem. It's been years since we've done anything in East Jerusalem other than drive through on the main drag, and this was a neighborhood we certainly didn't know, a hotel we'd never seen. Trying to find the right street in Arab East Jerusalem in the dark of night, I was reminded of that opening scene from *The Bonfire of the Vanities,* and hoped that things would end somewhat differently in this case. We did eventually find the hotel but, anxious not to have to park on one of the unlit side streets, decided to leave the car right in front of the hotel in flagrant violation of the parking rules. I figured that if we got a ticket, I'd contest it (if you can even do that here), and the judge would have to understand why we did what we did. (We didn't get a ticket.)

By the time we got there, the party was in full swing (the ceremony had been a few days earlier). The front of the hotel seemed pretty deserted, with no one in sight. We walked in, and still saw nobody, but we could hear the music coming from somewhere not too far away. Still, though, it wasn't clear where to go. So I walked up to the person sitting behind the registration desk and asked him where the party was. He just stared at me, and said nothing. Momentarily, I couldn't figure out what was going on, until I realized . . . he didn't speak Hebrew (or wouldn't speak Hebrew—I'm still not certain). So I tried English, and he told us how to find the party.

In the hall, the same thing. We had a gift with us, and I handed it to one of the hotel personnel, and told her it was fragile. Again, the blank stare. Again, I tried English, and again, it worked. Here we were, scarcely ten minutes from our house, and we might as well have been in a different country, a different world. More than thirty-five years after Israel conquered this territory in 1967, it's still not Israel. No matter what anyone says. It's a different universe, a universe where people like us are not particularly loved.

We were not the only Jews in the room, but I was certainly the only person wearing a *kippah*. As Elisheva and I made our way through the crowded room to get to the couple and to congratulate them, all eyes were on us. I don't know if people thought that we were Israeli security, or if we'd gotten hopelessly lost, but there were hundreds of eyes staring at us with a "what the hell are *you* doing here" kind of look. The plain and simple hatred on the faces of some was simply unmistakable. Elisheva, not easily rattled, reached for my hand and whispered to me, "If looks could kill . . ."

The music and the dancing continued, but for anyone who had seen us, we were suddenly the center of attraction. Not, shall we say, the most comfortable moment we've ever had in our lives. But we had already crossed the Rubicon, so we forged ahead to the bride, whom we spotted first. She greeted us very warmly, and then gave Elisheva a hug and a kiss. The crowd relaxed. Then the bride's father, whom I know from some research I've been doing in their village, came over and gave me a huge bear hug, thanked us for coming, and told us how pleased he was that we were there. Now, the people staring at us seemed a bit more relaxed, though no less perplexed. We chatted with the bride and groom for a few moments, and then went over to a table where there were a few empty seats.

The people at our table, mostly Arab men apparently married to European women—this was a pretty upscale Arab crowd, lots of very fine suits, and women in everything from the traditional headdress to very stylish European clothing—didn't have much interest in talking to us, to put it mildly. So for a while we chatted with a few other people whom we knew who'd come over to say hi, including the bride's sister-in-law, who's my Arabic tutor, and a few other family members. But after a while, we were left to our own devices, and I found myself studying the crowd and thinking about the situation we'd just walked into.

I realized, suddenly, that this was the first time in months that I'd gone into a hotel without being searched. There was, it dawned on me, no security at the hotel. The irony struck me. If you want to go to a place where you don't have to be worried about being blown up, just go to a completely Arab neighborhood in East Jerusalem. Those hotels don't blow up.

And I looked out at the men in the room, and realized that none of them had guns. We hadn't been to a wedding or Bar Mitzvah or any other celebration in years without having a good portion of the men (and the occasional woman) being very visibly armed, making what has always struck me as a particularly stupid political statement at these sorts of affairs. A few, perhaps, need to be armed to get home safely, but very few. Most are making a point. A point, by the way, that's not at all lost on the people in whose company we now found ourselves.

That *these* people weren't armed wasn't a choice, obviously. "We" don't allow "them" to carry guns. So, for a moment, with no visible security at the hotel and no guns at the party, it seemed like we'd finally left the war zone. But the truth was, we'd gone to its very center. The hatred on the faces of many of the people—even after the family had greeted us—made the point. There are two peoples here, and both are completely convinced that this is their home.

And that's why Yehiel Tchlenov was only mostly right. He was right that it didn't make any sense for us to try to build this country anywhere else, but he and his fellow founding Zionist ideologues did a remarkably lousy job of thinking through how to relate to the people who were already here. It's an unfortunate tradition that many Jews have continued, on both sides of the Atlantic Ocean.

Our kids weren't invited to the wedding, and I was partially relieved. I think they would have been petrified going to that hotel. But I also wish that they could have been there. To see another world that exists under our very noses. To see another people who also think this is home. To remember that when the movie at Rosh Hanikra quotes the verse that says "To your descendants will I give this land," it's a bit more complicated than that. There are all sorts of descendants here.

Generations after this all started, those generations are stuck here, still fighting it out. Most of us are stuck in our own worn-out narrative about whose "fault" this is, and no one's making any progress. They're waiting for us to get tired of dying so we just pack up and leave, and our government's policy is to hammer them so relentlessly that they give up and accept whatever solution we offer. But neither of those scenarios will come to be.

It's quiet these days, because we're all waiting for Iraq to happen. But Iraq either won't happen, or it will eventually end, and either way, we'll be back where we were before this "quasi-time-out." And then what?

Maybe what we all need to start doing is to remember that even when we're right, we're only mostly right. The challenge is to take seriously both Tzippori and the Ambassador Hotel, both Yehiel Tchlenov and the people whose hatred for us stems—at least in large part—from the fact that our society doesn't think about them, or their story, or the ways in which this place is also their history.

One thing is clear. Unless we start thinking beyond Tchlenov and his cronies, we'll soon be back to where we were a few months ago: back to the simmering cauldron of hatred, back to the killing, back to the dying. Our kids will continue to live in fear, the economy will collapse even further, and Israel's fragile democratic tradition will be put to tests it may not withstand.

And then, if we're not careful, the "Uganda Plan" won't have been the only plan not to have survived.

November 2002:
Olive Picking in the
Wild West (Bank)

On the off chance that you ever get bored in the Middle East—not likely, of course—you can always ask your kids what they're learning in history class. It's bound to elicit interesting conversation.

Micha's fourth-grade history class is now learning about the Hagganah, the Palmach, the Irgun, and the Lechi, all the Jewish armed groups that worked to get the British out of here a few decades ago. He had to memorize all of them, and as Elisheva reviewed them with him, she mentioned to him that the Irgun was the group that had blown up the King David Hotel in July 1946. Micha was suddenly perplexed. "But Ema, was that a good thing? I mean, I *love* the King David Hotel."

Ah, the miracle of ambivalence, a sentiment in short supply in this part of the world. Most people are so sure of themselves that large doses of righteous indignation are required to participate in political discourse these days. So I stay out of it. Indeed, when the government started to fall apart ten days ago, I decided that I would pay it no attention. If grown men (no sexism here—this time, all the relevant players were men) wanted to act like a bunch of turkeys, I figured, that's their right. But it's also my right to see this as a tempest in a teapot. After all, we have enough to be stressed out about already.

Then the government actually fell. Still, I decided, no big deal. We'll probably reelect more or less the same government we have now, so why stress? I had a lunch meeting with the elder statesman of our Foundation, a person with whom I work very closely, but whom I've never, ever heard make a political comment. As we were getting into the car, he asked how I was. "Fine," I responded. The response was icy. "Your country is committing suicide, and you're fine?"

I was almost certain he was kidding, and looked carefully for a smile, or glimmer in his eye, to let me know it was really OK to be fine. Neither came. Duly chastised, I got into the car; we dropped the subject and went to lunch.

The next morning, I met with yet another member of our faculty, also an elder-statesman type, the same one who for two years has been reassuring me that the dark moments here have to be taken in context. The country's seen hard times before, he often reminds me, and we'll get out of this one, too. So I was actually looking forward to this meeting, figuring he'd reinforce my determination not to let the current situation get to me. I asked him how he was. He looked up from his monitor and said, "I don't know how to be. I can deal with everything they do to us. But this stealing of olives is horrendous. We're becoming shameful. I don't remember things ever being this bad."

His reference was to a new phenomenon on the West Bank. A handful of settlers have been either stealing the olives from Palestinians' groves or, in other cases, shooting at and intimidating Palestinians so that they're afraid to go to their groves to harvest their olives. With the harvest season coming to an end, and since olives are in the case of many villages the primary or sole source of annual income, a small group of people has terrorized and incapacitated large segments of the Palestinian population. The phenomenon has been covered extensively in the Israeli press, less so (thankfully?) in the foreign news.

So now, having been chastised for feeling "fine" and having been told by my cheerleader-in-chief that we're shameful, my resolve began to crack. Therefore, it was with some greater interest than usual that I read an e-mail that came across my desk asking people to come to an olive harvest on Friday. The idea was that with Jews in the crowd, settlers certainly wouldn't shoot, and probably wouldn't harass. We could pick olives or just stand there, but our presence would make a difference. And as it had all been coordinated with the security forces, everything should be peaceful.

For a long time now, I've been ignoring these sorts of e-mails. They've been asking us to fill in trenches that the IDF has dug around Palestinian towns in order to enforce curfews, or to visit wounded Palestinians in Palestinian hospitals. Neither of those seemed to me particularly appropriate. Obviously, civilian Palestinians are suffering from the curfews, and often suffering terribly, but if the army decides that that's what it's going to take to stop our buses from blowing up and to make sure my kids get home from school in one piece, I'm not going to be the one to go fill in the trench. And if I wanted to visit more people in hospitals, there are plenty of mutilated Jewish kids I can find right here in Jerusalem hospitals—no need to go to the territories to find mutilated victims. We've got plenty of our own right here.

But this one seemed different. Filling in a trench or going to Palestinian hospitals always sounded like political statements—often even verging on self-hatred—that I didn't want to make. Helping people pick their olives—our government, to my knowledge, has not indicated that it's opposed to that—seemed pretty harmless, and given the state of things around here, I figured it might be good to at least do something proactive about something. So I requested and received spousal dispensation permitting me to travel to the territories, and replied to the e-mail saying that I'd go along.

I didn't pay much attention to where, exactly, we were headed, but threw together a backpack with a sandwich, a water bottle, a map, and a hat, and at the last minute, tossed my digital camera in for good measure. Friday morning, Elisheva drove me to the pickup spot with Avi in the car. Avi wanted to know where I was going, and why, so we told him. "So every year you're going to have to help them pick their olives?" he wanted to know.

Elisheva reassured him that this wasn't the case. "No, sweetie. It's only for now. As soon as this mess is over, they'll be able to harvest their own olives. For now, though, as long as the fighting goes on, we need to help them to make sure that a few Jews don't get in the way of their having enough money to live during the entire year."

Avi's response was immediate. "That's dumb. This will never be over."

"Yes, it will," his mother told him. "Probably sooner than you think."

"Ema," he replied with incredulity, "have you read any history? Have you heard of the Greeks, or the Romans? Do you know anything about the Crusaders, or the Turks? The British? The Palestinians are only the latest in a series. There's always someone who wants this place, and people are always fighting to have it. You're nuts if you think this is ever going to end."

I didn't know whether to be pleased that this kid, too, was actually absorbing something from his eighth-grade history class, or devastated by his sense of the futility of the whole thing. But, I figured, that's the good thing about being married. Elisheva would have to handle this after I got out of the car. She dropped me off and reminded me that Shabbat came in early, so I'd better get home on time.

A friend was driving to the harvest in his car, and I went with him. We set out of Jerusalem, and in the midst of our chatting, I suddenly noticed that he was taking the Modi'in road, into the middle of the territories, where there have been more than a few shootings and murders. "Where are we headed?" I asked. "Farata," he said.

"Where's that?" I asked, scanning the map I'd taken off his dashboard. He looked over, moved his finger way up high, searched for a moment, and then said, "Here."

Uh-oh. We were headed to a small village just a bit west of Shechem (Nablus in international terminology), deep in the heart of the Palestinian Authority, or whatever's left of it. Even in the "good old days," we never, ever went to these places. They're the big yellow blotches that are printed on all Israeli maps, meaning "No one in their right mind goes anywhere near here." The good news, though, was that now the Modi'in road didn't seem like such a big deal. That would be the least of it. Farata is not only deep in Palestinian territory. It's also right next to Chavat Gil'ad, the "illegal settlement," more like an outpost, that the army tried to remove a few weeks ago. That incident ended with several policemen being injured, and with the entire country worried that the settlement issue would lead to some sort of civil strife. We were clearly heading to the Wild West.

But the day was gorgeous, and even after we crossed the green line, the scenery was so beautiful that you could almost forget where you were. About two hours from Jerusalem, we got to "downtown Farata" (above five small storefronts on a main drag) and were met by three Palestinians, one of whom got in the car to show us where to go. We meandered through the village, then out through some fields, and drove way past the village until the road was so rough that the vehicles literally could go no further. So we parked on the side of the road as best we could, grabbed our stuff, and walked about a hundred yards. There, about fifty or sixty of the villagers were waiting for us, tarps and buckets in hand for the harvest. Some had hats, a few had cell phones. None had food or water—this is Ramadan, and they fast between sunrise and sunset.

Some casual greetings followed, and even with my rudimentary Arabic, I was able to understand that we'd walk another half a kilometer or so to the grove that they've been unable to harvest for fear of the "settlers," whoever they were. It was already hot, so this motley crowd of Jews and Palestinians walked slowly to the grove. It was quiet and deserted, and actually quite beautiful. Perfect, I thought.

Wrong.

Immediately, there was some upset among the elder Palestinians, who walked briskly to the trees and began to yell back to the rest of the group. Their olives, it turns out, were gone. They'd been stolen. The Palestinian elders showed us the trees. Any branches that could be reached from the ground were denuded of olives. At the tops of the trees, there were still thick bunches, giving a sense of how many olives had once been on each tree. In their eyes, you could see the devastation. The men muttered, a few of the women cried softly, but there was nothing to do. The olives were gone, and although they clearly had their theory about what had happened, there was nothing they could prove. They could make a scene, or get to work harvesting whatever was left. They chose the second option.

A group of us went over to a particularly large tree to get to work. The younger Palestinian men laid out the tarps under the tree, and then everyone climbed around (or some, into) the tree, and began picking the olives and dropping them onto the tarps. The tree was huge, and it took some time. Gradually, we got into a groove, and people began to chat as we were working. There were Palestinians, of course, and Israelis, both native and immigrant. So with time, one could hear in the tree idle chatting in Arabic, Hebrew, and English, and when I paused to listen for a moment, it actually sounded pretty idyllic. That chorus, with the sun, the clear skies, and the beauty of the surrounding hills, made it feel like a pretty perfect way to end the week.

We finished the tree after a while, gathered the olives into a large sack, folded the tarps, and went looking for another tree. Most of the trees had nothing left. The olives were gone before we got there. But we found another tree with some to pick, and set up the same system. We got to work, quietly rummaging in the branches for olives, and for a while, all you could hear was the rustling of the leaves and dropping of the olives onto the tarps.

A few minutes later, when I thought I heard barking, I figured I was wrong. So I kept picking. But then, it got louder, and couldn't be ignored. There was definitely some barking, and then some shouting. Curious, I left the group of pickers and made my way up the hill to where I thought it was coming from. The first thing that I noticed was someone, apparently a teenager, with a black and green cloth wrapped around his entire head so that his face was completely hidden, holding four or five menacing dogs on leashes. He was screaming uncontrollably at the group of Israelis who had in the meantime gathered. For a moment, given the black and green, I assumed he was a Palestinian—but I just couldn't figure out why a Palestinian would be angry with us. After all, we were here to help. Even if he didn't like Israelis too much, we were basically the good guys.

But then, I realized, his Hebrew was perfect, and native. This was no Palestinian. And from what he was saying, it was clear—this was one of the famed "settlers."

He ranted and raved that we should be ashamed of ourselves for helping them steal "his" land, though it wasn't at all clear to me why, if *they* were stealing from him, *he* had his face covered. Then I noticed the other two. One was a kid about seventeen or so, still wearing *tefillin* (phylacteries), also screaming at the top of his lungs. And behind him, a taller, very heavyset fellow, with long *pei'ot* (ear locks) and an M-16 at the ready. For a brief moment, it all looked like a scene from *Frisco Kid* gone horribly awry. One hoodlum and two religious kids, all worked up and armed, screaming at a bunch of people with backpacks and water bottles.

Somewhat bemused by all this, and perplexed by the soldiers on an armored personnel carrier about two hundred yards away who could certainly see this all through their binoculars but did nothing, I decided that this was too bizarre not to photograph. I took my camera out of the backpack and started taking pictures. Big mistake. For some reason, this enraged the three. The one with the dogs started toward me and the one with the *tefillin* went even more berserk. The *pei'ot*-meister in the back started waving his gun around. Several of the others in our group moved in to buffer between us, but it was clear that this was getting out of hand. The organizer of our group quickly pulled out his cell phone and called his police contact.

I continued to try to photograph, when I suddenly realized that the center of activity had moved elsewhere. It turns out that the kid with the *tefillin* had stolen the pack of one of our group's members, and run off with it. As all this was unfolding, two plainclothes policemen appeared out of nowhere from among the trees. They were filled in on the story, and promptly set out to arrest the two who had apparently taken the bag (which had been recovered when the thieves dropped it as members of our group chased them).

OK, a little excitement for the day. But all's well that ends well, and we went back to work. The Palestinians, by the way, had worked all the way through. They'd called this human rights group for a reason—they wanted to harvest, and our job was to run interference if anyone showed up for trouble. They seemed perfectly content to let us deal with the visitors, and throughout, moved from tree to tree, salvaging whatever was left for them to pick. We went back down the hill to join them, and worked for a while.

But the fun wasn't over. I heard some more shouting a short while later and, once again, scampered up the hill to see what was going on. This time, it was a different guy in a huge white *kippah* and an even bigger gun, and his wife, in a long skirt, long sleeves, hair covered—the full getup, right out of central casting. They were in their late twenties or so. He was screaming at police (the original two had remained on site, and had called in backups, so there was more than a bit of security) that this land belonged to Jews, that it was duly registered in Jews' names, and that it was the Palestinians who were stealing. And, pointing to me and one other person wearing a *kippah*, "You two should be ashamed of yourselves. You're killing Jews. We need these olives to live. You've got blood on your hands. . . ." This was a new one, and these guys were such classics that I couldn't resist. Out with the camera, and a couple of quick photos.

Another mistake. The wife was completely enraged by the camera, and started to try to grab it. She grabbed my arm and wouldn't let go. It wouldn't have been hard to shake her off, but as her husband was standing about ten feet away with a loaded gun, I didn't want to do anything even more stupid. So I just held her at bay until the police stepped in and pushed her aside. But now it was the police who were furious. One of them, wearing a bulletproof vest and armed to the hilt, came towards me screaming, "Why are you inciting her?" I genuinely had no idea what I'd done, so I asked him. They don't like to be photographed, he told me, in a tone that suggested that I should have known that. "Why not?" I wanted to know. He didn't appreciate the question, and didn't answer.

But one of the other policemen, not disturbed by my terribly rude behavior, came over and told me that he'd seen her attack me, and that if I agreed to file a complaint, he'd arrest her and take her to the pen in Ariel. I declined. *That,* it seemed to me, would be an unnecessary provocation.

I'll summarize the remaining hours of this mess quickly. Shortly after, as the police were trying to sort out the claim that this was actually Jewish land and that the Palestinians (who were still working quietly down the hill) were actually stealing, the army showed up. A tank rolled up with two jeeps, and now, we found ourselves with a tank, two army jeeps, two police jeeps, about fifteen soldiers, and ten policemen. (At least we were well protected!) The police and the army got into a bit of a tug-of-war about who was actually in charge, when a high-ranking army fellow rode up, everyone else kind of snapped to a quasi-kind-of-attention, and he pulled out a map, saying, "This whole area is a closed military area. No settlers, no Palestinians, no civilians. Everyone out."

Now this was a good solution to the immediate problem, but it also spelled defeat for the olive harvest. So the organizer of our group tried to cajole the army officer into checking with the police captain who'd authorized our presence there. Dozens of cell phones, calls back and forth—including two to a member of Knesset who tried to intervene from afar—but a stalemate had been reached. One of the Palestinian elders showed the police and the army the results of their work for the morning—two sacks of olives—and said, "Every year, this half of the grove yields eighty sacks. This is all we've got left. Can't we just collect the little that's here?" No answer.

The negotiations continued, and eventually, the army officer lost patience, and for some reason (this was definitely not my day) selected me and told me to go down into the field and tell the Palestinians and the civilians who were still working with them that they had to leave. But I wasn't responsible for any of this, and I had no intention of letting anyone think that I was. So I didn't move. Annoyed, he moved up to me, his bulletproof vest and M-16 now just about touching my chest, and said, "Move. Tell them to leave."

But his little show of force wasn't terribly convincing, and I knew that he wasn't going to shoot *me*. "I'm not in charge of any of this," I told him. "Tell someone who is."

"It makes no difference who's in charge," he told me.

"I think you've got that one wrong. It seems to me that if we knew who was in charge, we wouldn't be in this mess, would we?" I asked him. Another mistake.

He was clearly very annoyed, but he didn't want a scene, and the police were for some reason watching my back, and intervened on my behalf. He relented, and no one was sent to the field to get the people. About five minutes later, though, he remembered his idea . . . and me. "I thought I told you to go get the people out of the field," he said. "And I told you I'm not in charge," I told him back. "You want the people out of the field, send one of the soldiers. They're not doing anything."

A compromise emerged. The officer passed his bullhorn to one of the Palestinians who had meandered over to watch these negotiations, and told him—in no uncertain terms—to call everyone up. Palestinians, it seems, can't be quite as confident that they won't get into legal trouble, and so, unhappy as he was with his role, the man took the bullhorn and called to the villagers to stop harvesting and come up to the road. Not long thereafter, we were all shooed out of the grove.

The Palestinians wanted to know what would happen with their harvest. They were told that they could call the police on Sunday to arrange another time to come and get the remaining olives. But what would happen to their olive trees in the meantime? they wanted to know. No clear answer to that one. Finally, the ranking police officer said, "If anyone steals any of your olives, come to the police station to file a complaint."

"But how can we file a complaint if we won't know who did it?" Good question, no answer. Settlers 1, Harvesters 0.

We dispersed, with the villagers thanking us and shaking our hands. Most of our group headed back to Tel Aviv and Jerusalem, but five of us were instructed to appear at the police station in Ariel (about twenty minutes away by car). Two of the group wanted to file a complaint against the person who stole the bag and had been arrested, and as I was the only one who'd taken digital photographs (many others had taken pictures with regular film), I also had to go to show the photos to the investigating officer. The police took whatever information they needed, and we headed back to Jerusalem.

We made it back before Shabbat, with just enough time to shower and change before heading off to shul. In shul, in my regular spot, someone asked me where I got my tan. I hadn't realized that I'd gotten burned out in the sun, but this is the Middle East. Things burn quickly here; people too. So I quickly summarized the day's events, when the person sitting next to me began to explain what a terrible thing we'd done.

"They don't need those olives. They duped you, completely. The area's filled with thousands of olive trees. Why don't they just pick olives somewhere else? Don't you get it? They choose to pick olives right near settlements, and that way, they can scout out the territory as they plan their next attack. That's what happened in Chermesh recently—the settlers were uncomfortable about the harvest in their backyard, but they relented and let them keep picking, and sure enough, the next day, gunmen managed to sneak in and kill two teenagers out for a walk."

The truth is, I was momentarily taken aback. The eighty-year-old women out in the sun sure didn't look like cover for terrorists, but stranger things have happened here. And you couldn't really see Chavat Gil'ad from where we were working, so it didn't *seem* that that site would be much use for scouting out an attack, but who knows? And while the police clearly didn't see anything wrong with them picking there, and were anxious to help us help them, the army wasn't happy. A dose of Micha's ambivalence began to set in. So much for Middle Eastern certitude.

But still, I was far from convinced, and some of his argument was just plain wrong, of course. I could have explained that each family has its own grove, that they can't go just anywhere they want and pick olives as if they're all one big happy clan that shares everything, but I'd had enough of olive talk for the day, and just wanted to focus on the davening. But he wasn't done. "How much can those olives be worth, anyway? You find me a family or a village that needs the olives *that* much, and I'll give them five hundred bucks and they can just wait out the harvest and do it next year." Great. You've got to love a bit of imported American paternalism. That's quite a way to breed independence, quite a way of passing down a tradition they've had for generation after generation.

I didn't quite give in, and he realized he was quite unintentionally sounding a bit fascist. "Well, obviously it's sad that they're hurting, but this is a war, and we didn't start it. And given the choice between life [Palestinians scouting out attacks, disguised as harvesters] and livelihood, there's not much of a choice. Every moral tradition says you choose life."

What astonished me was how convinced he was that he was unquestionably right. The settlers are certain that they're right, too, as are the Palestinians. And so are the human rights workers who regularly accompany them out into the fields. And so are the soldiers, who don't intervene, because their job (as they've been trained to understand it) is to protect Jews from Palestinians, and no Jews are being threatened by Palestinians in this case. Everybody's right, everybody's certain. Some people are dead. And more and more are hungry. But no one's ambivalent.

Shul ended, and we all started the quiet walk home. Throughout the neighborhood, you could see in the windows families sitting down to their Shabbat meal. Up in Chavat Gil'ad, the same people who had been screaming at us earlier in the day were also sitting down to Shabbat dinner. As were the villagers from Farata, after a day's work in the fields and a long, hot fast. A kind of time-out, a much needed break with some quiet.

But the quiet won't last, I knew. This was only round one, and the battle's far from over. The harvesters will go back, as will the settlers. And the government, which has so far shown no interest in taking any of the painful and dangerous steps needed to defuse this Wild West, will almost assuredly be voted back into office, in some reasonably similar form, in a few short weeks. And then what?

It reminded me of my kids' history lessons. Avi, it suddenly struck me, may not have been overly pessimistic. This is an explosion waiting to happen, and no one seems to want to intervene. Everyone knows Israel can't survive as both democratic and Jewish unless we figure out something here, but no one wants to take a stand.

And as for Micha, who's only nine and who won't be an adult for a decade . . . I wondered whether, as he looks back on the story of this place one day, the King David Hotel will have been the only thing he loves that got reduced to a big pile of rubble.

"That's Why We All Hate You"

- - - - - - - - - - - - - - - - -

It's Hanukkah again, and we decide to take some time away from the pressure cooker that Jerusalem has become. We book a place in Eilat for the eight days, load up the van, and drive the kids down to the southern tip of Israel for a few days of relative warmth and, more important, relaxation. Eilat is so far from the territories that there's almost nothing to worry about there. Since the beginning of the war, there hasn't been a single terrorist incident in Eilat. Every Israeli knows: if you want to stay in the country but still get away from it all, Eilat's the place. It's Israel, true, but these days, it might as well be a different country.

We watch the kids decompress in front of our eyes. We're getting our old kids back. They're singing in the shower like we haven't heard in months, running around the hotel courtyard and the town so carefree that we scarcely recognize them. For a moment or two, the dramatic change makes me wonder what we've done to them by having them live such a different life most of the time, but they're so happy that even that worry evaporates quickly. This isn't the time to ponder, I tell myself. Just have fun. We've escaped.

We hike, swim, read. Walk and sleep. Go out to dinner. Surrounded by thousands of other people just trying to get away from it all, Eilat takes on a surrealistic quality. It's not as full as it would have been a few years ago, but it's far from deserted. On Friday, about six days into our stay, Eilat suddenly begins to fill up. It's strange. Usually, Israelis begin to head home towards the end of Hanukkah. I'd figured that the weekend would be quiet. But the town is filling up, and suddenly, I realize why. The masses of people filling Eilat aren't Jews, they're Israeli Arabs. They're here for Id el-Fitr, the Muslim holiday that celebrates the end of Ramadan. This is also their great getaway.

It's actually nice, I tell myself. Look how great this country is when people aren't scared. Jews and Arabs sharing the same hotels, the same boardwalk, the same beaches. Everyone getting along, no visible tension. Israel at its best. I make a point, of course, of pointing this out to the kids.

Friday afternoon, even though we've got to get showered and dressed for Shabbat, we decide to acquiesce to the kids' plea for one more water sport. We get towed out to sea on some inflatable something-or-other, while the guy driving the motorboat tries, with no difficulty, to flip us off and get us dumped into the not-nearly-as-warm-as-we'd-expected water. We climb back on, only to get dumped again a few moments later. And on it goes. The kids are delirious with laughter. Elisheva and I could definitely do without this. We eventually get towed back to the dock, and now, we've really got to rush for Shabbat.

We decide that Tali and I should go ahead and that everyone else will catch up and meet us at the hotel. We set off down the boardwalk and promenade, oblivious to the thickening crowds around us. About halfway back, we hear some yelling, but pay it no heed; we're in a rush. Shabbat is not far off. But the yelling escalates, and from the corner of my eye, I see three or four teenagers bothering two women in their early thirties. But the place is packed with people, there are police around, and it's clear that no one's in any danger. So Talia and I keep walking.

Then the shrieking. This scream you can't ignore, and we stop dead in our tracks. Now I notice more. The two women are clearly Jewish, and the teenagers are Arabs. It's not obvious, but you live here long enough, and you learn how to tell. The teenagers aren't touching the women, but they're clearly being thoroughly obnoxious. One of the women is screaming "Leave us alone" and then "You should be ashamed of yourselves." The boys just laugh, and continue provoking them. "Do you want me to call the police?" More leering and laughter. The screaming woman is enraged, on the verge of tears. And the boys are grinning, having a great time. Then, her self-control completely gone, the woman screams at them, "And then you wonder why we all hate you. . . ."

No one moves. You can virtually hear a pin drop. Even the boys stop their laughter, and now they look like they just wish they were anywhere else. There's a pain in their face that paralyzes even those of us who were disgusted with them. The truth's been told, and they know it.

Dozens of people all around, and no one budges. Because everyone is struggling with the awful truth. Even in Eilat, there is no escape. Yes, there's a veneer of coexistence in a resort town, but one group of obnoxious kids (who could just as well have been Jews, except these happened to be Arabs) finally gets a woman to tell it like it is. This is a society filled with hate. After all these years of fear, the Jews just hate the Arabs. She knows it, all the onlookers know it, and even the creeps know it.

Israel is a place where you can't escape hatred.

For what seems like an eternity, no one speaks, but the crowd slowly begins to thin. Tali and I start our walk back to the hotel, neither of us saying a word. I'm not sure what she's thinking, but I'm mortified. It's one of those scenes that parents desperately wish their children didn't have to see, didn't have to know about, because the truth it reveals is too painful to bear.

A moment or two later, Tali reaches for my hand, and holds it tightly as we walk. Sixteen years old now, she doesn't often reach for my hand like she used to. But now, she won't let go. And I know why. She doesn't want to feel alone. Part of her would like to be a little girl again; she'd like to be able to pretend that her father can make everything OK.

But she also knows I can't. The carefree vacation's over, the escape from the conflict is history. Not only for me, but for her, too. On the cusp of adulthood, she's mature enough to understand what that exchange really meant. And she's smart enough to be wondering about the long, dark, and frightening road that still lies ahead.

December 2002:
Houston Is Calling . . .

From:	"Ramon, Ilan (JSC–CB) (ASI)"
	⟨ilan.ramon1@jsc.nasa.gov⟩
To:	⟨Daniel Gordis⟩
Sent:	Wed, December 4, 2002 02:30 AM
Subject:	Houston is calling . . .

Hello Dan,

It was nice to meet you and moreover to listen to your speech—I got very touched and you had got me emotional the way I haven't been for years.

Anyway, I would appreciate it if you could send me some details of your [colleague] in New York.

Thanks and all the best,

ilan

From:	Daniel Gordis
Sent:	Tue, December 10, 2002 2:04 AM
To:	RAMON, ILAN (JSC–CB) (ASI)
Subject:	RE: Houston is calling . . .

Dear Ilan:

Thanks for the note and for your very kind comments about my remarks at the General Assembly. Coming from someone like you, they genuinely mean a great deal to me.

I apologize for not having gotten back to you last week—we were in Eilat for all of Hanukkah, and just came back after the weekend.

First of all, it was a real pleasure to spend some time chatting with you at the G.A. And on behalf of my kids, I want to thank you for the autographed "shuttle envelopes." They were thrilled, and will long treasure them.

The person [I recommend for your writing project] is ——.

Anyway, I hope that some of this is helpful. Again, it was a pleasure to meet you. In case we're not in touch before, allow me to wish you a "safe flight," though this is a somewhat more momentous version of that more usual wish! I look forward to remaining in touch, and hope you'll feel free to let me know if there's anything I can do to be of assistance.

Be-virkat kol tuv,
Daniel

From:	RAMON, ILAN (JSC-CB) (ASI) [mailto:ilan.ramon1@jsc.nasa.gov]
Sent:	Thursday, December 12, 2002 5:49 PM
To:	Daniel Gordis
Subject:	RE: Houston is calling . . .

Daniel,

Thanks for your reply, the useful and helpful information. As you can imagine I am pretty busy now in the last stage of preparing for the mission.

One quick question I must ask you after hearing you and reading just the first few pages in your book—why do you and your family still choose to stay and live in Israel??

All the best,
ilan

From:　　　Daniel Gordis

Sent:　　　Thu, December 12, 2002 9:54 AM

To:　　　　RAMON, ILAN (JSC-CB) (ASI)

Subject:　　RE: Houston is calling . . .

Dear Ilan:

　　Be-hatzlacha! We'll be following your successes from down here on earth, with great pride.

　　Obviously, the question is a complicated one, but I'll attach a copy of a piece I just wrote, which *partially* answers the question.* I look forward to discussing it further when you return to Earth!

> Wishing you safety
> and all success,
> Daniel

From:　　　RAMON, ILAN (JSC-CB) (ASI)
　　　　　　　[mailto:ilan.ramon1@jsc.nasa.gov]

Sent:　　　Saturday, December 14, 2002 12:31 AM

To:　　　　Daniel Gordis

Subject:　　RE: Houston is calling . . .

　　Thanks Daniel, and I am totally with you—especially as a second generation of a Holocaust survivor and after being here in the US for four and a half years. Israel is THE only place which we can call home and feel at home; although we need to make sure that it stays like that. Unfortunately lately there are more than a few Israelis who feel that "their" Israeli home is no longer what they had been used to and looking forward to be.

　　Any way—I appreciate your family decision a lot, it's

---

*The piece mentioned here, which was an attachment in the e-mail to Colonel Ramon, is the next chapter of this book, "There's No Place Like Home."

kind of like what the "Machalniks"* used to be in 1948, and this has always been appreciated by me more than any Israeli-born volunteering to the military.

> Best wishes,
>
> ilan

From:	Daniel Gordis
To:	RAMON, ILAN (JSC-CB) (ASI)
Sent:	Tuesday, December 17, 2002 11:05 AM
Subject:	RE: Houston is calling . . .

Dear Ilan:

I agree with YOU. The challenge is to preserve in Israel the kind of place of which we both dream. Our dreams of what this place can be may differ a bit one from the other, but "be-gadol" we envision the same thing. Yes, Israel is changing, and not always in ways that we'd like. That, I believe, is why being here and doing our share to make it into something that we can still love is so critical.

I look forward to talking with you about this more. Perhaps we could get together next time you're in the country. In the meantime, again, my wishes for safety—and even "she-yihyeh keif"†!!!

> Kol tuv,
>
> Daniel

---

*Between 1947 and 1948 about 3,500 Machalniks (an acronym for the Hebrew phrase *Mitnadvei Chutz L'Aretz*, which means "Volunteers from Outside Israel") came to Israel and fought alongside the Palmach and Hagganah after the State was declared—in the Israel Defense Forces.

†A Hebrew phrase that roughly translated means "Have a great time."

December 2002:
There's No Place Like Home

In New York last week, I had occasion to be interviewed on NPR. It still amazes me how many people listen to talk radio, and of those, how many find the time to search the Web in order to write e-mail comments on what they've heard. I was pretty flooded with responses to the interview and rather struck by one particular theme that appeared in many of the letters. The following is typical—I use it as the example because it was somewhat less inflammatory than many of the others:

331

"Listening to you on the Leonard Lopate show, I couldn't but be amazed at your disregard for the lives of your children. When the neighborhood we were living in deteriorated to the point that it was no longer safe to walk the streets, we moved. We could have stayed, worked with the neighborhood association, joined the block watchers, etc., but in the meanwhile we had images of our children coming home from school mugged, bloodied, or even killed. It wasn't worth it to be heroes. . . . How will you feel if one of those suicide bombers kills your child when you could have avoided it by moving back to the States? Israel does not need you, it has many, many people who will fight the good fight, and in any event the problems are caused by forces beyond your control. Doesn't your family come first? Richard."

Well, Richard, I didn't answer that e-mail until today, because I didn't really know where to begin. But today was the kind of day in Israel that clarifies everything—why we're here, why this isn't anything like the neighborhood that you left, and why we're not killing our children, but giving them something to live for.

We were at a Bar Mitzvah at the Kotel (the Western Wall) this morning. After the service was over, I grabbed a cab to head back to the office for a meeting. The news was prattling about something that "even we were unprepared for." In Israel, a comment like that on the news gives you that sinking feeling in your stomach that something else awful, something we'd never imagined could happen, has happened. And sure enough, that was the first I'd heard about the attack in Mombasa.

Details were sketchy, and the only way the news could get any information was to speak on cell phones to Israelis who were actually at the site. One woman, just shy of hysterical, told the story of the explosion, and recounted how it took just under two hours for the first Kenyan ambulances to arrive. (Tonight, Israelis still can't believe that. We get to these disaster sites in two to three minutes, though admittedly, we have a lot more practice.) When asked what she expected would happen next, she said, "I assume Israel will send doctors, medicine, and soldiers, and then they'll bring us home." And she was right. The news immediately cut to an airfield, where IAF planes were being loaded with the medical equipment and personnel that the Kenyans couldn't seem to amass, and shortly thereafter, the planes and their cargoes were on their way.

You see, Richard, this isn't some dumpy neighborhood somewhere in the States that makes no difference to anyone but those who can't get out of it. This is a place in which we know we matter. This is a place that will take care of us, no matter where we are. This is what we call home.

Getting out of here wouldn't necessarily make us any safer, by the way. Muslim extremist evil knows no borders. We've known that for a long time. Remember Munich? Remember New York? Muslim terrorism isn't about the settlements, or the "occupation" (which may or may not be a bad idea, depending on whom you ask, but certainly isn't the root cause of all this terrorism), but about Israel herself and about Israelis and Jews wherever they may be. (Truthfully, it's about a battle over Western civilization, which the Jews for some reason are seen to represent.) And when Jews end up butchered in Mombasa, they know one thing. Kenyan incompetence will not allow them to be stranded. We'll get there. And we'll bring whatever's left of them home.

And then we heard about the two shoulder-mounted missiles fired at the Arkia jet carrying 271 people, and how they missed. And on tonight's news, even CNN showed a home video one of the passengers had taken as the plane prepared to land. Outside the window, IAF F-15's were flanking the jet, making sure that it hadn't been damaged and was safe to land. They were so close that from the cabin window, the passenger was able to film the pilot and navigator relatively clearly. And as the plane landed, the video caught the clapping and spontaneous singing of "Heveinu Shalom Aleichem"—a kitschy old Israeli homecoming song that no one on that plane had sung for decades. But no matter. There was no reason to be embarrassed by the kitsch. Six decades ago, when people fired at Jews across the world, there was no one willing to do anything. Things have changed, Richard, because we have a home.

The F-15's outside the window showed our children, Richard, that we're not disregarding them or their safety—we've brought them to the only place on the planet where Jews can take care of themselves.

Of course, we're not always successful, Richard. You're right. Sometimes, they get us. In the past two years, there have been 14,500 terrorist attacks in Israel. No exaggeration. What's amazing is that relatively few have killed people. Still, when two terrorists shot up a Likud Party headquarters this afternoon killing six people (so far), it was the culmination (though the day's not over, so one hesitates to use that word definitively) of a rather horrible day. But no one's running away. The Likud Party primary didn't get canceled or delayed. The polls stayed open. The countries these terrorists "represent" don't have a single democracy to their credit (save Turkey, if you call that military-in-the-shadows-government sham a democracy), but we do. They blow up a hotel, try to shoot down a jet, shoot up a bus station, and still, we vote. Quietly, peacefully, democratically. And in the midst of all the sadness and grief, many of us are proud of that. I think we have a right to be.

You weren't proud of that neighborhood you left. Probably because it didn't stand for anything too important. Because it reeked of hopelessness.

So you left, and rightly so. But this place does stand for something important. And even on dark days like today, in which everyone I know was sullen, recovering from one bit of news only to hear another, this place pulses with hope. Those doctors flying to Mombasa are what this place is all about. The F-15's shadowing the 757 making its way home are what this place is all about. And the quiet, orderly voting is what this place is all about. What kind of a person in their right mind would leave this, Richard? This isn't a neighborhood. It's home. And with all its faults, and there are many, it's a dream come true. Walk away from that? How would we get out of bed in the morning and look in the mirror?

The chitchat over dinner tonight was fascinating. Micha, our youngest and nine years old, was trying to understand the difference between Sharon and Netanyahu. Apparently, today's Likud primary, a vote between Sharon and Netanyahu to see who will lead the party and be the one to run for prime minister, had been much discussed in his fourth-grade class. His older siblings were trying to explain. When they told him that Sharon has said that he's willing, in principle, to see a Palestinian state, Micha asked incredulously, "Give them *land*?" to which his brother and sister explained that "they" need someplace to live, too, which is why Sharon says that. But then, they continued, "the Arabs probably won't stop killing us for a long time, which is why maybe Netanyahu's right."

Elisheva and I didn't say much, and just listened to this rather lengthy discussion. They had most of it right, some of it wrong. But guess what, Richard? They were talking about the future, a future they believe in.

In just a couple of years, our daughter will get to vote, too. (That, of course, would not be the case if she lived in the Palestinian Authority. Or Lebanon. Or Syria. Or Jordan. Or Saudi Arabia. Or Egypt.) And she'll vote about stuff that really matters. The direction her country takes will be her choice, too. You're right that we can't completely stop the terrorism, and you're right that there's some danger here. But here's what our kids have learned: Life isn't about staying alive. It's about believing in something that matters while you're alive.

What our kids believe in, among much else, is the future. At the dinner table tonight, watching our kids balance the dangers of trusting people who've been doing this to you for two years, with the danger of what you'll have if you're not willing to risk anything, I realized that it works. They actually still believe in the future. There wasn't a grain of hopelessness in their conversation, Richard. I bet that wasn't true when people talked about your old neighborhood, was it? And that's what makes all the difference.

Yes, Richard, our family does come first. And that's why we're here. To raise our kids in a place that's all about them, about their history, their future, their sense of being at home. To live in a place that, unlike that old neighborhood you spoke of, matters very much. Not because we're heroes, for we're not. But because we know just a bit about Jewish history; and because we have no right to expect other Israelis to "fight the good fight" if we're not willing to.

On the news this afternoon, they interviewed some alleged aviation expert about the attempted attack on the Arkia 757. He explained how these missiles work, and gave a whole dissertation on the ease of operation of heat-seeking shoulder-launched missiles. When he was done, the interviewer asked him, "Then how did they miss? After all, a lumbering 757, barely off the ground? How do you explain this?"

His answer, I thought, was telling. He said, "I can't explain it. Either they fired without priming the heat-seeking element on the missiles, or they were faulty. But normally, there's no way to miss. It was a miracle."

He didn't mean anything theological by the comment, of course, but today's the day before Hanukkah. In your old neighborhood, and in your new one, too, it's Thanksgiving. I remember it well. College football during the day. Beer and pretzels, and chatting with friends. Turkey and stuffing at night. Not bad at all.

None of that here. Just a regular old dinner. But not so tomorrow night. Tomorrow night, when you look outside our living room window, in the windows of virtually every other apartment within sight, there are going to be Hanukkah candles flickering. Religious families, secular families. Left-wing families, right-wing families. Native families and immigrant families. American families and French families. Young families and old families. Sharon families and Netanyahu families. They'll all have candles in the window.

Because, Richard, somehow, in spite of everything, we still believe in miracles. Some of them happened a long time ago. But others are still happening. We understand them in different ways, and we disagree passionately about how to keep them going. But after a day like today, somehow we find ourselves still believing in them.

It's a crazy, dangerous place, this neighborhood of ours, Richard. But it's home. And it's a miracle. It really is. And from that, you see, you just don't walk away.

Now do you get it?

Happy Hanukkah.

Epilogues

Ethical Will

Dear Talia, Aviel, and Micha,

There's a tradition that Jewish parents have had for many centuries, called an "ethical will." It's a letter that we write to our children, so that when the time comes that we can't be with you anymore, we'll have put down in writing some of the things that it's most important to us that you know and remember. There are other kinds of wills that lawyers take care of, but this is something different—it's not about money or houses or anything like that. It's about us, and you, and what we want for you.

Ema and I have written ethical wills to you already. They're in the house where you'll find them if it's ever necessary, but there's no reason that we can't add another one, or many more, as the years go by. Now that we've been in Israel for just about four and a half years and have been bona fide Israelis for a bit more than three years, and now that so much has changed in your new country and your young lives, I think I owe you another letter.

The most important thing for you to know, of course, is that we love you, more than you know and more than we can tell you. We're incredibly proud of you, of how much you've grown up, of the good friends you are to the people you care about, and of the way in which you've made a life for yourselves in this new, strange, fascinating, and sometimes difficult place.

And that's what I want to write about now. About this place. About our having decided to live here and to raise you here. About the terribly sad things that have happened to our country in the past two and a half years. And about the sad things that have happened to you.

There are many nights after you've gone to sleep when Ema and I talk about this, about whether it was fair to do this to you, if we were right to take you from a wonderful life in the United States and Los Angeles to bring you to this mess, to this conflict, to the pain and the uncertainty that are now a part of your daily lives.

Do you know how sometimes you want something so badly that you actually convince yourself that you're going to get it, even if it's not a sure thing? I think that's what happened to us. We wanted so deeply to live in an Israel at peace that we convinced ourselves that the Palestinians also wanted it. And many Palestinians do, don't ever forget that. Don't ever let your frustration, your pain, your fear, get in the way of remembering that they are no more monolithic than we are—Palestinians disagree with each other and argue about this just as we Jews do. There are Jews of whom we're not proud, and there are Palestinians who are unwilling to stop killing. But there are also noble and peace-seeking Jews, and there are people just like that on the Palestinian side. One day, we hope, they too will have their state, and Jews and Palestinians will be able to live side by side in peace and security.

But at least for now, the Palestinians who dictate policy don't want to make the compromise that peace will require. Some of them want everything we have—the neighborhood where your school is, the street our house is on, even our house. Some of them want us to permit millions of refugees back into this country, turning us once again into a minority and undoing the very reason that we have this country.

As much as we want peace, you know that we can't give them all that they want. So, together with you, we've learned something important. We've discovered that when you finally understand what is important to you, you have to be willing to fight for it. Sometimes the things we have to fight for are little things, and sometimes they're big things. But nothing that's important comes easily. When you get older, you'll learn that good marriages don't come easily, and that satisfying work takes a lot of investment. And the same is true of having a homeland. Tragically, you've learned up close that the fight can be painful, frightening, and seemingly endless.

But do you know what's much worse than having to fight for something? It's not having anything to fight for. What's the point of all the years we have for living our lives if there's nothing so important to us that we wouldn't give everything—even our lives—for it? No one wants to have to give up their life for their home or their country, I think. But I wonder: If there's nothing in your life that's worth dying for, is there anything that's worth living for?

We think that the State of Israel is one of those things that is worth living our lives for. Aside from you and the other people we love, there's nothing that's more important to us. And that's because for us, Israel is not just a place—it's a story. And it's not just any story—it's our story, your story, the story of where we've come from, and the story of where we're going. It's a story that our people have been telling for a long time, and we feel a need to be a part of it.

All of the chapters of our story point to this land. Just like you, Abraham came here with his family and left everything else behind. Remember how when we drive down to the Dead Sea, Ema always asks you which of those little sand dunes you think Abraham walked on? Of course you're right that the wind has blown that sand about many thousands of times, and that he didn't walk on any of them. But you know what? That doesn't matter. He was here. So were the Maccabees. So were the rabbis of the Mishnah. And now, so are you.

Every year, as we sit at the Seder table and tell the story of the Exodus, this land is part of that story. The story that we tell at the Seder is not only the story of leaving Egypt, but of going somewhere specific, of wandering through the desert for forty years so we could end up . . . here. Every year we, like Jews across the world, sing *La-Shannah Ha-Ba'ah Birushalayim*—"Next Year in Jerusalem." But in the last few years, Ema and I began to feel that the song was sounding hollow. It wasn't enough just to sing it. If we were to sing it, we thought, we ought to mean it. And if we meant it, this was where we needed to be.

But we're here not only because of the past, but for the future as well. This is the first chance in two thousand years that the Jews have had to see if we can use our tradition to create a society that is different—and, yes, better—than the places we all left to come here.

If we build a fair and decent country, where people are treated well and where even people we disagree with are allowed to express their views, it will be our doing and we'll have the right to be proud of it. For the first time in centuries, it is Jews who will decide how to treat poor people, how we should take care of immigrants, what we will do with criminals, how we should run the schools and educate the next generation. Here, in this country, it's Jews who will decide how to treat the Arab minority fairly without losing the Jewish character of this country, how to use the power of the army in a just way, how to preserve the memory of what's happened to the Jews without becoming only bitter and angry.

This is a place where we can stop talking about what we'd do if only we were in charge; it's the place where we *are* in charge, and where we can put to the test all the texts that the Jews have been studying for so long.

Obviously we have a long way to go. Every day you see the Jewish and Arab beggars near our home and near your school who need our help. There are religious and secular people who need to learn to live together. There are Arabs who are citizens of Israel whom we have to learn to treat much better. There are Israeli soldiers who do terrible things, and I know that that sometimes makes you very sad, even angry or ashamed. That's why we're here—to be a part of the process of making this place even better than it is.

. . .

We'll love you no matter where you decide to live, but I hope that no matter what choice you'll make, you'll understand why we did this, why we *had* to do this. We hope you'll understand that in many ways, our coming here was less of a decision than it was a matter of giving in to gravity. The story that we were taught of who we are and who we are supposed to be pulled us here, in a way that is more powerful than most people can understand.

I know that some of your friends are leaving, that their parents are taking them away because they no longer think that this is a good place to raise kids. Ema and I watch the pain you feel as your friends pack up and leave, and hurt for you all over again, knowing how hard it must be for you to lose them so soon after you had to leave your Los Angeles friends behind. I wonder, sometimes, if you wish we would do the same, if you'd like to hear us tell you that we're packing up and heading out. You've never said anything of that sort, but I suspect that might be because you know it's not going to happen. You're right—it's not. I only hope that we're raising you in a way that helps you understand why.

I hope that as you grow older, you'll think you were fortunate that we brought you here. Fortunate to grow up in a country where kids are still freer and more carefree than in any other place we know. Lucky to be in a place where your history—your story—pops up every day and reminds you who you are. Lucky to be in a place that for thousands of years and for millions of Jews was merely a dream, but for you is home. Blessed to be in a place that's new enough that you can make a difference if you try. And lucky enough to be in a place that's important, that's even worth fighting for.

But whatever you decide, wherever you live, Ema and I hope that you'll learn important lessons from this childhood we've thrown at you. Find something you believe in, and make it yours. Decide what's worth hanging on to at all costs, what's worth being scared for, what's worth fighting for, what's worth giving everything for. If you can find that, you've found everything. And that, more than anything, is what we want for you.

You're wonderful. In ways that you don't yet understand, you've taught us much more than we've taught you. For that, and for much more—

We love you with all our hearts.

Abba

Perspective

- - - - - - - - - - - - - - - -

It's an old story, this biblical story we're living in. It starts with that strange command to leave home and to go to a new place. And then it's a story of unending conflict, a story that seems to suggest that to see the end of the battles, we're going to have to wait.

And it's true. We'll probably just have to wait.

A long time ago, the writer of the Book of Ecclesiastes said, "For everything there is a season, a time for every experience under heaven." We've seen a lot in the last two and a half years, but we've missed half the seasons. We've seen the time for dying, for uprooting the planted. There's been slaying and tearing down, plenty of weeping and throwing of stones. This has been, as our kids have seen, the time for hating, the time for war.

But what about the other times? For planting, for building up. For laughing and for building, for loving and for peace. When?

The hatred of Genesis will not be easy to overcome. It was a long time ago that Ishmael and Isaac went their separate ways, torn apart by a world that didn't seem to have enough for the two of them. Perhaps it was foolish, even audacious, to expect that we'd be the ones to see the rift healed. It was probably too much to ask. Why should ours have been the first generation to move to Israel in thousands of years and have it be conflict-free, to have peace reign when the story we tell about ourselves is one of jealousy, hatred, bloodshed, and conflict? Why? Where did we get the naïve idea that it would all end just for us?

But for how long? When? When will something change? We know that we have to wait, but without limit? Is there an end in sight? Patience, this world seems to say. Patience: the moral of this story we tell.

90 *O Lord. . . .*
²Before the mountains came into being,

before You brought forth the earth and the world,
from eternity to eternity You are God.

[3]*You return man to dust;*
You decreed, "Return you mortals!"
[4]*For in Your sight a thousand years*
are like yesterday that is past,
like a watch of the night.

—THE BOOK OF PSALMS

A thousand years in Your eyes are like a day in our lives. Living here requires superhuman patience, perspective that comes from a view that human beings simply don't have, cannot have. We will have to wait, and be satisfied with waiting. In all likelihood, we'll have to wait a long time. Jews have waited thousands of years. Could it be that waiting, and hoping, are what we're here for? Could it be that waiting and hoping will have to be enough?

. . .

Night has fallen now, and even this city has grown almost silent. For some strange reason, it's quiet outside tonight. No shelling, no screeching ambulances, no late-breaking news on TV shattering the still of night. Quiet, at last.

It won't last, of course. We've learned that, if nothing else. Something, sooner rather than later, will shatter this calm. But for now, for this one cherished moment, it's wonderful. It's all we want, all we need. So I head up the stairs to sleep, and check each of the kids in their rooms. Fast asleep, still as the night outside. Breathing softly, inaudibly, they look at peace, untroubled.

But are they? What dreams are raging in those seemingly peaceful bodies, what battles are being fought there in the depth of their sleep? What's the cost of all this going to be for them, for the innocent souls we brought here just a few years ago? Will all this breed strength and resolve, the sense that they can meet any challenge and make friends anywhere? Or will it just breed hatred and stubbornness, a sense that they've been wronged—by both their parents and their enemies—that will color the people they become? Will they see themselves as part of a wondrous story, a tale of thousands of years of which they're now a part, or has all that eluded them?

And I wonder. What are they dreaming of at this moment? War? Peace? And when they're all grown up, and their generation has inherited this land, will they still have the strength to dream?

Acknowledgments

Though this is in many ways a personal account of our family's story, neither the experiences described here nor the writing of this book would have been possible without the support and assistance of many other people. It is a pleasure to have an opportunity to thank them, however inadequately, for all that they have done for us.

My association with the Mandel Foundation and the Mandel Jerusalem Fellows has been more enriching and stimulating than I can describe. I am deeply grateful to Mr. Morton L. Mandel for the profundity of his vision for the Jewish People and for all that he does to make that vision a reality. It is no exaggeration to say that I learn from each of our encounters and from watching him give direction to the Foundation; it is a privilege and an honor to be associated with him and his work.

Ever since he invited me to a Mandel Institute Goals Seminar in July 1996, and then extended an offer to come to the Mandel Institute as a Mandel Fellow for the 1998–1999 academic year, Professor Seymour Fox has introduced me to a new world of educational thinking and Jewish communal engagement that has enriched me more profoundly than I ever anticipated. I am honored to have him as a mentor and teacher, and thank him for everything he has done to make the life described in this book a possibility.

To Annette Hochstein, president of the Mandel Foundation–Israel, my deep appreciation for having shaped a set of professional responsibilities and challenges that is engaging, challenging, and nurturing in every way. Her mentorship, guidance, and friendship have enriched my life and that of my family immeasurably during these past five years, and I look forward to many more years of working together.

To Varda Shiffer and Professor Mordecai Nisan, my thanks for their warmth, trust, support, encouragement, and guidance. One cannot ask for more thoughtful or caring colleagues and teachers.

Though I have been enriched immeasurably by all my colleagues at the Mandel School for Educational and Social Leadership, a few people have shaped this book in particularly profound ways. Professor Michael Rosenak patiently and lovingly offered a safe intellectual harbor as I made my way through my first serious encounter with Israeli post-Zionist thinkers. The course that Avi Katzman and Dr. Marc Silverman have taught on Israeli culture at the Mandel Jerusalem Fellows over the past several years has taught me much and forced me to think about this country in new and sometimes painful ways. Scott Copeland, a Jerusalem Fellow from 2000 through 2002, is one of the most capable and knowledgeable tour guides I have seen in action. His willingness to answer my questions about places and events, even late at night, went far beyond the call of duty or friendship. More than once, after he answered a question for me at the end of the day, when I awoke the next morning and checked my e-mail, I found that he had sent several more documents to fill in the picture he had already capably described. I am deeply grateful.

To Sharon Gonnen and Dikla Klein-Marcus, my thanks for all they do on a daily basis to ensure that our office, and thus my life, runs smoothly and efficiently. The writing of this book would have been infinitely more difficult without their dedication and talents.

When I first decided to try to turn the e-mails about Israel into a book, I had lost most of the original material. I'd changed computers too often and had moved apartments too frequently to have any "sent files" or hard copies of those letters. Fortunately, several people had kept copies of various letters, and within a few weeks I was able to reconstruct the entire original set. For their organization, their willingness to hunt these letters down, and their encouragement to proceed with the project, my thanks to my father, to my brother Elie (who also forwarded them far and wide), to my sister-in-law and brother-in-law, Sharon Waxman and Daniel Rosenblum, and to Ellen Anreder.

I am very grateful to a variety of people who afforded me an opportunity to share some of this material publicly in the past few years and thus to benefit from a great deal of response and many sorts of reactions. To Robert Bleiweiss of *Jewish Spectator,* and to Robert Eshman of the *Los Angeles Jewish Journal,* my thanks for publishing portions of original versions of several of the letters as they first appeared. To Susan Berrin of *Sh'ma* magazine, my thanks for the publication of "When the Heart Trumps the Mind," which appears here in a slightly modified form. And finally, to Adam Moss and Ilena Silverman of the *New York Times Magazine,* my deepest possible thanks for their interest in these letters and the extraordinary wisdom and skill with which they crafted this story in their pages.

Rabbis Nathan Laufer and Shoshana Gelfand afforded me an opportunity to work through some of this material at a Wexner Heritage Foundation conference in Vail, Colorado, in June 2001 and again in Jerusalem later that summer. The responses that I received were extremely helpful, and I am grateful to them for their friendship and collegiality. To all my friends at the WHF, my thanks for all they did to disseminate these e-mails early on.

Because these e-mails originated as more private communications to friends and family during our first years here, it did not immediately occur to me to try to convert them into a book. Two people pressed me—gently but consistently—to think about bringing this material to a wider audience. To my brother Elie and to Kathi Shaivitz Rosenberg, many thanks. The ice cream sandwiches from fourth grade are more than paid back.

To Saul Singer of the *Jerusalem Post,* many thanks for assistance with research on many matters included herein, both major and minor.

It is unusual for the photographer who takes the "author photo" to be mentioned in a book's acknowledgments, but Zion Ozeri is more than just a world-class photographer. He is a close friend, and someone with whom I've spent many hours talking about these letters and about Israel. I'm honored that he was willing to take the photo for this book, for the issues discussed in these pages weigh on his heart no less than they do on mine.

Translations from the Hebrew Bible are taken from *Tanakh–The Holy Scriptures* by the Jewish Publication Society, often with minor modifications on my part.

Twenty-five to thirty years later, I hope that it is not too late to thank two teachers from my youth whose inspired teaching has left a profound imprint on me to this very day. It is in large measure to Mr. Samuel Butler Grimes III, my eighth-grade English writing teacher at the Gilman School, that I owe my love of writing. Thirty years later, I still recall him patiently reviewing poems I had written, and occasionally poems on which I'd gotten hopelessly stuck. When he once nonchalantly said to me, "Some poems just aren't meant to be finished," I doubt that he suspected I'd recall that remark decades later. But I do, and I think of him often when I throw out a page or clear the screen and start over. For that and much more, thanks I cannot fully express.

Though it is in some ways a pure coincidence that several elements of this book make use of French, I suspect that there is more to it. I was fortunate to study French throughout my high school years with Mme. Winifred O'Connor, a masterful and gifted teacher who did much more than get me to speak French relatively well for an American high school student. Mme. O'Connor used the medium of language to teach us how to observe and appreciate a culture radically different from our own, and I have thought of her teaching more than once in this mysterious, fascinating, and sometimes frightening place called the Middle East. Decades later, and from thousands of miles away, my most profound thanks and appreciation.

Richard Pine is the finest literary agent imaginable, and I've been privileged to work with him on all of my books. Few people outside my family and my closest teachers have had such an impact on my work and career, and I'm deeply grateful. This book could not have come to be without his faith in the possibility of the project and his critical guidance as it first assumed a shape and a voice. I look forward to many future projects under his tutelage.

Douglas Pepper, my editor at the Crown Publishing Group, brought a sympathetic eye and a critical pen to the project, and transformed it from a clumsy assortment of letters into a much more refined narrative. I cannot imagine a more gifted and professional editor with whom to work. For his wisdom, his conviction that this book could speak to a wide audience, and his warm support throughout this project, I am deeply grateful.

And now, closer to home. I had been teaching at the Brandeis-Bardin Institute and its Brandeis Collegiate Institute (BCI) for some time already when the then executive vice-president of the Institute, Dr. Alvin Mars, invited a new faculty member to join us. I'd heard of Rabbi Levi Lauer before he joined our ranks, but had never met him. From our very first encounter, we began to develop a friendship that has impacted me and enriched my life far beyond anything words can describe. For years we debated in front of the students at BCI questions related to Zionism, Levi arguing that Jewish life could be lived more meaningfully in Israel than anywhere else, while I maintained that the Diaspora was no less a vibrant and viable Jewish community. To this day, Levi insists that my living here is tacit admission that I lost those debates. Perhaps, perhaps not. But either way, we're here due in no small part to him and the hours of conversations that he and I had in the California desert, and Elisheva and I are grateful to Levi and Chaya for everything they did to bring us here and to make our landing as smooth and successful as it has been.

Pinchas and Sandy Lozowick have done far more than even a deep friendship should entail to make our lives here not only pleasant, but possible. In ways large and small, they have helped make Israel a home for us as no one else could have. They would certainly deny that they have been so thoughtful, helpful, and generous of spirit with us, but that modesty is precisely what makes them the treasured friends they are. Not a day goes by without our feeling deeply indebted to them.

And finally, since this is a memoir of a family saga of sorts, to my family. My parents were the ones who first modeled for us a passionate love for Israel, a love that I hope is expressed in these pages. And when it came our turn to move here, no one could have been more supportive or loving than my parents have been. Their intellectual acuity, moral seriousness, and passion for Jewish life are only a few of the many qualities that we love and admire about them.

I've dedicated this book to my brothers, Elie and Yonatan, and their families, all of whom have afforded us constant support and encouragement during the past few years. Yonatan and Robbie were still living in Israel when we arrived, and did much to show us the ropes and help us make a life here. Elie and Avra also share our love for Israel, and have offered a steadying hand and a sensitive ear during even the most difficult moments. Now that we no longer have a home in America, Elie and Avra's apartment on the Upper West Side has become my American pied à terre. Their hospitality and graciousness know literally no bounds.

Though we're now separated by many thousands of miles, with one of us in Vancouver, one in New York, and one in Jerusalem, my relationship with my brothers is deeper and means more to me than I ever imagined it could or would. To both of them, and to their families, unbounded love.

Elisheva knows that it is no exaggeration to say that we're here because of her, and I can't imagine having lived this adventure—with its glorious moments as well as its devastating ones—without her. One simply cannot ask for a more insightful, passionate, and wise person with whom to share a journey like this, and a life. Jewish tradition claims that the air of the land of Israel makes one wiser. I'm not sure about that, but if my experience is any indication, it certainly enables one to fall even more deeply in love than you ever thought possible.

And to Talia, Aviel, and Micha, my thanks not only for their patience with a father whose hands often seem tethered to a keyboard and for their willingness to have much of their lives of the past few years shared so widely, but even more important, for living through this wonderful and devastating five years with us. I don't know how many parents derive strength from their children, or are in awe of their children even at such early ages, but you have given Ema and me more than we could ever have dreamed. We love you, and still hope—even after everything that we've lived through together—that one day yours will be the first generation to live in this land, in peace.

JERUSALEM

JULY 2003

TAMMUZ 5763

About the Author

- - - - - - - - - - - - - - - -

DANIEL GORDIS is vice president of the Mandel Foundation–Israel, and director of its Jerusalem Fellows Program. He is the author of, among other books, *God Was Not in the Fire: The Search for a Spiritual Judaism* and *Becoming a Jewish Parent: How to Explore Spirituality and Tradition with Your Children*. He immigrated to Israel with his wife and three children in 1998 and lives in Jerusalem.

Readers can subscribe to these dispatches, which still appear regularly, by visiting www.danielgordis.org.